Think Outside THE Lunchbox
COOKBOOK

By **Jyl Steinback**
"America's Healthiest Mom"
Ashley Arpel Greenwald
& **Friends**

INTRODUCTION BY
Dr. Scott Stoll
FOREWORD BY
Keegan Kuhn

Shape Up Us Inc.
501c3 nonprofit
Tax ID - 26-0051941

Think Outside The Lunchbox
By Jyl Steinback, Ashley Arpel Greenwald & Friends

Editor: Carol Allen and Caitlin Keniston
Cover and Text Design by Ken Minniti and Jacqueline Davila of Target Market Media Publications, Inc.
Cover Photo: Steve Meier Photography
Introduction by Dr. Scott Stoll
Foreword by Keegan Kuhn

Copyright 2020 by Shape Up Us, Inc. an Arizona Corporation
Nutrition Analysis: Julie Salmen MS RD
First Edition
ISBN number 978-1-893694-22-4 - $19.95

Visit our website at
www.ThinkOutsideTheLunchbox.today

Please share your favorite success story, favorite recipes or any questions to: Jyl@ShapeUpUs.org.

Jyl's Books
The Busy Mom's Slow Cooker Cookbook
The Busy Mom's Make It Quick Cookbook
Supermarket Gourmet
Countertop Magician
Cook Once, Eat for a Week
Superfoods- Cook Your Way To Health
The Fat Free Living Super Cookbook
The Fat Free Living Family Cookbook
Fat Free Living Cookbook from Around the World
Recipes for Fat Free Living 4: Breads
Recipes for Fat Free Living 3: Desserts
Recipes for Fat Free Living Cookbook 2
Recipes for Fat Free Living Cookbook

The recipes in this book are to be followed exactly as written. Neither the publisher nor the author is responsible for your specific health or allergy needs that may require medical supervision, or for any adverse reactions to the recipes contained in this book.

Printed in the United States of America

Table of Contents

Acknowledgments
❖ ❖ ❖

I want to thank all of you from the bottom of our hearts to yours for helping me make this world a healthier place. Please enjoy all of these delicious recipes that I know you and your families will love. I am so grateful for your letters and emails. You make my day, and I appreciate all of your wonderful support and energy. Each and every one of you makes a difference and that is what it takes to create change. Thank you!

To all of our incredible friends that shared your beautiful quotes: You make our mission to create a healthier world so enjoyable and exciting. Thank you so much for your words of encouragement and fabulous support. Please keep those cards and letters coming (as my dad always said). I love them all!

To my beautiful children Jamie, Adam, Scott and Ashley . . . AMAZING YOU ALL ARE and I am so incredibly lucky. Thank you for being YOU!

I have been blessed in so many ways in my life. I want to personally thank you for your unconditional kindness, love, friendship and hard work. You are all extraordinary, creative and as I always say brilliant!

Ashley Arpel Greenwald – One word sums you up AMAZING! You are my ROCK STAR and I am so grateful you met Scott so I could meet YOU! OMGosh you are a beautiful gift on so many levels and I count them every day. You are full of life, love and as I always tell Scott, "Sweet as sugar" or in our world "Date Sugar" Thank you for being YOU!

Julie Salmen—I absolutely love working with you! This is our first book together and you are brilliant! Thank you Susan Benigas for the beautiful introduction. Julie you bring so much to our "table." Your support is amazing and you are an incredible nutritionist and special friend! I love all of your updated materials on all of the latest information to keep us all "Thinking Outside The Lunchbox." Thank you so much for you and your driven passion to a healthier world all in moderation. Keeps us balanced.

Dr. Scott Stoll – I loved meeting you at your International Plant-Based Nutrition Health Conference. You are my personal Hero and Rock Star for living your dream to change the world one person at a time. You make such an incredible impact on the world through your work. I love your "Keys to Abundant Living": A plan for Healthy Living, Healing the Body and the Science of Health" and how you help each of us "Thrive and excel to be our best through a healthier lifestyle encompassing it all mind, body and emotion. https://drscottstoll.com

Keegan Kuhn – We are so blessed to have you write our foreword. Your passion, mission, vision and drive is extraordinary! I loved how you say in your introductory, "The solution to these problems and so many others hangs on the end of our forks" and I totally agree! I so enjoyed your documentaries, "Cowspiracy" and "What the Health." Phenomenal! Together We All Change the World! Thank you for being YOU! https://www.firstsparkmedia.net

Paige Ohliger—You are a miracle in progress! I am so grateful that I met you at the International Plant-Based Nutrition Health Conference. How lucky for me! You are talented and creative beyond words. I thank you for your gentle kindness and loving heart. All of your hard work helped us to create and make Think Outside The Lunchbox possible.

Ken Minniti – President & CEO of Target Market Media Publications Inc. I am so lucky the day I called you to work with us on Thinking Outside The Lunchbox" and you said YES! You made my day! You are always positive, uplifting, full of energy and so talented. Thanks for saying YES! You are extraordinary! Thanks for YOU! and helping us orchestrate this memorable book that helps create change and our future.

Jaqueline Dávila – Production Manager at Target Market Media Publications – AMAZING! You sat with us on the phone for hours to we all felt is was magnificent! Thank you for your brilliance, perfection, creativity ("Thinking Outside The Lunchbox") and patience my beautiful friend. You got our vision and did a glorious front and back cover and layout of our cookbook.

Caitlin Keniston – final editor with Target Market Media Publications – you are outstanding and kept us focused and consistent. Thank you so much for your hard work and patience. BEYOND AMAZING!

Steve Meier and Steve Meier Photography – YOU are my ROCK STAR. I say it only takes one "Great" picture and YOU did it my friend. Beautiful! Phenomenal! And painless!! The front cover photo is beyond spectacular!

Harold Sims – Thank you so much for your beautiful photography. We loved all the laughter you brought to our kitchen.

Thank you Cindy Muhleman for the photo of Ashley and I! You are AMAZING! I love you!

To all of our "Rock Star" Friends - Thank you so much for photographing your amazing recipes. You are each so incredibly creative and talented. We are so grateful to you for bringing your delicious recipe into our kitchens.

Carol Allen – What a blessing you are and a fabulous editor. Thank you for all your detail touches and your amazing support. You never stopped giving and we are so blessed.

FRIENDS you are breathtaking! EACH and EVERYONE one of you made this book possible.

Michelle Allen and Madi Page – you both ROCKED our index! INCREDIBLE you both are! Thank you so much for you hard work!

Sean Deblat – YOU ARE BEYOND AMAZING! Dynamic! Driven! Walk your talk! Thank YOU!

John Duarte – your photo of Ashley and her beautiful creation of her yummy blue cake is amazing!

Caryn Dugan –Congratulations on your new plant-based education center – "Center for Plant-based Living" in St. Louis, MO. We are so grateful to you in joining us as one of our beautiful friends. Your incredible knowledge, wisdom and passion to help other to transition to a plant-strong diet though all of your classes, events and programs are extraordinary. Thanks for you!

Neeme Liivlaid – Love your smoothies! Thank you for being a beautiful new friend. I love your wife!

Nele Liivlaid – You are unstoppable! You are so sweet and soft-hearted and a master at creating habits! You educate through research and your incredible knowledge of nutrition. We are so honored to have you part of this cookbook. Thank you for all of your hard work and generosity. We so love your son and husband being part of our cookbook. A circle of health, family and love that keeps on giving! I love waking up to you each morning (on-line) with our glass of celery juice in our Waterford wine glass toasting . . . To Health!

Carolina Maturana – You never stop! You are my personal hero! Not only do you create amazing recipes, walk your talk and live the lifestyle and also our phenomenal taste tester. WOW! INCREDIBLE! Thank you for being you!

Sharon Palmer – You are amazing. I love how you make your entire recipes from your garden. That is so inspiring! Also your passion to connect plant base to sustainability and connect the soil to whole foods is the circle that keeps on giving back to our bodies, our souls and our earth. Beautiful. Thank you so much for you.

Neil Popp – I so enjoyed working with you! You are so correct, "We are the Future" and your passion for Plant-based culture, and your love of ripe, fresh ingredients is the secret to our healthy future.

Reuel Rodriguez – We are so blessed to work with you! Your talent, experience, your zest for life is contagious. I absolutely loved what "Think Outside The Lunchbox" means to you, "Being mindful being creative and thinking from the Heart about our choices and to you that starts with healthy homegrown foods and recipes that feed our soul. Thank you are full of life and energy.

Laura Salyer – You are an extremely creative expert chef and love everything you have shared with Think Outside The Lunchbox. Thank you for being our recipe taster, expertise chef and everything in-between. You were always there to share and support. Thank you!

Aspen Sims – I just love how you and your dad work together – that is what "Shaping Up" is all about. Working together through love and laughter and of course in the kitchen. You are so talented and your recipes are beyond delicious! Thank you!

Diane Smith – What I absolutely love about you is your gentleness and passion to live life by your golden rule "Eating a plant-based diet is one of the best ways to gain optimum health – it could save your life." Nothing more needs to be said. You are a blessing in our lives. Thanks for you and joining us on our journey to living a healthier life! https://www.plantbasedcooking.com

Kiana Varner – You MASTER Juicer! Love it ALL! It is so dear to my "Heart" - Just got addicted to Juicing and love it! Thanks for all of your expertise!

Kelley Williamson – You are magnificent! Talented! Changing the future of our children! You are a phenomenal chef. "Nibbles in the Classroom" is so dear to my heart and so are you! Spectacular. Thank you for your hard work, delicious recipes, beautiful pictures and "Thinking Outside The Lunchbox!"

Introduction

By Dr. Scott Stoll

Have you ever stopped to consider that your breakfast, lunch and dinner plates are one of the most powerful and influential forces in the world today? The food choices that you make each day have a far-reaching, cumulative effect over your lifetime and will dramatically impact more than just your health. But all too often we eat without conscious intention and so our food choices are driven by unconscious forces like habits, cravings, insecurity, convenience and/or emotional pain.

Did you know that the average person will eat about 2000 pounds of food this year and consume approximately 58 million calories a lifetime? Bite by bite, these daily decisions add up to impact your cells, organs, brain, mood, relationships, work, goals, accomplishments, service, the health of the soil we are stewarding for future generations, and precious environmental resources like land and water. Every day we are individually and collectively shaping our future with what we put on our plate. And the world today has rapidly shifted in the wrong direction with the billions of bites of unhealthy food reflecting a larger cultural reliance on processed foods which has led to what is commonly referred to as the "Standard American Diet." Also known as S.A.D., typically consists of primarily highly processed or refined and empty calorie foods full of sodium, added sugar and saturated fat and devoid of foods like fruits, vegetables, legumes, nuts, seeds and whole grains.

During the past 100 years, cultures around the world have disengaged from healthier traditional eating patterns, ancient wisdom, and meals prepared at home. Swayed by the need and desire for convenience, hyper-tantalizing tastes, abundance, and affordability, they have unconsciously embraced a new "westernized" diet that is ultra-processed, calorie dense, rich in animal products, and nutrient poor. Decades of this dietary shift have elevated lifestyle related diseases, like heart disease, Type 2 diabetes and many cancers, to the leading cause of death and disability globally. And this same diet has crept into the daily food choices of our children. They too are experiencing epidemic levels of obesity and the same diseases, like cardiovascular disease and Type 2 diabetes at shockingly young ages.

There is a solution; the overwhelmingly body of research evidence substantiates the benefits of a whole food, plant-based diet to prevent, suspend, and reverse lifestyle related diseases. I don't want you to miss that key word in the last sentence because it is so important. A whole food, plant-based diet can in many cases reverse some of the most common diseases like type 2 diabetes and heart disease. And this same diet preserves key environmental resources and helps to regenerate every aspect of the food ecosystem. It is not a new dietary pattern, but rather a return to the predominantly plant-based diet that has sustained the longest lived and healthiest people groups around the world for a millennia.

However, not all plant-based foods or diets are created equally. Some are much richer in essential vitamins, minerals, and regenerative phytochemicals that have the ability to optimize the function of your cells throughout your body, like improve the resiliency of your immune system. Supportive research has demonstrated that a whole food, plant-based diet composed of nutrient rich foods like dark leafy greens, berries, beets, Brussels sprouts, broccoli, and beans significantly reduces inflammation. Research has also demonstrated that only 3% of the population is meeting the minimum daily recommendation for fiber intake, largely because they are not eating enough of the sole source – plants!

The real interface of the science of health and the experience of renewed health is your kitchen. The art of preparing delicious healthy meals has been largely ignored over the past several decades and many don't know where to even begin creating a nutritious lunch or dinner. Today, you are holding in your hand a guide to prepare delicious, meals from plant-nutritious ingredients. This is the key to a sustainable, healthy diet; create delectable mouth-watering meals everyone can enjoy. When the children in you life taste delicious food they will ask for more.

Cooking healthy food at home may be a lost art but this team of talented chefs and their friends are helping you "Think Outside The Lunchbox" and reclaim mealtime with fun, and tasty recipes that please your whole family. And through this process these recipes will also help you rediscover the joy of preparing life-giving food.

To your health – Scott!

Foreword

By Keegan Kuhn

We stand at a pivotal time in human history. Faced with the looming impacts of global climate change, mass species extinction, deforestation and desertification, the solution to these problems and so many others hangs on the end of our forks. Almost no other lifestyle choice we make has a greater impact on the planet than the foods we choose to eat everyday.

Animal agriculture (the raising of animals and their feed crops for human consumption) has a greater impact on climate change than the entire global transportation sector and is the primary driver of rainforest destruction, species extinction, top soil erosion, water pollution, water consumption, ocean dead-zones and virtually any other issue you could care about in the environmental world.

Raising animals for their flesh, milk or eggs is incredibly land and resource intensive. The land needed to raise animals and the crops fed to them occupies 45% of the earth's ice free land, by far the largest single use of any industry on the planet, compared to only 2.7% for all the world's cities combined. Making room for the 70 billion land animals raised each year for human consumption means that huge areas of the world's forests must be cleared. 91% of Brazilian Amazon destruction to date has been animal agriculture. When forests are cleared we loss wild species at an alarming rate. An estimated 100 animal, plant and insect species go extinct every day due to habitat destruction, the primary driver of which is animal ag. We are currently in the largest mass extinction the planet has seen in 66 million years in large part due to our desire to eat other animals.

When forests and native ecosystems are cleared, they are often burned to make room for grazing or feed crops, which not only releasing a tremendous amount of carbon but also hinders the ability of the planet to absorb carbon from the atmosphere. The animals that are then places on that land produce a even more emissions in the form of methane from their digestion, which has the global warming potential 86x greater than CO_2 on a 20 year timeframe.

Land converted for raising animals suffer from higher rates of erosion, further depleting our dwindling top soil. The run off erosion from factory farms and fields makes its way into our streams, river and eventually ocean, choking the waterways with nutrients that cause massive dead-zones; areas of coastal waters that are completely void of life.

But it's not just water pollution, it's also water consumption. Animal agriculture is responsible for 56% of all water consumption in the USA, where all household domestic water use from washing dishes, flushing toilets, cleaning clothes, etc. is only responsible for 5%. To produce 1lbs of beef takes upwards of 2500 gallons of water, the equivalent of 2 months worth of showering. To produce 1 gallon of milk takes up to 1000 gallons of water to produce.

But there is something we can do about this! We can switch from a diet based on animal protein to a diet based on plant protein. Switching to a plant-based diet we can reduce our dietary emissions by 50%, use 1/11 the fossil fuels, use 1/13 the water and 1/18 the amount of land needed! That is the equivalent of everyday saving 1100 gallons of water, 45lbs of grain, 30sqft of forested land, 20lbs of CO2e and 1 animals life, every day!

According to an analysis from Dr. Sailesh Rao and the University of Illinois if we allowed land cleared for animal agriculture to revert back to forests we would be able to sequester more carbon from the atmosphere that we have emitted since the beginning of the industrial era began. We could STOP climate change by simply switching how we eat.

No other choice we make will have a bigger impact on our planet, our health and other animals than switching to a plant-based diet. Won't you join me? Source material can be found at: www.cowspiracy.com/facts

Meet Our Nutritionist
Julie Salmen, MS, RD

My life began in a small farming community with a very large family garden, more fruit trees than a kid cares to count and daily chores outdoors. In addition to teaching me the challenges that farmers face with the seasons to grow food, it also taught me to appreciate the texture and flavor of truly fresh produce. Most of our meals were eaten together as a family and were balanced with the major food groups (including dessert). I credit my parents with building this foundation and knowledge of how to balance life with health and helping me become who I am today.

I am a registered dietitian, mom of a spunky 8-year-old and veggie gardener who loves to balance health with fun. Looking at eating habits of the average American today drives my desire and mission to make the foods we eat better for us. I have taken on the food industry from every angle, including working with manufacturers, restaurants and home chefs to drive better nutrition into the foods we eat. I am here to find a way to match what the consumer wants to eat with what they need to eat. And, the consistent message that comes up time and time again with my work is how we are eating too few plants!

Do not confuse my interest in promoting plants with veganism or vegetarianism. I want EVERYONE to have access to health through plants. There is a lot of research to point to the benefits of increasing plants in our diet, which is why I have always said, "Eat More Plants!" And from the nutrition I've provided for each recipe in this cookbook, you will certainly see why. I am proud to work with this collection of friends to help you think outside the lunchbox when it comes to the meals you make for your family and friends. We are all in this together to live life to the fullest.

For more fresh ideas on how I can help you or your company further, visit my website at www.nutritiousideas.com

Meet Dr. Scott Stoll, Introduction

Dr. Stoll is the co-founder of the Plantrician Project, the International Plant Based Nutrition Healthcare Conference, the International Journal of Disease Reversal and Prevention, and the Regenerative Health Institute, a unique collaborative project with the Rodale Institute. He serves on the advisory board at Whole Foods for their healthcare clinics and served as a member of the Whole Foods scientific and medical advisory board. Dr.Stoll is the Chairman of the board for the Plantrician Project and chief medical director for the Rouxbe cooking school.

Every year Dr. Stoll hosts the very popular one-week health immersion, Dr. Stoll's total health immersion in Naples Florida and helps attendees recover lost health, overcome addictions, and restore emotional balance. In addition to authoring several books, hosting his own daily TV and radio programs, Dr. Stoll has appeared on numerous national shows including the Dr. Oz show, a 2018 PBS special, and numerous documentaries including Eating You Alive, Wait till its Free, and The Game Changers. As well as being a published author and member of the 1994 Olympic Bobsled Team, he is a highly sought-after international speaker. Dr. Stoll resides with his wife and six children in Bethlehem, Pennsylvania.

Meet Keegan Kuhn, Foreword

Keegan Kuhn is the award-winning co-director of the highly acclaimed documentary films Cowspiracy (executive produced by Leonardo DiCaprio) What The Health (executive produced by Joaquim Phoenix) and director of Running For Good: The Fiona Oakes Documentary. Kuhn is the owner and operator of First Spark Media, a digital film production company tailored to creating films for social justice. For more information, visit www.firstsparkmedia.net.

Meet Our Friends

Michelle Allen Hello, my name is Michelle Allen! I am currently a senior studying nutrition communication, however, I am returning from a semester off where I earned my esthetics license and laser certificate. I am passionate about all things health, wellness, and beauty, and I hope to exude healthy and positive energy to those around me. Having the chance to work with Jyl and her amazing team has been a wonderful learning experience for me and I feel incredibly lucky to have been given this great opportunity! Think Outside The Lunchbox is a great resource for families and young children to find their excitement for healthy food and delicious recipes, and I hope that everyone enjoys it as much as I do!

Kayli Dice, MS, RD

As a registered dietitian and food and nutrition expert, Kayli Dice has devoted her entire career to helping people shift toward eating more plants. She believes food should be enjoyable, simple, and nourishing. Kayli authored the Plant-Based Nutrition Quick Start Guide, chairs the American College of Lifestyle Medicine Registered Dietitian Member Interest Group, and is Director of Nutrition & Healthcare at Lighter, Inc.

Caryn Dugan

Caryn Dugan is St. Louis, Missouri's leading expert in plant-based culinary nutrition and education. She adopted this way of eating after losing her dad to cancer and only weeks later also receiving that diagnosis. She helps others transition to a plant-strong diet through classes, events and programs she designs. You can also find her doing regular cooking segments on local affiliates of NBC, CBS and FOX morning shows. Most recently Caryn opened The Center for Plant-based Living the nation's first plant-based nutrition and culinary education center.

Cardo Hendrik

Cardo Hendrik – "Cardo" for short – Nele Liivlaid's son – Cardo means "thistle" in Spanish. His name is plant! Cardo is a curious and kind-hearted 9-year-old boy who's been loving his plants for as long as he can remember. He's very much into robotics as well as arts and crafts. Additionally, he has solid grey belt in Brazilian Jiu-Jitsu -- so, you better eat your plants! :)

Nele Liivlaid

Nele Liivlaid is author of Plant-Based Made Easy: Th e Complete Practical Guide to Healthy Whole Food Diet. She is also plant-based certific ate g raduate f rom eCornell and a featured blogger. On her blog nutriplanet.org Nele shares easy-to-follow recipes, video tutorials, regular and Candida/blood sugar meal plans, and articles about healing Candida naturally. Read Nele's Story p. 354.

Carolina Maturana

Hi I am a Los Angeles born Chilean plant-based chef that's all about positive thinking, kindness and healthy living. Growing up in Chile I was exposed to a wide variety of vegetables and fruits at an early age. This created a solid foundation for me to be able to sustain a plant-based vegan diet as an adult. My enthusiasm towards this lifestyle and love for others have encouraged me to share my message. Through music, food photography, writing and healthy recipe development I hope to inspire other families to bring light to their best selves as well.

Madison Page

My name is Madison Page but most people call me Madi! I am currently a 22 year old senior at Arizona State University studying Nutrition. My ultimate goal in life is to become a Physician's Assistant but plan to implement much of what I've learned being a nutrition major into my future career. Being able to contribute to the making of this cookbook was a life changing experience and I thank Jyl and the rest of her team for allowing me to learn so much. I hope that this cookbook will inspire people to learn to cook in new ways and to make people better understand how to incorporate plant nutritious dishes into their diet!

Sharon Palmer, RDN, MS

Sharon Palmer, RDN, MS in Sustainable Food Systems, is known as The Plant-Powered Dietitian. She is an award-winning journalist, author, and plant-based and sustainability food and nutrition expert based in Los Angeles. Her books, The Plant-Powered Diet and Plant-Powered Life, have met with critical success, and she writes extensively in national publications, as well as for her popular blog at SharonPalmer.com. In addition, she serves as the nutrition editor for Today's Dietitian, nutrition advisor for Oldways, and ambassador for Meatless Monday.

Neil Popp

Neil Popp is extremely passionate about plant-based culture, and loves using ripe, fresh ingredients to create dishes that can surprise anyone's taste. "We are the future, and the future is vegan"!

Reuel Rodriguez

Reuel Rodriguez has worked as a professional chef for over ten years. With his unwavering compassion for others and positive leadership skills becoming a chef was a no-brainer. His passion for veganism and healthy eating began eight years ago when he decided to prioritize the planet. He dreams of going back to his roots and starting his own Hawaiian-fusion restaurant that not only tastes good but is good for you. His passion for healthy eating comes out in each delicious meal he prepares by using only the best ingredients To me Think Outside The Lunchbox means being mindful being creative and thinking from the Heart about our choices.

Laura Salyer

I am a professionally trained musician, passionate health and wellness advocate, weight lifter, and an avid animal lover. I have been making healthy, delicious plant-based foods for my family and myself for over five years, and I love to experiment with desserts. I dream of opening my own fully plant-based restaurant and café in the future as I enjoy sharing my tasty treats with others. To me, Think Outside The Lunchbox™ means being original and creative with what you eat; it means being diligent and purposeful about what you put into your body, and striving to make healthful choices.

Aspen Simms

For the past 2 1/2 years Aspen Sims has been cooking creative and delicious dishes at Binkley's Restaurant. However, starting as a dishwasher at Ciao Grazie, is what kicked off her culinary jobs. Born in Phoenix, Arizona, Aspen Sims was always an adventurer, constantly looking for things to do to keep busy. She enjoyed many things, but her main thing was always food. At 4 years old whether being posted on the countertop watching her mother cook, or watching Food Network, Aspen was all about food. She was outgoing as well, so outgoing that she opened her own baking business at 8 years old, called Jade's Tasty Treats (or JTT for short). People all over her neighborhood knew about it, and supported her. As she grew older school became a priority, and later sports were introduced, leading to a retirement of JTT. As Aspen grew older, she started to see how harsh, and challenging people, and growing up could be. She began to lack confidence to pursue Sports and/or Cuisine because of it. She later suffered a sports career ending injury, and was stuck in a really dark place. Luckily her parents took notice, and helped her to see the beauty in the world. Her father had a friend of a friend, named Chef Binkley who was willing to sit down with Aspen and tell her the truth about the restaurant industry, which were definitely not rainbows and chocolate mountains. Somehow that made Aspen want to be a Chef even more, and in a joking matter she asked Chef Binkley if she could intern there, just knowing he would say no. Only he said yes, and she nearly fainted. Aspen was still in high school so Sundays were the only day available, however once she graduated from high school, she was there everyday. That led to Chef Binkley offering her a job, knowing she had no culinary experience, and wanted to teach her himself. This helped her develop an interest and passion for cooking all over again. And she started her first job in the fine dining side of the restaurant industry as a prep cook at 17, in 2017. Although she had no culinary experience, Chef Binkley quickly noticed how easily it came to Aspen, and how she had a Knack for taking on challenges, and trying to improve her time when executing prep. Soon after she was in charge of her own dishes, and not long after that she was promoted to Chef De Partie at 18. Now at 19, she has traveled to experience multiple cuisines, and has made new connections. In spring of 2020, Aspen will be moving to Japan to further her Japanese Cuisine studies under a famous sushi chef in Akibane, Japan. She plans to continue on this journey, and hopes to open her own successful restaurant that will bring people together from far and wide.

Diane Smith

Diane Smith shares whole food plant-based recipes, science-backed articles and tools to help people make the dietary change that could save their lives on her website plantbasedcooking.com

Kiana Varner

I am a currently a student majoring in Nutrition and Health in Texas. When I'm not studying, I am either with my daughter traveling or trying out different recipes together. I also work with my parents at our juice bar called Pure Juice. I am always incorporating a healthy lifestyle into lives.

Think Outside The Lunchbox means to me is to have fun and mix up different fruits and vegetables in ways you would have never thought of doing.

Kelley Williamson

Kelley Williamson is a Chef and a Certified Food for Life Instructor through Physicians Committee for Responsible Medicine (PCRM) specializing in low fat plant based (vegan) cooking under the name Plant Based Kitchen. Kelley focuses on facilitating cooking classes, offering personal chef services and sharing food information, recipes and ideas through all of the classes that she teaches. Kelley has taught over 2000 individuals on plant based nutrition and has a passion for helping people heal through food. Kelley has classes at Tagawa Gardens, Whole Foods, Natural Grocers and her own "cook with me" cooking School. To find out more please go to: https://www.meetup.com/Denver-Healthy-Plant-Based-Cooking-Classes/

Kelley has most recently formed a non-profit, Healthy Living thru Nutrition, in May 2015 which will focus on establishing relationships with schools, students, families, and volunteers across the state of Colorado. The essential purpose of this non-profit will be to fulfill the Healthy Living thru Nutrition mission by teaching cooking classes that focus on proper nutrition, which helps families build the skills and knowledge to cook meals and make healthy choices on their own. Professional Credentials: Chef * Food for Life Instructor Certification* Forks Over Knifes Certification* Plantrician Certification* Plant Powered Lifestyle Coach

Introduction
by Jyl Steinback

For as long as I can remember everyone asks me how did you get started? Why are you so passionate about "Building A Healthier Future for Our Children"? What is your story? And in this book which is so "Life changing" on so many levels of our being I decided to share my story."

My journey-started way back when I was in grade school. I was in the fifth grade. It was quite challenging for me as a child. I had a really tough time reading no matter how many hours I spent practicing with my parents and teachers. I actually flunked 5th grade spelling. Thank goodness now for spell check! Maybe it doesn't sound so bad right now as you are reading this but it changed the course of my life, as I am sure some of you can relate. When I was in 5th grade for spelling you had to stand up in front of the whole class and if you missed a word you had to sit down in front of all of your classmates – it was devastating– spelling was a "BIG" thing back then.

I am not feeling sorry for myself at all because it was really a blessing and became a mission within myself to share with others that are having a hard time with life - that these challenges are really a gift. Each and everyone of us excel and it is our life lesson to seek what is "your magic," what is your "passion" and why are you "SO AMAZING! Because WE ALL ARE . . .SO AMAZING! When I look back today I realize this all happened with a purpose and reason. . So I could help educate children through an education program that we created that support children to learn in the way they need to learn. Is that visual? Audio? Do they need to touch it and be shown? How about smelling it? Using all 5 senses is the BEST way to be educated so everyone is successful in the way they need to learn and feel great about themselves. This is how the Hip Hop Healthy Heart Program for Children™ was born. We ALL have a story. Good, bad or indifferent it is "Our story", our journey and our life lessons. And this is ALL OK! Because what I learned from this incredible journey is I can change "My story" anytime I want. I love that about life. WE ALL HAVE A CHOICE!

Then I went to college at Arizona State University passionate about education and how I was going to "Change the world." I could not wait to get started! I was walking to my class the first week of school and sitting on the wall were eight men with cards to "rate" the women that walked by . . .YIKES! I was weighing thirty pounds more than I am today not in great shape physically and those numbers weren't real sexy! I was once again devastated. Again another beautiful lesson in life that uprooted the way I lived. I was again on a mission to eat healthier and how do you do that with all of the "Diets" out there. Well I tried them ALL!! And the bottom line I didn't want a diet . . .I wanted a "Lifestyle" a "Way of Life" that made me feel great from the inside-out. HUGE difference!! Yes I wanted to loose weight, but that was a side benefit. I wanted to be healthy with lots of energy so I had the stamina to do all of my passions and dreams. I wanted to feel good about me and know that I could also go into my closet and fit into any pair of jeans I put on. We have all had those days trying on the whole closet before you went out to find one outfit you liked. I didn't want to worry about what I ate – that was to time consuming and so much negative energy.

So I had to start "Thinking Outside The Lunchbox." What will this take and what do I want to accomplish? Once again, I started "Reshaping" my life.

Instead of living to eat, I wanted to eat to live – and eat well - with the approach laid out in this cookbook. We call it "Thinking Outside The Lunchbox" because it's not just about the food. "Thinking Outside The Lunchbox" means you'll not only be healthier on the inside but so will our planet (please enjoy our forward by Keegan Kuhn and his amazing documentary "Cowspiracy: the Sustainability Secret (2014)" and "What The Health (2017)."

Everyone wins.

Our focus in this book is on a totally plant nutritious lifestyle. These recipes utilize only vegetables, whole grains, legumes, nuts and fruits. A totally plant nutritious lifestyle eliminates all animal products, including beef, pork, poultry, dairy and eggs. It's a kinder, gentler approach to eating.

Also, the ingredients in these recipes are minimally processed, which means less sugar and fewer preservatives.

A full-fledged plant nutritious lifestyle provides solid health benefits. Study-after-study shows that plant nutritious can help you improve blood pressure, reduce the chance of heart disease, lower cholesterol, and even help prevent Type 2 diabetes.

A plant nutritious lifestyle also can help you lose weight. In fact, a study from Loma Linda University found that – on average - people on a plant nutritious lifestyle had a lower body mass index than meat eaters.

Some other benefits of a plant nutritious lifestyle include that it:
• Decreases the risk of cancer, even slowing the progression of certain types
• Prevents or halts the progression of some auto-immune diseases
• Enhances longevity
• Increases energy
• Improves mood and mental clarity

Who doesn't want to pass these benefits along to their families and reap the amazing life changing benefits as both Dr. Scott Stoll and Keegan Kuhn will share?

There are some common myths about plant nutritious lifestyle, such as whether your family will get enough protein. The answer is a resounding yes. The average American consumes double the amount of protein needed for health purposes. As long you include a variety of grains, legumes, and vegetables, your body will obtain all the amino acids necessary for it to flourish.

You may be thinking, "but what if I'm an athlete? Won't a plant nutritious lifestyle hurt my performance?" Not according to the American Council of Exercise and the American Dietetic Association. Your little gymnasts and dancers will thrive on a plant nutritious diet.

There's an environmental factor to consider, too. If you are interested in reducing your carbon footprint, there's no better way than to stop eating animal products.

A United Nations study determined that animal agriculture produces 14.5% of the world's greenhouse emissions, compared to 13.5% for all forms of transportation combined. And, by adopting a totally plant nutritious lifestyle globally, scientists estimate that food-related emissions could be cut by 70%.

Never mind the huge amount of natural resources necessary to raise animals to maturity. Did you know it takes eight gallons of water and 10.6 pounds of feed to produce one pound of edible beef?

Clearly, a plant nutritious lifestyle is healthier and provides environmental benefits. But Thinking Outside The Lunchbox also is more ethical. Animal agriculture is not only harmful to the livestock being raised. It also is responsible for the deaths of three million animals, killed to eradicate animals, which might attack livestock.

So, for a healthier family, a better way of life for our animal friends, and an improved planet, try Thinking Outside The Lunchbox.

Now that's food for thought!

What does "Thinking Outside The Lunchbox" mean to you? I would love for you to e-mail me: Jyl@ShapeUpUs.org and share what that means to you.

To me it is changing your habits; it's a cultural change and getting educated. It is rolling out of bed on the other side in the morning (don't knock it till your try it – it will change your whole day – you will think differently). It is clasping your hands – moving one finger over - - it's different, it feels strange possibly uncomfortable but wonderful. I now do it all the time. If you are a walker or biker and you always go on the same trail – go the trail another way and "Think Outside The Lunchbox."

Thinking Outside The Lunchbox is my nature - it is the puzzle of life that keeps us having fun- connecting the dots and deciding what is best at hand. Life is extraordinary and meant to be just as it is- as it unfolds beautifully for all. Serendipitous! - Perfect timing for everything.

So I must add my full circle experience to my story at the top of the page . . .about my fifth grade teacher and flunking spelling. When I went back to St. Louis in June of 2019 one of my beautiful friends since I was 10 years old (in the same fifth grade class) was book signing her first book and I flew in for our "Shape Up Missouri" event and to celebrate my grade school friend. When I got to the bookstore about 15 minutes later- in walks "our" fifth grade teacher. When someone told me who she was – It was just such a serendipity moment and full circle of my life. I had to laugh out loud. I had just written this intro sharing for the first time "my story." My friend had her join her at the book signing because her fifth grade teacher had "shaped" her life to be a brilliant writer. I was devastated because I flunked spelling and started my journey of creating our curriculum. I had to stop in my tracks for a minute because when this teacher and I started talking. This is not how she remembered me– she thought of me as a huge celebrity for writing cookbooks, exercise programs and creating Shape Up Us nonprofit. She mentioned how she had followed my career and was just so proud of me. WOW! I had to sit back to see the two very different stories of how we each perceived "me." A life changing "Aha" moment. I believe there are no accidents. I believe I was suppose to be at this book store to celebrate my friend and to see this teacher again and sit next to her to celebrate both my friend and me for two similar reasons but so different in my eyes. I always say there are three sides to every story, your side, their side and the "real" side and all equally are as important to the mind of the side "YOU" believe is true. What a life changing moment.

But, then to leave you with one more thought to ponder . . ."in my mind" this all happened because of eating cleaner and healthier and allowing more intuitive moments into my life, I allowed this seren-dipitous moment to happen in my life to heal on another level of my being. At the same breath, I LOL as I write my story . . .I could not spell serendipitous so I spoke it into my phone for the correct spelling. I love spell check! And I now love me!

It has been a journey my friends and I would be honored to hear all of your beautiful stories and journeys. What and who, "Shaped" your life. Please write me at: Jyl@ShapeUpUs.org

I always say it only takes one person to believe in you to help "Shape Up" your life.

I am always here for you.

I have two now four extraordinary children that I am so proud of and honored to be their mom. I can't even begin to share how they have "shaped" my life on so many levels. I love you Jamie, Scott, Adam and Ashley. Thank you for you! and all of incredible support in believing in me and all of my dreams. You are my Heroes! I am so extremely blessed for each and every one of you. I love you all with all my heart and soul to yours.

I love to hike in the desert with my amazing family, friends and new pal "Kona" a black wolf mala-mute as I listen to Shape Up RADIO – high-energy music that lasts the whole mountain (a free app to download on both Apple and Android phones). Love it! Dance like nobodies watching you that is my motto! My favorite movie is Field of Dreams, "Build it and they will come" and here YOU are! You have arrived and I am so grateful.

Thanks for joining us – perfect timing as I always say . . . serendipity. Don't you love your magic?

Light and love always,

Thanks for being YOU!

Jyl

Resources:

https://www.ncbi.nlm.nih.gov/pmc/articles/PMC3662288/
https://jamanetwork.com/journals/jamainternalmedicine/fullarticle/1710093
https://spectrummagazine.org/article/loma-linda-university/2013/10/05/vegetarians-tend-be-slimmer-meat-eaters-new-loma-linda-stud
https://www.acefitness.org/education-and-resources/lifestyle/blog/86/are-vegetarian-diets-safe
https://theconversation.com/more-than-one-good-reason-for-eating-mainly-plant-foods-38378
https://theconversation.com/going-veggie-would-cut-global-food-emissions-by-two-thirds-and-save-millions-of-lives-new-study-56655
http://www.beefresearch.ca/blog/cattle-feed-water-use/
https://navs-online.org/articles/veganism-animal-rights/

Introduction
by Ashley Arpel Greenwald

As I stare at the blank page before me, I am overcome with overwhelming nerves. I've probably gotten up to get coffee 6 times, and it's only 9:02am. How do I convey my relationship with food? Where did my incredible love and passion for baking come from? Was it making pasta with my dad as a child? Baking mini apple pies with my mom? Maybe it was the tea parties every Tuesday with grandma Janie or dipping frozen bananas into chocolate with Grandma Adrien and my big brother. I guess we will never know officially, but for as long as I can remember I have had a divine love for food, the culinary arts, and of course, eating.

My introduction to the culinary world was through sugar, eggs and butter; pretty much everything you won't find in this book. Hailing from New York, pizza and donuts were a staple in my life while salads and most vegetables were overlooked. It wasn't until I moved to Los Angeles and met Jyl that I started to "think outside the lunchbox" and develop an interest in healthy living. But before I take you down my plant-based road, I should probably start at the semi-beginning.

When I was 18 years old, I moved to Los Angeles, like so many others, with a dream and a wish. I auditioned for and was accepted into the prestigious American Academy of Dramatic Arts, but upon graduating I was plagued with the ever so common questions: Will I make it? What will my contribution to society be? What will it look like? At 21 years old, I simply did not know. For two years auditions came and went. Finally, at age 23 I landed my very first movie role alongside Nicolas Cage and Wendell Pierce. I got to fly to New Orleans, eat all the beignets I want, and perform next to some of the world's most famous actors. To say that I was on cloud 9 would be a severe understatement...I don't know what "making it" means per-say, but I swear, for a brief moment, I thought I had.

When I came back to L.A., and subsequently back to reality, I was once again plagued with life altering questions: Where is my next role? When will I work again? Why isn't Nicolas Cage calling me back? (Joking...I don't have his number...I swear) I was turning 24 and I desperately needed an outlet that sparked not only my excitement but creativity; a performer is still a performer, even without a stage or camera, after all.

I opened my own online bakery, That's Ashley's Kitchen, in 2015. What started out as a small entre-preneurial side-gig, quickly grew into a respect and admiration for the field. In order to grow and learn more I took odd jobs here and there. At one point, I was a private chef for a food delivery app.

After about two years of selling sugary cakes and cupcakes both online and at farmers' markets, I felt ready for more. I started to include treats that catered to certain dietary restrictions; gluten free, vegan, paleo, etc...When I met Jyl in 2018, I was quickly introduced to a world that I never even knew existed. Plant based cooking. The term sounds simple enough, yet, I myself, a professional baker of several years, didn't know the full definition of a plant nutritous lifestyle. With the guidance and understanding that Jyl and Julie so graciously provided me, I was able to grow and learn more about being plant nutrious every day. I am now happy to say that not only has my lifestyle changed, but my business has also flourished with the delectable additions of plant nutritious goodies.

Take a look at my bakery's website www.ThatsAshleysKitchen.com and follow me on Instagram using the handle @ThatsAshleysKitchen!

Whole Food, Plant-Based Solutions for You

By Julie Salmen, MS, RD

You have now heard that there are old studies, new studies and most likely future studies to come that demonstrate the need for us to consume plant nutritious foods to support optimum health. Food, after all, is the best medicine. But what does it mean to eat a "whole food, plant-based diet?" Is this book just for vegans? Vegetarians? Absolutely not!

We went to our friends at the American College of Lifestyle Medicine (ACLM) to help us explain the whole food, plant-based diet. The official position statement on the role of diet in lifestyle medicine from ACLM is as follows, "For the treatment, reversal and prevention of lifestyle-related chronic disease, the ACLM recommends an eating plan based predominantly on a variety of minimally processed vegetables, fruits, whole grains, legumes, nuts and seeds." Sounds great ACLM!

So, all of our recipes focus on the goodness of plants in all forms, including fresh, frozen (unsweetened), canned (no salt added and unsweetened) and dried (no added salt and unsweetened). We think beyond salt to flavor dishes with herbs, spices and seasonings, as well as limit the amounts of salt and oils used in all recipes. When we use added sugars, we focused on those that are minimally processed (think date paste, molasses, maple syrup). We do not use highly processed or artificial ingredients, refined flours or anything animal-based, but we have provided basic substitutions for those recipes that call for things that you would expect to come from dairy ingredients or animals. That is thinking outside of the box or lunchbox in our case.

When it comes to the nutrition of our recipes, we've made sure that the nutrition is balanced with healthy fats, complex carbohydrates and plant protein to keep you going and support optimal health. Because we use fresh plant ingredients in every recipe, you are getting the most out of each ingredient with vitamins, minerals and other nutrition that mother nature provides. We can't forget about fiber, which most Americans are not eating enough of today. Our recipes all include fiber, which should be no surprise since plants are THE source of fiber in our diet. And why is fiber so important you ask? Here are just a few reasons...

- High intakes of fiber were linked to a reduced risk of heart disease, stroke, hypertension, diabetes, obesity and certain gastrointestinal diseases.
- Increasing fiber intake lowers blood pressure and cholesterol levels.
- Increased fiber intake helps with a feeling of fullness and weight loss.

So, we hope you enjoy the variety and creativity our chefs bring to plant-based eating. All recipes conveniently include the nutrition for each serving. We also let you know which recipes do not contain any natural sources of gluten and recipes that are easy for kids to get into the kitchen and help out.

PLEASE NOTE ... You should consult your physician to learn more about how changing your diet can change your life. Do not stop taking medication or make changes until you've spoken with your physician as this is not intended to be medical advice. Want a physician who is trained in promoting health through lifestyle changes? The American College of Lifestyle Medicine is a great place to find like-minded doctors who treat your chronic disease with lifestyle changes, including how to eat for optimal health. Visit their website at https://www.lifestylemedicine.org/ACLM/ACLM/About/Membership_Directory_ListingView.aspx.

BELL PEPPER

CHERRY

CHILI

MUSHROOM

CORN

TOMATO

RED ONION

PUMPKIN

BUTTERNUT
SQUASH

CARROT

DRIED
APRICOT

BEETROOT

RED
BEANS

ALMOND

SWEET
POTATO

GINGER ROOT

JUBILEE

KUMATO

RADISH

RED KRAUT

ONION

WHEAT

BELL PEPPER

EGGPLANT

TURNIP

GARLIC

CHANTERELLE

YELLOW SQUASH

Definitions

A bit more about the terms, recommendations and equipment used in our recipes...

- **Kid-Friendly:** While all of our recipes are great for the whole family, kids included, recipes designated "kid-friendly" are also easy for kids to get into the kitchen to help create these delicious dishes.

- **Gluten Free:** Recipes designated as gluten free do not contain any wheat, rye, barley or triticale ingredients (natural sources of gluten). Depending on your level of sensitivity to gluten, always check ingredient statements for any gluten-containing ingredients on products not labeled gluten free.

- **Level of Difficulty:** Each recipe is designated as easy, medium or challenging to indicate recipes that are for beginners versus those recipes that may require a little more experience to complete.

- **Food Processor versus Blender:** For our recipes that reference a blender or food processor, our chefs have assured us that you can use one or the other for the recipe. Always start with the kitchen tool listed, but defer to the backup in cases where the original one is not available.

- **Storage Containers:** We commonly refer to storing your finished recipes or leftovers in glass storage containers. We recognize the strain on our environment when using disposable packaging, and we encourage you to keep this in mind too. If you do not have glass, any reusable container will do.

- **Tips or Facts:** Each recipe will include an interesting fact or tip for making the recipe. Enjoy these extra fun facts and helpful tips!

- **Salt to Taste:** Some of our recipes include a statement "salt to taste." That means, we believe the recipe is flavorful on its own, but some may want a pinch of salt. A 1/8t of salt is about 190-250mg sodium, depending on the type of salt, and is included in the nutrition analysis unless marked optional. If you choose not to add salt, the total sodium will be lower in the final recipe.

Basics, Flavor
Boosters &
Condiments

Brown Sauce

by Caryn Dugan

Easy | **Gluten Free** | **6 Servings**

Whether a topper or a dip, this brown sauce is sure to make a statement at your dining table!

Ingredients

2 ½ c unsweetened almond milk
½ c old fashioned oats
⅓ c nutritional yeast
⅓ c unsalted raw cashews
1 ½ Tbsp baking soda
½ Tbsp smoked paprika
1 tsp mustard powder
1 tsp onion powder
½ tsp garlic powder
½ tsp turmeric powder
⅛ tsp salt

Directions

1. Gather ingredients.
2. Place all ingredients in a high speed blender or food processor.
3. Blend for 3 minutes until creamy.
4. Transfer to a saucepan over medium-high heat, stir continually for 7-8 minutes or until the sauce thickens up.
5. Serve warm.

Nutrition Per Serving Serving Size: 1/4 cup, 50 calories, 2.5g total fat, 0g sat fat, 0mg cholesterol, 540mg sodium, 5g carbohydrates, 1g fiber, 0g total sugar, 2g protein

Tip or fact: Use as a sauce over potatoes or grains.

Shopping list

Packaged
□ old fashioned oats
□ nutritional yeast
□ unsalted raw cashews

Baking Ingredients
□ baking soda

Refrigerated or Frozen
□ unsweetened almond milk

Seasonings and Spices
□ smoked paprika
□ mustard powder
□ onion powder
□ garlic powder
□ turmeric powder
□ salt

Cashew Cream
by Caryn Dugan

Easy | Kid Friendly | Gluten Free | 8 Servings

Cashew cream is very versatile. Add it to soups and sauces to thicken them.

Ingredients
1 c raw unsalted cashews
1 c water

Directions
1. Gather ingredients.
2. Place cashews in container and cover with water. Soak for a few hours or overnight. The longer they soak, the easier they will blend.
3. Drain and rinse.
4. Place soaked cashews in blender with ¼ cup of water. Blend until smooth adding a little water at a time until you get the consistency you would like.

Nutrition Per Serving Serving Size: 1/4 cup, 90 calories, 7g total fat, 1g sat fat, 0mg sodium, 4g carbohydrates, 2g fiber, 1g sugar, 3g protein

Storage: Store in airtight glass container in the refrigerate for up to 5 days or freeze for up to 3 months.

Tip or fact: Cashews are 21% protein, 46% fat and 25% carbohydrates. The high fat content of cashews is the reason why they are great for boosting the flavor and creamy texture for plant-based sauces.

Basics

Shopping list

Packaged
☐ raw cashews

Cashew Parmesan Sprinkle by Laura Salyer

Easy | Gluten Free | 16 Servings

A simple, delicious substitute for parmesan cheese.

Ingredients

¾ c raw cashews
3 Tbsp nutritional yeast
¼ tsp garlic powder
¼ tsp onion powder
¾ tsp sea salt
2 Tbsp hulled hemp seeds

Directions

1. Gather ingredients.
2. Place cashews, nutritional yeast, garlic powder, onion powder and salt in the bowl of a food processor or blender. Process briefly until crumbled into a loose meal.
3. Stir in hemp seeds until well combined.

Nutrition Per Serving Serving Size: 1 tablespoon, 45 calories, 3.5g total fat, 0g saturated fat, 110mg sodium, 2g carbohydrate, 1g fiber, 0g sugar, 2g protein

Ingredient Swaps: You may substitute another type of nut for the cashews, or even try it with seeds. Seeds such as sunflower and shelled pumpkin (aka: pepitas) work well in this recipe.

Storage: Store in an airtight glass container in the refrigerator for up to 2 months.

Tip or fact: If you are searching for hulled hemp seeds, look in the health foods or supplements section of most grocery stores. If you still cannot find them, don't worry – this recipe is tasty with or without them! You can also try adding your favorite herbs and seasonings to different batches to create new flavor combinations. Herbs like rosemary, thyme, sage, cayenne, and others will give your version a unique and delicious kick! Just add them during processing to combine.

Shopping list

Packaged
☐ unsalted raw cashews
☐ nutritional yeast
☐ hulled hemp seeds

Seasonings and Spices
☐ garlic powder
☐ onion powder
☐ sea salt

Cashew Sour Cream

by Caryn Dugan

Easy | Kid Friendly | Gluten Free | 8 Servings

You can't have a baked potato without sour cream!

Ingredients

1 c prepared cashew cream
(recipe p. 3)
½ Tbsp lemon juice, to taste

Directions

1. Gather ingredients.
2. Prepare cashew cream recipe according to recipe on page 3.
3. Mix 1 cup of prepared cashew cream and 1/3 tablespoon lemon juice. Add additional lemon juice until you've reached our desired "sourness."
4. Serve cold.

Nutrition Per Serving 90 calories, 7g total fat, 1g sat fat, 0mg sodium, 4g carbohydrates, 2g fiber, 1g sugar, 3g protein

Storage: Store in an airtight glass container in the refrigerator for up to 5 days or in the freezer for up to 3 months.

Tip or fact: Cashew Sour Cream adds rich flavor and fiber.

Basics

Shopping list

Produce
☐ 1 lemon

Packaged
☐ raw cashews

Dry Beans

Preparing dry beans is a lot easier than you think. Here we give you two different ways to accomplish this task – one requires a little more time but less effort. Enjoy!

Ingredients
1 c dry beans

Directions
Method 1: OVERNIGHT
1. In a large bowl, cover beans with 3 inches of cold water, cover and set aside at room temperature for 8 hours or overnight.
Method 2: QUICK SOAK (1 to 1 ½ hours)
1. In a large pot, cover beans with 3 inches of cold water, cover and bring to a boil. Boil for 1 minute, remove pot from heat and set aside, covered, for 1 hour.
2. Drain soaked beans and transfer to a large pot.
3. Cover with 2 inches of cold water and bring to a boil.
4. Skim and discard surface foam. Reduce heat, cover, and simmer, stirring occasionally until beans are tender.
5. Drain beans and serve warm.

Nutrition Per Serving Depends on the type of bean.

Ingredient Swaps: 1 cup dry lentils (makes 2 1/2 cups cooked lentils)

Storage: Store in the refrigerator up to 5 days.

Tip or fact: Here are nine amazing beans to consider... chickpeas (also known as garbanzo beans), kidney beans, black beans, soybeans, navy beans, pinto beans, cannellini beans. Beans are a great way to boost plant protein and fiber.

Shopping list

Packaged
☐ Any variety of bean

6

Indian Spice Mix

by Nele Liivlaid

Medium | **6 Servings**

Here's an aromatic mix of dry-roasted and ground Indian spices ready to be used in soups, stews, curries, rice dishes or even sprinkled on top of salads. Be ready for explosion of flavors!

Ingredients

2 Tbsp coriander seeds
1 Tbsp cumin seeds
1 Tbsp caraway seeds
1 Tbsp fennel seeds
1 Tbsp yellow mustard seeds
Seeds from 10 green cardamom pods or ½ tsp ground cardamom

Directions

1. Gather ingredients.
2. In a medium non-stick pan dry toast cumin seeds separately for 30 seconds until they become toasty and fragrant.
3. Toast all remaining spices together for 2-3 minutes until they start to brown and you can smell the fragrances. NOTE: If you want to be meticulous, add the mustard seeds first. After a few minutes, toss in the coriander and fennel seeds followed by cardamom and caraway seeds a minute later.
4. Let the seeds cool completely before you grind them with mortar and pestle or with grinder.

Toasting Times

Different spices need different times for toasting. Here are the time ranges for the most common Indian spices:
- Mustard seeds: 2-5 minutes, until fragrant and lightly browned. Remove from heat when the seeds start to pop.
- Coriander seeds: 3-4 minutes, until you can start seeing a light golden-brown tinge to the seeds and they start "dancing" and popping in the pan.
- Fennel seeds: 3-4 minutes.
- Caraway seeds: 2-3 minutes.
- Cardamom seeds: 2-3 minutes (remove from pods first).
- Cumin seeds: 30 seconds to 1 minute, until your nose gets a whiff of smoke and fragrance.

Basics

Nutrition Per Serving Serving Size: 1 tablespoon, 20 calories, 1g total fat, 0g sat fat, 0mg cholesterol, 0mg sodium, 3g carbohydrates, 2g fiber, 0g total sugar, 1g protein

Tip or fact: You definitely can use pre-ground spices and blend them together. However, you'll have much more fragrance when you dry-roast whole seeds and then grind them yourself.

Shopping list

Seasonings and Spices
- ☐ coriander seeds
- ☐ cumin seeds
- ☐ caraway seeds
- ☐ fennel seeds
- ☐ yellow mustard seeds

Mango Salad Dressing
by Jyl Steinback

Easy | **Gluten Free** | **16 Servings**

This is going to be a staple in your fridge. It's that good!

Ingredients
2 c mango, cut in chunks
½ c lime juice
⅓ c orange juice
⅓ c cider vinegar
1 tsp ground ginger

Directions
1. Gather ingredients.
2. Combine all ingredients in a food processor or blender and blend until smooth.
3. Refrigerate several hours or overnight before serving.

Nutrition Per Serving Serving Size: 2 tablespoons, 20 calories, 0g total fat, 0g sat fat, 0mg sodium, 4g carbohydrate, 0g fiber, 3g total sugar, 0g protein

Storage: Store in an airtight glass container in the refrigerator for 5-7 days.

Tip or fact: When the mango is green the amount of vitamin C is higher, as it ripens the amount of beta carotene (vitamin A) increases.

Shopping list

Produce
☐ 2 lbs mangos
☐ 3 limes
☐ lime juice

Packaged goods
☐ 3 oz. cider vinegar

Refrigerator or Freezer
☐ 6 oz. orange juice

Seasonings and spices
☐ ground ginger

One Flax Egg

by Ashley Arpel Greenwald

Easy | Kid Friendly | Gluten Free | 1 Serving

Quite possibly one of the greatest egg substitutes around! Flax eggs are a great source of moisture for baked goods and cakes!

Ingredients

1 Tbsp flaxseed meal
3 Tbsp water, room temperature

Directions

1. Gather ingredients.
2. Mix flaxseed meal and water together in a small bowl.
3. Let mixture sit for 5 minutes before using.
4. Double recipe to create 2 flax eggs, triple for 3 flax eggs, etc.

Nutrition Per Serving Serving Size: 1 flax egg, 30 calories, 2g total fat, 0g saturated fat, 0mg sodium, 3g carbohydrate, 2g fiber, 0g sugar, 2g protein

Ingredient Swaps: Replace flaxseed meal with chia seeds for a thicker egg substitute.

Tip or fact: Loaded with fiber and omega-3 fatty acids, flaxseeds have been known to reduce inflammation in the arteries and improve digestive health.

Basics

Shopping list

Packaged goods
☐ flaxseed meal

Pita Crisp Crackers

by Jyl Steinback

Easy | **18 Servings**

Perfect crispy dippers!

Ingredients

6 loaves of whole wheat pita
  bread, 4 in. each
cooking spray, optional
seasonings of choice, see below

Directions

1. Preheat oven to 350°F.
2. Gather ingredients.
3. Line baking sheets with foil and spray with cooking spray.
4. Cut pita breads into 8 wedges.
5. Split pieces (12-16 wedges per pita).
6. Arrange pita wedges in single lawyer on baking sheets.
7. Spray lightly with cooking spray and sprink with 1-2 tablespoons of your choice of seasoning.
8. Bake 10-15 minutes, until crisp and golden brown.
9. Pita wedges can be served immediately.

Nutrition Per Serving 40 calories, 1g total fat, 0g sat fat, 75mg sodium, 8g carbohydrate, 0g fiber, 0g sugar, 1g protein

Tip or fact: Choose from a variety of flavors for pita crisps: Italian—sprinkle with Italian seasoning; Southwest—sprinkle with cumin and cayenne pepper; garlic—sprinkle with garlic powder

Shopping list

Packaged goods
- 6 loaves whole wheat pita, 4 in. each
- cooking spray, optional

Seasonings and Spices
- Italian seasoning, optional
- cumin, optional
- cayenne pepper, optional
- garlic powder, optional

Red Pepper Vinaigrette
by Jyl Steinback

Easy | Gluten Free | 8 Servings

Roasted red pepper brings a richness to this Italian style dressing.

Ingredients
½ c water
¼ c red wine vinegar
2 tsp dried basil
1 tsp garlic powder
15 oz. roasted red peppers,
   drained

Directions
1. Gather ingredients.
2. Combine all ingredients in a food processor or blender and process until smooth.

Nutrition Per Serving 15 calories, 0g total fat, 0g sat fat, 310mg sodium, 2g carbohydrate, 0g fiber, 2g sugar, 0g protein

Storage: Store in airtight glass container in the fridge.

Tip or fact: To reduce the sodium, consider making your own roasted red peppers!

Basics

Shopping list

Canned Goods
☐ 15 oz. jar roasted red peppers

Packaged goods
☐ red wine vinegar

Seasonings and Spices
☐ dried basil
☐ garlic powder

Tahini-Chickpea Dressing
by Nele Liivlaid

Easy | **Gluten Free** | **8 Servings**

Here's an easy and quick salad dressing with tahini and chickpeas that effortlessly makes your meals complete. You just need a blender and 10 minutes.

Ingredients

8.5 oz. chickpeas, unsalted or no salt added
3 Tbsp tahini, unsalted or no added oil
3 Tbsp lemon juice
½ tsp garlic powder
1½ tsp turmeric
½ tsp mustard seeds, crushed
¼ tsp black salt
⅛ tsp Himalayan salt
4 Tbsp nutritional yeast
2 tsp date sugar, optional
1 c water

Directions

1. Gather ingredients.
2. Blend all ingredients in a blender or use immersion blender.

Nutrition Per Serving 70 calories, 4g total fat, 0g sat fat, 0mg cholesterol, 70mg sodium, 7g carbohydrates, 3g fiber, 2g total sugar, 4g protein

Storage: Store in an airtight glass container in the fridge for up to 4 days.

Tip or fact: If you don't have tahini, use any additive-free nut or seed butter, e.g. peanut butter, sunflower seed butter, almond butter, cashew butter, hazelnut butter.

Shopping list

Produce
☐ 2 lemons

Packaged
☐ tahini
☐ nutritional yeast
☐ date sugar, optional

Canned
☐ 8.5 oz. can chickpeas, unsalted or no added salt

Seasonings and Spices
☐ garlic powder
☐ turmeric
☐ mustard seeds
☐ black salt
☐ Himalayan salt

Tofu Sour Cream

by Caryn Dugan

Easy | **Gluten Free** | **6 Servings**

Sour cream for all of your sour cream needing dishes. You'll never know the difference.

Ingredients

12 oz. package of medium firmness silken tofu
¼ lemon, juiced
1 Tbsp red wine vinegar
½ tsp garlic powder
½ tsp onion powder

Directions

1. Gather ingredients.
2. In a blender, mix all ingredients well.
3. Chill for at least one hour and serve.

Nutrition Per Serving 40 calories, 2g total fat, 0g sat fat, 0mg cholesterol, 0mg sodium, 2g carbohydrates, 1g fiber, 0g total sugar, 4g protein

Storage: Store in an airtight glass container in the fridge for 3-4 days.

Basics

Shopping list

Produce
☐ 1 lemon

Packaged
☐ 12 oz. medium firmness silken tofu
☐ red wine vinegar

Seasonings and Spices
☐ garlic powder
☐ onion powder

Whipped Coconut Cream

by Laura Salyer

Easy | **Kid Friendly** | **Gluten Free** | **4 Servings**

A refreshing, cool snack topper for summer days.

Ingredients

14 oz. canned full-fat coconut milk
½ tsp vanilla extract

Directions

1. Gather ingredients.
2. Refrigerate the canned coconut milk for at least 6 hours. Overnight is preferable to separate the cream from liquid.
3. Carefully remove can from fridge and opening without shaking or turning upside down. This could cause the liquid and cream to mix again and you'll have to start over.
4. Scoop the solid coconut cream and place in a medium mixing bowl or standing mixer.
5. Whip the cream at low speed until creamy, then increase to high speed for 5 minutes or until fluffy and holding soft peaks.
6. Refrigerate until ready for use.

Nutrition Per Serving 100 calories, 11g total fat, 9g sat fat, 5mg sodium, 1g carbohydrate, 0g fiber, 0g sugar, 1g protein

Storage: Although it is best immediately after whipping, the coconut whipped cream will keep in the refrigerator for 3 days in an airtight glass container. Try leftovers on pie, brownies, on top of bananas, or with granola!

Tip or fact: Do your best to keep any liquid out of the coconut cream as it will hinder the whipping process. However, I do suggest saving it to use as a delicious base for smoothies or shakes, or you can even drink it by itself!

Shopping list

Packaged
☐ vanilla extract

Canned
☐ 14 oz. canned full-fat coconut milk

Parsley

Amazing
Appetizers &
Snacks

Avocado Corn Tostadas

by Laura Salyer

Easy | **Kid Friendly** | **Gluten Free** | **4-6 Servings**

Guacamole-topped corn tortillas.

Ingredients

Homemade Corn Tortillas:

2 c masa harina (corn flour, not corn starch)
½ tsp salt
1 ½ c warm water

Avocado Topping:

2-3 ripe avocados
1 medium tomato, diced
½ medium red onion, diced
1-2 cloves garlic, minced
½ c cilantro, chopped
1 lemon, juiced
Pink Himalayan sea salt
Pepper to taste
Red pepper flakes, optional
Fresh lettuce or microgreens, optional
Pickled onions, optional

Shopping list

Produce
☐ 2-3 ripe avocados
☐ 1 medium tomato
☐ 1 medium red onion
☐ 1-2 cloves garlic
☐ 1 bunch cilantro
☐ 1 lemon
☐ fresh lettuce, optional
☐ microgreens, optional

Packaged
☐ masa harina
☐ pickled onions, optional

Seasoning and spices
☐ pink Himalayan sea salt
☐ pepper
☐ red pepper flakes

Directions

Instructions for Corn Tortillas:

1. Add 2 cups of masa harina, ½ teaspoon of salt, and 1 cup of warm water to a large bowl and stir until water is absorbed.
2. Slowly add the remaining water until dough forms.
3. Knead the dough into a ball. Use more water if dry or more corn flour if too sticky.
4. Separate dough into golf-ball-sized portions and flatten using a tortilla press or any flat-bottomed dish lined with parchment paper to avoid sticking.
5. The tortillas should be approximately 4 inches in diameter.
6. Heat a skillet to medium-high heat and add a tortilla, flipping after 10 seconds.
7. Cook each side for 1-2 minutes or until light brown spots are forming.
8. Continue cooking the rest of the tortillas.

Instructions for Avocado Topping:

1. Combine the pitted and peeled avocados in a large bowl with diced tomato, onion, garlic, and cilantro.
2. Sprinkle with pepper, to taste.
3. Add fresh lemon juice and mix well.
4. Scoop guacamole onto tortillas and top with red pepper flakes, lettuce or microgreens, pickled onions, sliced cherry tomatoes, your favorite salsa, or anything else you might like.
5. Serve immediately as tortillas lose their crispness after topping.

Nutrition Per Serving 310 calories, 15g total fat, 2g sat fat, 240mg sodium, 40g total carbohydrates, 10g fiber, 2g total sugar, 7g protein

Ingredient Swaps: If you cannot find masa harina at your grocery store, feel free to use store-bought corn (or even flour) tortillas. I love the taste of freshly made, still-warm corn tortillas, but any premade ones should do. If using store-bought, simply heat the tortillas in a skillet until browned and crispy.

Storage: Store any extra cooked tortillas in an airtight glass container in the fridge for up to a week.

Tip or fact: These guacamole-topped corn tostadas are my version of a classic side dish or snack often enjoyed in Mexico and other parts of Latin America.

"Cheese" Fondue

by Sharon Palmer

Medium	Gluten Free	8 Servings

Fondue is traditionally made with cheese, but that doesn't mean plant-powered eaters have to skip this tradition altogether. Yellow, waxy potatoes are used to create a healthy, plant-based "cheesy" fondue perfect for dipping with vegetables, tofu, and bread cubes.

Ingredients

1 lb. small yellow potatoes (Yukon gold, fingerling), peeled and quartered

2 medium carrots, chopped

1 yellow onion, diced

2 cloves garlic, minced

2 Tbsp ground flax

½ c reserved potato water

½ c unsweetened, plain plant-based milk

¼ tsp white pepper

¼ tsp turmeric

Pinch nutmeg

2 Tbsp nutritional yeast

2 Tbsp Dijon mustard

salt, to taste

Directions

1. Gather ingredients.
2. Place potatoes and carrots in medium covered pot, cover with water and cook for 10 minutes until tender.
3. Drain, reserving 1/2 cup of water and place cooked vegetables in a blender container.
4. Add onions and garlic to a large skillet. Sauté for 8 minutes until tender.
5. Add onions and garlic to the blender container.
6. In the same skillet (don't clean), add flax and broth. Stir with a whisk over medium heat.
7. Stir in reserved potato water and plant-based milk until smooth.
8. Add pepper, turmeric, nutmeg, nutrional yeast, and mustard. Heat until thickened and bubbly.
9. Pour mixture into the blender container and process until smooth. Adjust with salt as desired.
10. Transfer fondue mixture to a fondue pot and heat until bubbly.
11. Serve with dipping options like fresh vegetables and tofu.

Apps & Snacks

Nutrition Per Serving 70 calories, 0.5g total fat, 0g sat fat, 0mg cholesterol, 110mg sodium, 15g carbohydrates, 3g fiber, 3g total sugar, 3g protein

Tip or fact: Serve this fondue with your favorite plant-powered dipping items such as: cubed tofu, bell pepper chunks or strips, mushrooms, broccoli florets, cauliflower florets, cucumber slices, asparagus spears, snow peas.

Shopping list

Produce
- 1 lb. small yellow potatoes
- 2 medium carrots
- 1 yellow onion
- 2 cloves garlic

Packaged
- ground flax

Refrigerated or Froz.en
- unsweetened plain plant-based milk

Seasonings and Spices
- turmeric
- nutmeg
- nutritional yeast
- Dijon mustard
- Salt

Egg Salad

by Nele Liivlaid

| Easy | Gluten Free | 4 Servings |

This gluten free plant-based egg salad sandwich is super easy and quick to make as you'll only need one bowl, a fork and 10 minutes of your time.

Ingredients

8.5 oz can unsalted chickpeas
1 medium avocado
2 Tbsp lemon juice
½ tsp turmeric
¾ tsp Indian black salt
½ tsp crushed mustard seeds
½ tsp garlic powder
2 Tbsp nutritional yeast
4 Tbsp plain plant yogurt
black pepper, to taste

Directions

1. Gather ingredients.
2. Rinse and drain the chickpeas.
3. In a bowl or on a plate, mash the chickpeas with the avocado using a fork or a potato masher.
4. Mix in lemon juice and add turmeric, black salt, pepper, mustard seeds and garlic powder. Mix well before adding in nutritional yeast and yogurt. Make it creamier or leave it coarser – it's up to you.
5. Give it a final stir. Taste and adjust if necessary.
6. Spread it on a slice of bread or cracker or top your salad with this yummy egg-flavored creaminess.

Nutrition Per Serving 140 calories, 7g total fat, 1g sat fat, 460mg sodium, 15g carbohydrate, 4g fiber, 3g sugar, 6g protein

Tip or fact: Plant-based folks love black salt (also known as Himalayan black salt) as a replacement for eggs as it has this pungent smell. The sulfur compounds cause the salt to smell like hard-boiled or rotten eggs. But don't worry, the finished dish won't smell like rotten eggs at all!

Shopping list

Produce
☐ 1 avocado
☐ 1 lemon

Packaged
☐ 8.5 oz. can unsalted chickpeas
☐ plain plant yogurt
☐ nutritional yeast

Seasonings and spices
☐ Turmeric
☐ Indian black salt
☐ mustard seeds
☐ garlic powder
☐ black pepper

Guacamole

by Carolina Maturana

| Easy | Gluten Free | 4-5 Servings |

This mouth-watering guacamole is creamy, flavorful, just a bit spicy and great with veggies, crackers or chips.

Ingredients

4 ripe avocados
¼ c red onions, finely chopped
¼ c cilantro, finely chopped
½ serrano pepper, minced
1 lime, juiced
¾ tsp pink Himalayan salt

Directions

1. Gather ingredients.
2. In a medium-size bowl, smash avocados, leaving a couple of chunks if you'd like.
3. Add onions, cilantro, salt, serrano peppers and combine well.
4. Add lime juice and mix well.

Nutrition Per Serving 260 calories, 24g total fat, 3.5g sat fat, 240mg sodium, 15g carbohydrate, 11g fiber, 2g sugar, 3g protein

Ingredient Swaps: You can use 1/3 or less jalapeño pepper instead of serrano peppers.

Storage: It's best to eat right away, but can be store for one day in an airtight glass container. To avoid its getting dark, use cotton wrap on the guacamole making sure there's no contact with air and cover using the lid.

Tip or fact: Want to know if your avocado is overripe? Check under the stem. Peel it back. If it is green, the avocado is good. If you find brown underneath, the avocado is likely overripe and you will find brown spots inside the fruit.

Apps & Snacks

Shopping list

Produce
☐ 4 ripe avocados
☐ 1 medium red onion
☐ 1 bunch cilantro
☐ 1 serrano pepper
☐ 1 lime

Seasoning and spices
☐ pink Himalayan salt

Heart of Palm Salsa

by Laura Salyer

| Easy | Gluten Free | 2-3 Servings |

Chunky salsa dip packed with fresh veggies.

Ingredients

15 oz. jarred heart of palm
1 English cucumber, roughly diced
1 c fresh cherry tomatoes, chopped
2 green onions, finely chopped
1 lemon, juiced
⅓ c fresh cilantro, roughly chopped
1 jalapeño pepper, finely chopped
Pink Himalayan sea salt to taste
1 pinch red pepper flakes

Directions

1. Gather ingredients.
2. Drain and rinse the hearts of palm, then roughly chop.
3. Add hearts of palm to a medium bowl with the diced tomatoes, cucumber, green onion, jalapeño, and lemon juice.
4. Toss to combine.
5. Add cilantro and red pepper flakes.
6. Serve with escarole, crostini, tortilla chips, or crackers.

Nutrition Per Serving 60 calories, 0g total fat, 0g sat fat, 570mg sodium, 11g total carbohydrates, 3g fiber, 5g total sugar, 4g protein

Ingredient Swaps: In this recipe, the jalapeño and red pepper flakes are optional, but they add a nice heat to the salsa. Also, if you do not like the flavor of cilantro, you may wish to swap it for fresh parsley or leave it out altogether. As for the cucumber, I prefer to use English cucumbers to regular ones. Unlike other cucumbers, the English breed generally has a wax-free skin, a limited amount of or smaller sized seeds, and they are much less bitter. However, if you have trouble finding English cucumbers, you may substitute regular ones in its place.

Storage: This salsa is best served immediately, but you may store it in an airtight glass container for up to 24 hours. Any longer and the tomato will begin to lose its flavor.

Tip or fact: When preparing the jalapeño, it is best to wear gloves to protect your skin from capsaicin burns. If you do not have any, you may want to use reusable bags or thick towels to cover your hand holding the pepper. Avoid the seeds as they contain the highest concentration of heat. Also, you may want to pulse the ingredients in a food processor depending on what consistency of salsa you generally prefer.

Shopping list

Produce
- [ ] 1 lemon
- [ ] 1 bunch cilantro
- [ ] 1 jalapeño pepper
- [ ] 2 green onions
- [ ] 1 cucumber
- [ ] cherry tomatoes

Packaged
- [ ] 15 oz. jarred heart of palm

Seasoning and spices
- [ ] Pink Himalayan sea salt
- [ ] red pepper flakes

Heirloom Tomato Olive Bruschetta
by Carolina Maturana

Easy | Gluten Free | 4 Servings

This bruschetta recipe is so colorful and flavorful. Great for parties or a healthy snack.

Ingredients

3 large or 4 medium size heirloom tomatoes

2 cloves garlic, minced

¼ c fresh Italian basil, finely chopped

½ c black olives, finely chopped

pink Himalayan salt, to taste

black pepper, to taste

fresh Italian basil leaves, garnish

Directions

1. Gather ingredients
2. Wash and dice heirloom tomatoes and put them in a mixing bowl.
3. Add garlic, chopped basil, olives, salt and pepper and combine well.
4. Serve on flax crackers and garnish with basil leaves and olives.

Nutrition Per Serving 45 calories, 2g total fat, 0g sat fat, 130mg sodium, 6g total carbohydrate, 2g fiber, 3g total sugar, 1g protein

Ingredient Swaps: You can also use green or kalamata olives. For more flavor add chopped fresh oregano.

Storage: Store in the an airtight glass container for up to 4 days in the fridge.

Tip or fact: Try using different colored heirloom tomatoes to bring even more color to this dish.

Apps & Snacks

Shopping list

Produce
- [ ] 3-4 medium size heirloom tomatoes
- [ ] 2 cloves garlic
- [ ] fresh italian basil

Canned
- [ ] black olives

Seasoning and spices
- [ ] himalayan salt
- [ ] black pepper

Hummus
by Carolina Maturana

Easy | Gluten Free | 2 Servings

This simple yet scrumptious hummus recipe takes only minutes to make but is delicious for days!

Ingredients

1 clove garlic, crushed
2 tsp cumin
1 Tbsp tahini
1 can garbanzo beans, keep liquid aside

Directions

1. In a blender or food processor, combine all ingredients.
2. Blend on low speed.
3. Slowly add garbanzo bean liquid until desired consistency.

Nutrition Per Serving 110 calories, 3.5g total fat, 0g sat fat, 430mg sodium, 16g total carbohydrates, 4g fiber, 3g total sugar, 5g protein

Ingredient Swaps: To reduce sodium, consider using dry garbanzo beans. Recipe p. 6.

Storage: Store for 5 days in the fridge.

Tip or fact: Make sure tahini is mixed before using so it has a creamy consistency.

Shopping list

Produce
☐ garlic

Packaged goods
☐ tahini

Canned
☐ 1 can garbanzo beans (or chickpeas)

Seasoning and spices
☐ cumin

Mississippi Caviar

by Sharon Palmer

| Easy | Gluten Free | 12 Servings |

Here's one of my favorite, delicious, plant-based recipes. Bon appetit!

Ingredients

15 oz. cooked black-eyed peas, rinsed, drained (recipe p. 6)

15 oz. cooked black beans, rinsed, drained (recipe p. 6)

15 oz. low sodium canned corn, drained

2 small plum tomatoes, diced

1 medium bell pepper (green, red, orange, or yellow), diced

3 cloves garlic, minced

1 small jalapeño pepper, finely diced

½ c fresh cilantro, chopped

1 small onion, diced

1 lemon, juiced and zested

2 Tbsp white vinegar

¼ tsp paprika

½ tsp oregano

½ tsp ground cumin

Directions

1. Gather ingredients.
2. Mix together peas, beans, corn, tomatoes, bell pepper, jalapeño, cilantro and onion in a medium bowl.
3. Whisk together lemon juice and zest, vinegar, paprika, oregano, cumin and salt. Drizzle over the vegetable mixture.
4. Toss together.
5. Chill until serving time.

Nutrition Per Serving 120 calories, 1g total fat, 0g sat fat, 75mg sodium, 23g carbohydrate, 7g fiber, 4g sugar, 7g protein

Tip or fact: Using dried beans versus canned reduces sodium dramatically. If you are in a time crunch, use canned beans, but look for unsalted or low sodium.

Apps & Snacks

Shopping list

Produce
- 2 small plum tomatoes
- 1 medium bell pepper
- garlic
- 1 small jalapeño pepper
- 1 bunch cilantro
- 1 small onion
- 1 lemon

Packaged
- white vinegar
- dried black-eyed peas
- dried black beans

Canned
- 15 oz. can low sodium cooked corn

Seasonings and Spices
- paprika
- dried oregano
- ground cumin

Nutty Pesto Dip

by Laura Salyer

Easy | **Gluten Free** | **8 Servings**

Creamy and rich this pesto dip pops with the nutty flavor of walnuts and pine nuts. Serve as a dip or yummy spread for a sandwich.

Ingredients

½ c fresh basil leaves
1 c arugula
2 cloves garlic, peeled
½ c pine nuts
½ c walnuts
1 c Great Northern beans, cooked and drained (recipe p. 6)
⅓ c water

Directions

1. Gather ingredients.
2. Add the basil, arugula, garlic, beans, pine nuts and walnuts to a food processor.
3. Slowly add water to the mixture until it becomes creamy.
4. Serve with whole wheat baguette slices or raw or steamed vegetables.

Nutrition Per Serving 270 calories, 19g total fat, 2g saturated fat, 30mg sodium, 19g total carbohydrate, 8g fiber, 1g total sugar, 8g protein

Ingredient Swaps: Any type of white bean would work for this recipe.

Storage: Store in an airtight glass container in the refrigerator for up to a week.

Tip or fact: This pesto also makes an amazing spread on sandwiches or – my favorite – broiled tomato toasts. To make toasts, set your oven broiler to low and place thick slices of sourdough, seeded, or whole wheat bread on a baking sheet. Spread a generous layer of pesto on bread, then top with sliced tomato or avocado. Broil until edges are golden brown and bubbly, then enjoy sprinkled with red pepper flakes and sea salt.

Shopping list

Produce
□ bunch fresh basil
□ arugula
□ garlic

Packaged
□ pine nuts
□ walnuts

Canned
□ 1 can Great Northern Beans

Ooh La La Nachos

by Kelley Williamson

Easy | **Gluten Free** | **2 Servings**

There is no better day than a day with nachos. This is a favorite of many who are looking for a savory dish that is filling.

Ingredients

6 corn tortillas (6 inch round), cut into triangles
1 Tbsp black olives, sliced
½ avocado, diced
1 medium tomato, rough chopped
½ small yellow onion, rough chopped
1 Tbsp juice from lime
1 Tbsp fresh cilantro, roughly chopped
½ c canned black beans
1 Tbsp canned green chiles

Directions

1. Preheat oven to 350°F.
2. Gather ingredients.
3. Slice corn tortillas into triangles and spread out on a baking sheet.
4. Bake for 10-15 minutes or until a nice golden brown.
5. Chop the tomato and onion.
6. Mix together in a large bowl. Add the lime juice to the salsa and mix well. Top with chopped cilantro.
7. Slice the black olives and set aside.
8. In a small saucepan, heat beans, green chiles, and salsa on low.
9. Dice the avocado.
10. To assemble, you can place in small serving dishes and add each ingredient as wanted or you can place baked chips on a plate and top with beans, avocado, salsa and the rest of the ingredients. Enjoy.

Nutrition Per Serving 320 calories, 10g total fat, 1.5g sat fat, 240mg sodium, 54g carbohydrate, 5g fiber, 4g sugar, 9g protein

Apps & Snacks

Ingredient Swaps: Add any ingredient that you would like to your nachos.

Storage: Store the extra chips in a large glass container with a lid.

Shopping list

Produce
☐ 1 tomato
☐ 1 small onion
☐ 1 lime
☐ 1 avocado

Packaged
☐ 1 bag corn tortillas

Canned
☐ 1 can black olives
☐ 1 can black beans

Roasted Red Pepper Hummus
by Jyl Steinback

Easy	Kid Friendly	Gluten Free	5-6 Servings	

Delicious and refreshing hummus with fresh vegetables

Ingredients

- ½ c roasted red peppers, in jar with no oil
- 2 Tbsp tahini
- ½ tsp sea salt
- 1 Tbsp parsley, fresh or dried
- 1 15oz. can low sodium garbanzo beans, rinsed and drained
- ¼ c celery, sliced into sticks
- ¼ c carrots, sliced into sticks

Directions

1. Gather ingredients.
2. Add all ingredients to a food processor and blend until smooth.
3. Using a spatula, scrape all the hummus out of the food processor bowl and place in a bowl.
4. Slice fresh vegetables and place in a circle around the bowl. Enjoy.

Nutrition Per Serving 110 calories, 4g total fat, 0.5g sat fat, 350mg sodium, 14g carbohydrate, 5g fiber, 3g sugar, 5g protein

Ingredient Swaps: Add any type of flavors to the hummus base. You can add basil or different herbs, nuts, sesame seeds, etc.

Storage: Store in a glass bowl with a lid in the refrigerator.

Tip or fact: Make hummus (two or three different flavors) on a Sunday and chop your vegetables and enjoy all week. You can also use the hummus on a whole wheat wrap and add the vegetables.

Shopping list

Produce
- ☐ celery
- ☐ carrots

Packaged
- ☐ tahini

Canned
- ☐ jar roasted red peppers with no oil
- ☐ 15 oz. can low sodium garbanzo beans

Seasonings and Spices
- ☐ sea salt
- ☐ parsley

Summer Bruschetta

by Carolina Maturana

| Easy | Kid Friendly | Gluten Free | 6 Servings |

This summer bruschetta is very simple yet delicious.

Ingredients

- 2 c sugar plum or cherry tomatoes halved
- 1 c organic strawberries, quartered
- 1 c arugula, chopped
- ¼ c basil
- 1 Tbsp date syrup or coconut nectar
- 3 Tbsp balsamic vinegar
- 1 Tbsp or more of toasted pecan pieces, to garnish
- 1 Tbsp balsamic glaze, to garnish

Directions

1. Gather all ingredients.
2. In a small bowl, combine 3 tablespoons of balsamic vinegar with date syrup (or coconut nectar) and salt.
3. In a large bowl, gently combine tomatoes, strawberries, basil, arugula and the mix of sweetener and balsamic vinegar.
4. Serve on flax crackers, drizzle with balsamic glaze and top with toasted pecan pieces.

Nutrition Per Serving 50 calories, 1g total fat, 0g saturated fat, 135mg sodium, 9g total carbohydrate, 1g fiber, 7g total sugar, 1g protein

Tip or fact: To make balsamic reduction (balsamic glaze) heat a small pot and add balsamic vinaigrette. Simmer on low continuously stirring until it reduces to 70%.

Apps & Snacks

Shopping list

Produce
- ☐ sugar plum or cherry tomatoes
- ☐ strawberries
- ☐ arugula
- ☐ basil

Packaged
- ☐ balsamic vinegar
- ☐ date syrup or coconut nectar
- ☐ pecans

Watermelon Pizzas

by Laura Salyer

Easy | **Gluten Free** | **4 Servings**

A refreshing, cool snack for summer days.

Ingredients

1 Tbsp whipped coconut cream (recipe p. 14)
1 small or personal watermelon
½ c blackberries
½ c blueberries
5 mint leaves, en chiffonade
½ c walnuts
3 Tbsp slivered almonds
2 Tbsp raw cacao nibs
2 Tbsp Goji berries
agave nectar or maple syrup, optional

Directions

1. Gather ingredients.
2. Set oven to low broil and spread walnuts evenly on a baking sheet. Place walnuts on the top rack and watch closely to avoid burning.
3. Remove when walnuts are sizzling, fragrant and golden-brown. Chop roughly to prepare for pizzas.
4. Prepare whipped coconut cream recipe from p. 14. Refrigerate until ready to use.
5. Wash and slice off the ends of both sides of the watermelon to make flat. Cut the watermelon in half lengthwise, then again to quarter.
6. Lay the quartered sections on their rind and slice approximately 4-6 triangle-shaped pieces into each quarter.
7. Arrange triangles flat on a serving tray and cover with coconut whipped cream, berries, nuts, mint and a light drizzle of agave nectar or maple syrup, if desired.

Nutrition Per Serving 290 calories, 24g total fat, 12g sat fat, 15mg sodium, 18g total carbohydrate, 5g fiber, 9g sugar, 5g protein. Without Whipped Coconut Cream: 190 calories, 13g total fat, 2.5g sat fat, 10mg sodium, 17g total carbohydrate, 5g fiber, 9g total sugar, 4g protein

Ingredient Swaps: If you are allergic to coconut, or you simply do not enjoy the taste, feel free to try using a dairy-free yogurt or other creamy, plant-based alternative. Also, certain stores now sell premade coconut and soy milk whipped cream. Look for them next to the regular whipped cream or in the frozen dessert section.

Storage: Although it is best immediately after whipping, the coconut whipped cream will keep in the refrigerator for 3 days in an airtight glass container.

Tip or fact: En chiffonade refers to a specific way to cut an herb or vegetable as a garnish. For the mint in this recipe, cut the leaves into very thin ribbons.

Shopping list

Produce
☐ 1 small or personal watermelon
☐ blackberries
☐ blueberries
☐ 5 mint leaves

Packaged
☐ walnuts
☐ slivered almonds
☐ raw cacao nibs
☐ Goji berries
☐ Agave nectar or pure maple syrup

Wonderful Tortillas

by Nele Liivlaid

Easy | **Gluten Free** | **14 Servings**

These Mediterranean-inspired, gluten free tortillas are made with soaked buckwheat and are perfect for making wraps, tacos, and more!

Ingredients

- 7 oz unroasted buckwheat groats
- 8.1 oz water
- 1 Tbsp + 1 tsp ground chia seeds
- 1 tsp dried oregano
- ¼ tsp garlic powder
- ¼ tsp Himalayan salt
- dash black pepper
- 1½ Tbsp nutritional yeast
- 2-3 unsalted sundried tomato halves

Directions

1. Gather all ingredients.
2. Soak buckwheat groats overnight or at least 4-6 hours.
3. Rinse and drain the buckwheat groats well before pouring into regular or immersion blender.
4. Add all the other ingredients (except tomatoes) and process the ingredients into smooth batter.
5. Blend in the tomato halves – if you use the dry ones, soak them in hot water for 5-10 minutes. Whether you prefer them fully incorporated or with some chunks is up to you! Don't leave too big chunks though as they'd stick out from your thin tortillas.
6. For Frying: Pour 1-2 tablespoons of batter (depending how large tortillas you want to make) onto hot non-stick pan and spread it out into as thin circle as you can. Once it's cooked on top, flip the tortilla over and fry for another minute or so. Place the tortilla on cooling rack and repeat until the batter is finished. Swipe the pan clean with slightly oiled kitchen paper between the tortillas. You can use coconut oil, olive oil or avocado oil.
7. For Baking: Heat oven to 375°F. Pour some batter on a baking sheet lined with parchment paper and shape your tortillas with circular movements. How round-shaped you get them depends on your skills and practice. Bake them for 7-8 minutes and let cool before you try to separate them from the paper – you'll need some patience, but they definitely come off in the end.

Apps & Snacks

Nutrition Per Serving 60 calories, 1g total fat, 0g sat fat, 0mg sodium, 11g carbohydrates, 2g fiber, 0g sugar, 2g protein

Ingredient Swap: Use 2 tablespoons of ground flax seeds instead in chia seeds.

Tip or fact: Always grind your own chia seeds and store in a sealed container or glass jar in the fridge.

Shopping list

Packaged
- ☐ unroasted buckwheat groats
- ☐ ground chia seeds
- ☐ nutritional yeast
- ☐ unsalted sundried tomato halves

Seasonings and Spices
- ☐ dried oregano
- ☐ garlic powder
- ☐ Himalayan salt
- ☐ black pepper

Parsley

Thyme

Delicious
Dips, Spreads
& Sauces

Eggplant Caviar

by Jyl Steinback

Easy | **Gluten Free** | **6 Servings**

Creamy roasted eggplant. Yum. If you like eggplant, this is your dip.

Ingredients

1 ½ lbs eggplant
3 Tbsp lemon juice
1 ½ tsp garlic powder
¼ tsp cayenne pepper
⅛ tsp black pepper

Directions

1. Preheat oven to 400°F.
2. Gather all ingredients.
3. Wrap whole eggplant(s) in foil, place on baking sheet and bake 1 hour, until very soft.
4. Remove from oven, unwrap and let cool 15 minutes.
5. Cut eggplant in half. Scoop pulp from shell and place in food processor or blender.
6. Add remaining ingredients and process until smooth.
7. Transfer to a bowl, cover and refrigerate 2-4 hours, before serving with pita crisp crackers (recipe p. 10).

Nutrition Per Serving 35 calories, 0g total fat, 0g sat fat, 0mg sodium, 8g carbohydrates, 3g fiber, 4g sugar, 1g protein

Tip or fact: When choosing an eggplant, look for a firm, glossy-skin eggplant that is heavy for its size with a bright, mold-free top. Younger, smaller eggplants are usually less bitter than larger or older ones. Since eggplants are quite perishable, store them whole in the refrigerator for 2 to 4 days.

Shopping list

Produce
☐ 1 ½ lbs eggplant
☐ 2 lemons

Seasonings and Spices
☐ garlic powder
☐ cayenne pepper
☐ black pepper

Exotic Mango Salsa

by Jyl Steinback

Easy | Gluten Free | 4 Servings

Not just a dipping salsa! Try tossing this refreshingly mango salsa with mixed greens and then sprinkled with toasted macadamia nuts.

Ingredients

2 c mango, peeled, seeded and chopped
¼ c green onions, sliced
¼ c yellow bell pepper, chopped
1 tsp dried basil
2 tsp jalapeño peppers, chopped
2 Tbsp lime juice

Directions

1. Gather all ingredients.
2. Combine all ingredients in a medium bowl and toss until well mixed.
3. Refrigerate until chilled before serving.

Nutrition Per Serving 60 calories, 0g total fat, 0g sat fat, 0mg sodium, 14g carbohydrates, 1g fiber, 12g sugar, 1g protein

Tip or fact: Mangoes are one of the most popular fruits in the world, and it is a symbol of love in India.

*Dips &
Sauces*

Shopping list

Produce
☐ 1 mango
☐ 1-2 green onions
☐ 1 small yellow bell pepper
☐ 1 lime
☐ 1 large jalapeño pepper

Seasoning and spices
☐ dried basil

Ginger Pineapple Salsa

by Jyl Steinback

Easy | **Gluten Free** | **6 Servings**

A zing of ginger with the sweetness of pineapple makes this a great pairing with a seasoned pita chip or cracker.

Ingredients

1 ½ c fresh pineapple, chopped
1 c cucumber, chopped
¾ c sweet onion, minced
4 tsp fresh cilantro, chopped
2 Tbsp green chiles, chopped
1 tsp garlic, minced
1 tsp ground ginger
¼ c lemon juice

Directions

1. Gather all ingredients.
2. Combine all ingredients in medium bowl and mix well.
3. Cover and refrigerate at least 2-3 hours or overnight.
4. Serve over chicken or fish, or with baked pita chips or crackers.

Nutrition Per Serving 35 calories, 0g total fat, 0g sat fat, 20mg sodium, 9g carbohydrates, 1g fiber, 6g sugar, 1g protein

Tip or fact: Vidalia and Walla Walla onions, named for the areas they come from, are two of the most popular sweet onions available. Other varieties include the Texas 1015, Imperial, Oso Sweet, Maui, Bermuda, and Italian red.

Shopping list

Produce
☐ pineapple
☐ 1 large cucumber
☐ 1 sweet onion
☐ 1 bunch cilantro
☐ 1 lemon
☐ garlic

Packaged
☐ 4 oz. can chopped green chiles

Seasoning and spices
☐ ground ginger

Hot and Spicy Tomato Salsa by Jyl Steinback

Easy | **Gluten Free** | **16 Servings**

Perfect topper for your burrito. The hint of apple juice adds a little sweetness to the heat.

Ingredients

3 tomatoes, chopped
15 oz. can tomato puree, unsalted
2-3 tsp garlic, minced
4 oz. can chopped green chilies
3 Tbsp onion, chopped
⅓ c unsweetened apple juice
¼ c lemon juice
½-1 tsp cayenne pepper
½ tsp ground black pepper
¼ c fresh cilantro, chopped

Directions

1. Gather all ingredients.
2. In a medium saucepan, combine all ingredients except cilantro.
3. Bring to a boil over high heat. Reduce heat to medium, and cook uncovered for 15 minutes, stirring occasionally.
4. Stir in cilantro.
5. Serve with baked tortilla chips or on top of your burrito.

Nutrition Per Serving 20 calories, 0g total fat, 0g sat fat, 35mg sodium, 5g carbohydrates, 1g fiber, 3g sugar, 1g protein

Storage: Freeze up to 2 months.

Tip or fact: To reduce the heat of this recipe, buy mild green chilis and skip the cayenne pepper. You may want to boost the flavor with a pinch of salt.

Dips & Sauces

Shopping list

Produce
☐ 3 tomatoes
☐ 6 medium garlic cloves
☐ 1 onion
☐ 2 lemons
☐ 1 bunch cilantro

Packaged
☐ 15 oz. can tomato puree, unsalted
☐ 4 oz. can chopped green chiles
☐ apple juice

Seasoning and spices
☐ cayenne pepper
☐ black pepper

Kiwi Pineapple Salsa

by Jyl Steinback

Easy | **Kid Friendly** | **Gluten Free** | **4 Servings**

This is salsa is always a showstopper with its sweet tart and slightly savory flavor. Serve over a wedge of watermelon for a unique side salad.

Ingredients

4 small kiwi fruit, peeled and diced

½ c pineapple, diced

1 mango, diced

¼ c red or green bell pepper, diced

2 Tbsp red onion, diced

¼ c chives, minced

2 c homemade vegetable broth (recipe p. 124)

1 tsp ground black pepper

2 Tbsp scallions, chopped

Directions

1. Gather all ingredients.
2. In medium mixing bowl, combine ingredients and toss together.
3. Cover bowl and refrigerate until chilled.
4. Serve with baked tortilla chips or on top of watermelon wedges as a unique side salad

Nutrition Per Serving 140 calories, 1g total fat, 0g sat fat, 30mg sodium, 33g carbohydrates, 6g fiber, 23g sugar, 3g protein

Tip or fact: Kiwifruit has two times more vitamin C than oranges.

Shopping list

Produce
- ☐ 4 small kiwi
- ☐ 1 small pineapple
- ☐ 1 mango
- ☐ 1 red or green bell pepper
- ☐ 1 small red onion
- ☐ 1 bunch chives
- ☐ 1 scallion
- ☐ vegetable broth ingredients (p. 124)

Seasoning and spices
- ☐ black pepper

Papaya Tomatillo Salsa

by Jyl Steinback

Easy | **Gluten Free** | **4 Servings**

This out of the ordinary salsa combo will be sure to bring smiles.

Ingredients

- 1 large papaya, peeled, seeded and diced
- 2 medium tomatillos, diced
- ½ small red onion, diced
- 2 red jalapeño peppers, seeded and diced
- 4 green onions, diced
- ¼ bunch cilantro, cleaned and chopped
- ¼ c orange juice
- salt, to taste
- black pepper, to taste

Directions

1. Gather all ingredients.
2. Combine all ingredients in a medium bowl and mix well.
3. Serve with pita crisps (recipe p. 10).

Nutrition Per Serving 110 calories, 1g total fat, 0g sat fat, 95mg sodium, 27g carbohydrates, 5g fiber, 18g sugar, 2g protein

Tip or fact: Green jalapeños work too if you can't find red.

Dips & Sauces

Shopping list

Produce
- ☐ 1 large papaya
- ☐ 2 medium tomatillos
- ☐ 1 small red onion
- ☐ 2 red jalapeño peppers
- ☐ 4 green onions
- ☐ 1 bunch cilantro

Refrigerator or Freezer
- ☐ orange juice

Seasoning and spices
- ☐ salt
- ☐ black pepper

Pineapple Salsa
by Carolina Maturana

Easy | **Gluten Free** | **4-5 Servings**

This refreshing salsa is perfect for potlucks and gatherings.

Ingredients

1 pineapple, diced
5 radishes, thinly sliced and quartered
¼ c cilantro, finely chopped
½ serrano pepper, seeded and minced
⅓ small red onion, finely chopped
2 Tbsp lime juice
2-3 Tbsp pumpkin seeds
pink Himalayan salt, to taste
black pepper, to taste

Directions

1. Gather all ingredients.
2. Combine all ingredients and top with pumpkin seeds.
3. Let this recipe sit overnight to develop the flavor.
4. Serve cold with flax crackers or as a salad.

Nutrition Per Serving 120 calories, 2g total fat, 0g sat fat, 45mg sodium, 26g carbohydrates, 3g fiber, 18g sugar, 3g protein

Storage: Store in an airtight glass container in refrigerator for up to 4 days.

Tip or fact: The smaller you cut the ingredients, the easier to serve with crackers. Consider a sliced baguette if you leave the ingredients in larger chunks.

Shopping list

Produce
☐ 1 pineapple
☐ 5 radishes
☐ 1 bunch cilantro
☐ 1 serrano pepper
☐ 1 red onion
☐ 1-2 limes

Packaged
☐ pumpkin seeds

Seasonings and Spices
☐ pink Himalayan salt
☐ black pepper

Sauce Vert

by Apen Sims

Medium | 4-5 Servings

This multipurpose sauce is delicious, plantricious, and nutritious. You can use it as a dip, a spread, or a salad dressing.

Ingredients

¼ c fresh parsley
1 bunch fresh watercress
2 sprigs Tarragon
⅛ c fresh dill
½ Tbsp capers
3 cornichons
1 Tbsp Dijon mustard
2 Tbsp lemon juice
3 Tbsp chervil
¾ c water
pinch salt, to taste
2-4 garlic cloves
1 c raw cashews
2 tsp Dijon mustard

Directions

1. Gather all ingredients.
2. First puree cashews, 2 teaspoons of Dijon mustard, garlic cloves, and ¾ cup of water in a blender.
3. Then add all other ingredients, and water out until desired viscosity.

Nutrition Per Serving 130 calories, 9g total fat, 1.5g sat fat, 140mg sodium, 7g carbohydrates, 2g fiber, 2g sugar, 4g protein

Storage: Store in an airtight glass container in refrigerator.

Tip or fact: Add water carefully. If you just dump it in, it could ruin your emulsion.

Dips & Sauces

Shopping list

Produce
☐ 1 lemon
☐ 1 bunch parsley
☐ 1 bunch fresh watercress
☐ tarragon
☐ dill
☐ chervil
☐ garlic cloves

Packaged
☐ Dijon mustard
☐ cashews
☐ capers
☐ cornichons

Seasoning and spices
☐ salt

Ratatouille Pasta Sauce

by Jyl Steinback

Easy | **Gluten Free** | **4 Servings**

This easy Mediterranean flavored pasta sauce goes so well with al dente pasta or cooked rice and even serves as a dressing on top of salad bowls.

Ingredients

2 Tbsp water
1 large bell pepper, chopped
1 c onion, chopped
1 c celery, chopped
2 medium zucchini, cut into cubes
2 tsp garlic powder
1½ Tbsp dried oregano or Mediterranean herb blend
2 16 oz. cans diced or chopped tomatoes
6 oz. can unsalted tomato paste
¼ c water
black pepper, to taste
1 c fresh basil, chopped
½ Tbsp date sugar, optional

Directions

1. Gather all ingredients.
2. Finely chop bell pepper, celery and onion.
3. In a large skillet or pot, heat 2 tablespoons of water and sauté the chopped veggies for 5 minutes, stirring occasionally.
4. While celery/onion/bell pepper is cooking, cut zucchini into smaller cubes. When the 5 minutes is up, add them into pot and cook covered for additional 3 minutes.
5. Now, add garlic power and oregano/herb blend as well as diced tomatoes, tomato paste and ¼ cup of water and stir well. Bring to boil and let simmer (covered) on low heat for 15 minutes, stirring occasionally.
6. Let the pasta sauce cool a bit before you stir in fresh basil and season with black pepper and date sugar.
7. Serve with your favorite pasta or cooked whole grains (rice, millet, buckwheat, quinoa) and complement with lettuce and/or cooked leafy greens.

Nutrition Per Serving 120 calories, 1g total fat, 0g sat fat, 150mg sodium, 25g carbohydrates, 7g fiber, 15g sugar, 5g protein

Storage: Store in a sealed glass container in refrigerator for up to 4 days. For longer keeping, divide the sauce into smaller portions and freeze for up to a month.

Ingredient Swaps: Use red or yellow onions. For extra flavor opt for fresh garlic instead of powder – when the sauce is done cooking, stir in a few crushed cloves.

Tip or fact: To save time, keep frozen pepper strips on hand; simply grab the amount needed and cook from frozen or thawed state (1 large bell pepper = 3/4 to 1 cup sliced peppers).

Shopping list

Produce
☐ 1 large bell pepper
☐ 1 medium onion
☐ 1 small bunch celery
☐ 2 medium zucchini
☐ fresh basil

Packaged
☐ 1 16 oz. cans diced or crushed tomatoes
☐ 6 oz. can unsalted tomato paste
☐ date sugar

Seasonings and Spices
☐ dried oregano
☐ Mediterranean herb blend
☐ garlic powder

Roasted Red Pepper Dip
by Diane Smith

This roasted red pepper dip is a great base to build on. You can certainly add some green veggies to the dip for added dimension and just to change it up.

Ingredients

- 1 c jarred roasted red peppers in water, rinsed and drained
- 2 slices whole grain bread
- ½ c chopped walnuts
- 1 Tbsp fresh lemon juice
- ½ tsp ground cumin
- 2 cloves garlic, roughly chopped
- ¼ tsp red pepper flakes
- ½ tsp sea salt

Directions

1. Gather all ingredients.
2. Combine all ingredients in a food processor including the bread. Pulse until smooth.
3. Transfer to a serving bowl and serve with pita, crackers or sliced raw vegetables like carrots, jicama, and celery.

Nutrition Per Serving 107 calories, 7g total fat, 0.6g sat fat, 130mg sodium, 9g carbohydrates, 1g fiber, 2g sugar, 2g protein

Tip or fact: Walnuts contain more ALA omega-3 fatty acids than any other nut.

Dips & Sauces

Shopping list

Produce
- ☐ 1 lemon
- ☐ 2 cloves garlic

Packaged
- ☐ 1 jar roasted red peppers in water
- ☐ whole grain bread
- ☐ chopped walnuts

Seasonings and Spices
- ☐ ground cumin
- ☐ red pepper flakes
- ☐ sea salt

Spicy Hummus

by Jyl Steinback

Easy | **Gluten Free** | **6 Servings**

Green chilies add just the right amount of heat to this hummus. Makes a perfect dip or spread it on a sandwich for added spice and nutrition!

Ingredients

15.5 oz. can low sodium garbanzo beans, drained
2 Tbsp low sodium vegetable broth
2 Tbsp water
4 oz. can chopped medium to hot green chiles
¼ tsp garlic powder
1 Tbsp tahini
¼ c lemon juice

Directions

1. Gather all ingredients.
2. Combine garbanzo beans, vegetable broth, water, chiles, garlic powder, tahini and lemon juice in food processor or blender; mix until smooth and creamy (if too thick, add a little more water).
3. Serve with veggies or toasted pita chips or as a spread to add zest to a grilled veggie or hummus sandwich.

Nutrition Per Serving 90 calories, 3g total fat, 0g sat fat, 100mg sodium, 13g carbohydrates, 4g fiber, 3g sugar, 4g protein

Storage: Store in airtight glass container in the refrigerator up to 3 days.

Tip or fact: Capsaicin is the compound in chili peppers that makes your mouth feel hot, but it is also being used in creams and patches to help relieve pain.

Shopping list

Produce
☐ 2 lemons

Packaged
☐ 15.5 oz. can low sodium garbanzo beans
☐ 4 oz. can chopped medium to hot green chiles
☐ low sodium vegetable broth
☐ tahini

Seasonings and Spices
☐ garlic powder

Super Salsa

by Jyl Steinback

Easy | Kid Friendly | Gluten Free | 10 Servings | 📷

We call it Super Salsa because it is packed with fiber rich black beans and corn. Use it as a dip or pour it over leafy greens to make a Super Salad!

Ingredients

2 14.5 oz. cans petite-cut diced tomatoes with jalapeños, drained

14.5 oz. can stewed tomatoes with bell pepper and onion, drained and chopped

5 ½ c boiled black beans (recipe p. 6)

2 ½ c frozen corn kernels, thawed

1 c green onions, chopped

Directions

1. Gather all ingredients.
2. Combine all ingredients in a large bowl. Cover and refrigerate overnight.
3. Serve salsa with baked tortilla chips or sliced raw Zucchini and yellow squash.

Nutrition Per Serving 270 calories, 1g total fat, 0g sat fat, 330mg sodium, 54g carbohydrates, 15g fiber, 5g sugar, 15g protein

Storage: Store in airtight glass container in the refrigerator up to 3 days.

Dips & Sauces

Shopping list

Produce
☐ green onions

Packaged
☐ dry black beans

Refrigerated or Frozen
☐ frozen corn

Sweet N Sour Sauce

by Ashley Arpel Greenwald

Easy | **Gluten Free** | **2 Servings**

Move over plain soy sauce, we're adding some pizzazz to our edamame with this quick and easy Sweet N Sour sauce!

Ingredients

¼ c unsweetened applesauce
2 Tbsp soy sauce
½ Tbsp malt vinegar
1 large lemon, juiced

Directions

1. Gather all ingredients.
2. Place all ingredients into a small saucepan and mix over low heat.
3. Cover and let simmer for 8 minutes, mixing occasionally.
4. Enjoy with your favorite veggies like edamame.

Nutrition Per Serving 25 calories, 0g total fat, 0g sat fat, 580mg sodium, 6g carbohydrates, 0g fiber, 4g sugar, 2g protein

Tip or fact: This is a great sauce for boosting the flavor of steamed vegetables.

Shopping list

Produce
☐ 1 lemon

Packaged
☐ unsweetened applesauce
☐ soy sauce
☐ malt vinegar

Sweet Potato Sauce

by Ashley Arpel Greenwald

| Easy | Gluten Free | 4 Servings |

The perfect pairing to our Sweet Potato Meatballs on p. 216.

Ingredients

½ c sweet potato puree
3 Tbsp unsalted tomato paste
1 Tbsp malt vinegar

Directions

1. Gather all ingredients.
2. Place all ingredients in a small saucepan over low heat and mix.
3. Let simmer on low heat for 10 minutes.
4. Serve immediately. Best paired with Sweet Potato Meatballs (recipe on p. 216).

Nutrition Per Serving 35 calories, 0g total fat, 0g sat fat, 15mg sodium, 8g carbohydrates, 1g fiber, 3g sugar, 1g protein

Ingredient Swap: Swap in fresh sweet potatoes by boiling them and pureeing them after cooled.

Storage: Store in an airtight glass container in the refrigerator.

Tip or fact: North Carolina produces more sweet potatoes than any other state. Sweet potatoes are not the same as yams. Sweet potatoes taper to a point at the ends while yams have rounded ends.

Dips & Sauces

Shopping list

Packaged
☐ sweet potato puree
☐ unsalted tomato paste
☐ malt vinegar

Tomato Dipping Sauce

by Nele Liivlaid

Easy | **Gluten Free** | **3-4 Servings**

This tomato dipping sauce is hearty and yet has a nice and fresh taste – perfect with raw veggies or falafels.

Ingredients

3 Tbsp unsalted oil-free tahini
1½ Tbsp lemon juice
¾ c unsalted tomato puree
¼-½ tsp turmeric
¼ tsp smoked paprika
¼ tsp garlic powder
⅛ tsp Himalayan salt
black pepper, to taste

Directions

1. Gather all ingredients.
2. Blend all ingredients in a blender or use immersion blender.
3. Serve with baked falafels, as dressing over a salad or use as dipping sauce for raw veggies.

Nutrition Per Serving 90 calories, 7g total fat, 1g sat fat, 60mg sodium, 8g carbohydrates, 3g fiber, 3g sugar, 3g protein

Storage: Store in a sealed glass container in the fridge for up to 4 days

Shopping list

Produce
□ 2 lemons

Packaged
□ unsalted oil-free tahini
□ unsalted tomato puree

Seasonings and Spices
□ turmeric
□ smoked paprika
□ garlic powder
□ Himalayan salt
□ black pepper

Touch o' Spice Lentil Dip

by Jyl Steinback

Medium | **Gluten Free** | **8 Servings**

This perfectly spiced creamy lentil dip is also great spread on whole grain toast as side to soup or a snack.

Ingredients

- 1 c dry red lentils
- 1 c chopped red onion
- 2 ½ c water
- 2 tsp curry powder
- 1 tsp whole cumin seeds
- ¾ tsp hot pepper sauce
- 2 tsp crushed garlic

Directions

1. Gather all ingredients.
2. Combine lentils, onion, and water in a medium saucepan. Cover and bring to a boil over high heat. Reduce heat to low and simmer 20 to 25 minutes until lentils are soft.
3. Place lentil mixture in food processor or blender and process until smooth (don't overprocess or it will be runny).
4. In a nonstick skillet add curry powder and cumin seeds and cook over medium heat 1 to 2 minutes.
5. Add hot pepper sauce and crushed garlic. Cook over medium heat for 1 minute.
6. Stir spicy mixture into lentils.

Nutrition Per Serving 100 calories, 0.5g total fat, 0g sat fat, 0mg sodium, 17g carbohydrates, 3g fiber, 1g sugar, 6g protein

Tip or fact: An excellent way to get fiber in your day, lentils help balance blood sugar levels, promote regulatory and may even help lower cholesterol levels.

Dips & Sauces

Shopping list

Produce
- ☐ 1 medium red onion
- ☐ garlic

Packaged
- ☐ dry red lentils
- ☐ hot pepper sauce

Seasonings and Spices
- ☐ curry powder
- ☐ whole cumin seeds

Spinach Dip
by Nele Liivlaid

Easy | **Gluten Free** | **3-4 Servings**

This creamy spinach dip combines the simple but divine flavors of onions and garlic with the subtle sweetness of coconut and saltiness of spinach.

Ingredients

1 small onion, diced
3 garlic cloves, minced
2.5 oz. coconut milk
¼ tsp turmeric
16 oz. frozen chopped spinach
⅛ tsp Himalayan salt
black pepper, to taste
chilli pepper flakes, to taste

Directions

1. Gather all ingredients.
2. Thaw spinach. Squeeze out and discard any excess water.
3. In a small skillet or pot heat 2 tablespoons of water. When it starts to sizzle, add onions and garlic, mix briefly, cover and sauté over medium heat for 3 minutes.
4. Add turmeric, stir and pour in coconut milk.
5. Bring to boil before adding spinach. Stir, bring to boil and simmer until spinach is cooked, about 3 minutes.
6. Season with Himalayan salt, black pepper and garnish with some chili flakes.

Nutrition Per Serving 60 calories, 1.5g total fat, 1g sat fat, 140mg sodium, 8g carbohydrates, 4g fiber, 2g sugar, 4g protein

Ingredient Swaps: In place of coconut milk you can use cashew sour cream (recipe p. 5).

Tip or fact: Spread on a slice of bread, serve as a side, pour it over pasta, use as a component of a Buddha bowl or use as a dip for raw veggies.

Shopping list

Produce
☐ 1 small onion
☐ garlic

Refrigerated or Frozen
☐ 2.5 oz. coconut milk
☐ 16 oz. frozen spinach

Seasonings and Spices
☐ turmeric
☐ Himalayan salt
☐ black pepper
☐ chili pepper flakes

Parsley

Thyme

Anise

Bountiful
Breakfast

No Scrambling Necessary

You roll out of bed, dreading the thought of scrambling around to get breakfast on the table. Your body has essentially been fasting for at least eight hours (hopefully at least 8 hours) and you know you need to feed the machine. If you and the family skip this important meal, you will be running on fumes until the next meal. We know time is short in the morning – the number one reason to skipping breakfast – and we are here to tell you all about the benefits to trying one of our plant-powered breakfasts to fuel your body right!

Science tells us that eating a healthy breakfast is linked to numerous benefits

- Eating essential nutrition in the morning means you are more likely to meet all of your needs throughout the day
- Energy from food wakes up your mind and body to get them running as fast as you need them to
- A filling breakfast with whole ingredients, like whole grains, milk alternatives and cut fruit, provides fiber to keep you full until lunch. Plus, if you fill up on plant-nutritious meals, you will have less room for empty calories, like what you may find in the vending machine.
- Research has shown that breakfast eaters tend to weigh less than those who always skip breakfast. It's not completely clear why. Some nutritionists believe that hunger gets the best of you if you skip breakfast. So, you tend to eat more at lunch and dinner. As far as I'm concerned, why isn't important if it helps keep your weight in check!

For kids, according to the Academy of Nutrition and Dietetics, breakfast is even more important. The benefits for kids include:

- better classroom performance
- more mental clarity
- increased problem-solving skills
- better hand-eye coordination

But you're probably thinking I don't have the time to fix a healthy breakfast. Wrong. There are plenty of quick-fix breakfast ideas, as well as a number that can be prepared ahead of time and even kept for several days.

The recipes we've developed are so tasty, your family won't believe they are healthy. So, don't tell them. Just plate up these healthy, tasty breakfast ideas.

No scrambling necessary.

Sources:

https://www.todaysdietitian.com/newarchives/090111p44.shtml

https://www.eatright.org/food/nutrition/eatright-at-school/breakfast-in-schools-healthy-nutritious

https://www.eatright.org/food/nutrition/eating-as-a-family/breakfast-key-to-growing-healthy

Apple Cinnamon Porridge

by Ashley Arpel Greenwald

Medium | **Gluten Free** | **2 Servings**

A delicious grain-free porridge to start your day.

Ingredients

- 1 c water
- ¾ c raw cashews
- 4 small red delicious apples, about 2 c chopped
- 1 ½ tsp ground cinnamon
- ¼ tsp ground nutmeg
- ⅛ tsp ground cloves
- ¼ tsp almond extract

Directions

1. Gather all ingredients.
2. Place raw cashews into a small bowl and pour 1 cup cold water on top. Cover and place in refrigerator to soak for at least 4 hours OR pour 1 cup piping hot water over cashews and let soak for 30 minutes.
3. While cashews are soaking, chop all apples and place in a large skillet. Add 1 cup water and all remaining ingredients. Use a bamboo spatula to stir over low heat.
4. Cover and let simmer for 20-25 minutes, uncovering to stir occasionally. The water will have been reduced into a thick syrup by the end.
5. When done, remove apple mixture from heat and carefully transfer to the bowl of a food processor or blender. Blend until completely smooth and pour into a medium mixing bowl. Set aside.
6. When cashews are done soaking, drain them over the sink and place them in the bowl of a food processor or blender. Blend until cashews are very small, but not too much as to turn them to butter. They should look chopped.
7. Pour cashews into apple mixture and mix until completely combined.
8. Top with bananas, sliced almonds and extra cinnamon and dig in! Best served hot!

Nutrition Per Serving 430 calories, 22g total fat, 3g sat fat, 5mg sodium, 55g carbohydrates, 13g fiber, 34g sugar, 8g protein

Ingredient Swap: Swap almond extract for vanilla extract.

Tip or fact: Bananas are known as the "happy fruit" because they contain tryptophan. Tryptophan is an amino acid that gets converted to 5-HTP in the brain. The 5-HTP is then converted to serotonin which is known to promotes relaxation and puts you in a good mood.

Shopping list

Produce
- ☐ 4 small red delicious apples

Packaged
- ☐ raw cashews

Baking Ingredients
- ☐ almond extract

Seasonings and Spices
- ☐ ground cinnamon
- ☐ ground nutmeg
- ☐ ground cloves

Banana Blueberry Bread

by Kelley Williamson

Easy | Kid Friendly | 7 Servings

Delicious fruit bread with a touch of sweetness.

Ingredients

1 ½ c hot water
1 c unsweetened applesauce
½ c coconut sugar
2 c whole wheat flour
1 ½ tsp baking soda
1 tsp cinnamon
2 ripe bananas
1 c fresh blueberries

Directions

1. Preheat the oven to 350°F.
2. Gather all ingredients.
3. In a large bowl, add in the water, applesauce and coconut sugar and let set for 5 minutes.
4. Combine all the other ingredients into a large bowl and mix well. Then add the wet ingredients to the dry ingredients and mix but don't overmix.
5. Pour into two large size bread pans (non-greased) and bake for 30 to 35 minutes or until a knife comes out cleanly.
6. Let cool and then remove from the bread pan and slice.

Nutrition Per Serving 210 calories, 1g total fat, 0g sat fat, 280mg sodium, 49g carbohydrates, 5g fiber, 19g sugar, 5g protein

Storage: Store in a glass dish with a lid on the countertop or refrigerator.

Ingredient Swap: Swap gluten free flour for the whole wheat flour.

Tip or fact: Use any fruit that you want to make this bread. Substitute in peaches for the bananas or pumpkin when it is close to Thanksgiving. If you substitute in pumpkin, remember to add pumpkin pie spice. A quick tip on bananas, when your bananas turn black or dark spotted, peel the banana and place in a freezer Ziploc bag and freeze. About 1 hour before you make your bread, thaw the bananas and the bread will be even tastier or moister.

Shopping list

Produce
☐ 2 ripe bananas
☐ blueberries

Packaged
☐ unsweetened applesauce

Baking Ingredients
☐ coconut sugar
☐ whole wheat flour
☐ baking soda

Seasonings and Spices
☐ cinnamon

Banana Bread

by Ashley Arpel Greenwald

Easy | Gluten Free | 8 Servings

Delicious? ✓ Soft inside, crispy outside? ✓ Packed with flavor and healthy goodness? ✓✓✓

Ingredients

2 Tbsp chia seeds
¼ c + 2 Tbsp oat milk
2 c oat flour
½ c brown coconut sugar
2 tsp baking powder
1 tsp baking soda
3 large ripe bananas
¼ c cashew cream (recipe p. 3)
1 tsp apple cider vinegar
1 tsp almond extract

Directions

1. Preheat the oven to 350°F.
2. Gather all ingredients.
3. Place chia seeds and oat milk in a small bowl. Set aside and let soak for 10 minutes.
4. In a large mixing bowl combine oat flour, coconut sugar, baking powder and baking soda. Set aside.
5. Peel bananas and place in the bowl of a food processor or blender and process until pureed. Add cashew cream, apple cider vinegar and almond extract. Process again.
6. Pour wet mixture into dry mixture and whisk.
7. Pour batter into a nonstick loaf pan. Mine is 3.09 inches (H) x 7.25 inches (W) x 3.25 inches (D).
8. Bake for 45 minutes, or until the top of the bread is golden brown and crispy.
9. Best served warm, however, can be served at room temperature.

Bountiful Breakfast

Nutrition Per Serving 190 calories, 4g total fat, 0.5g sat fat, 170mg sodium, 36g carbohydrates, 4g fiber, 15g sugar, 5g protein

Storage: Seal in an airtight glass container for up to three days. Does not need to be refrigerated.

Ingredient Swap: Swap oat milk for nut milk of choice or rice milk. Swap brown coconut sugar for maple sugar.

Tip or fact: One of Ashley's favorite breakfast recipes.

Shopping list

Produce
☐ 3 large ripe bananas

Packaged
☐ chia seeds
☐ raw cashews
☐ apple cider vinegar

Baking Ingredients
☐ oat flour
☐ brown coconut sugar
☐ baking powder
☐ baking soda
☐ almond extract

Brown Rice Fruit Bread

by Ashley Arpel Greenwald

| Easy | Kid Friendly | Gluten Free | 8-10 Servings | 📷 |

Delicious and soft inside with a crispy crust. Packed with flavor and healthy goodness.

Ingredients

1 flax egg (recipe p. 9)
2 c brown rice flour
½ Tbsp baking powder
1 tsp baking soda
1 c almond milk
½ c + 2 Tbsp maple syrup
2 Tbsp olive oil
½ c blueberries
¼ c raspberries, optional

Directions

1. Preheat the oven to 350°F.
2. Gather all ingredients.
3. Create the flax egg (recipe p. 9). Set aside and let soak for at least 5 minutes.
4. In a separate large bowl, whisk brown rice flour, baking powder and baking soda together.
5. Add almond milk, maple syrup, and olive oil. Mix again.
6. Finally, add the flax egg and mix for the last time.
7. Pour entire mixture into a 9 in. nonstick springform pan.
8. Place blueberries on top of mixture, distributing evenly. If using raspberries, do the same.
9. Place in the oven and bake for 20 minutes.
10. Let cool for 10 minutes before slicing and eating. Best eaten warm or cold!

Nutrition Per Serving 200 calories, 4g total fat, 0.5g sat fat, 170mg sodium, 40g carbohydrates, 2g fiber, 13g sugar, 3g protein

Storage: Store in an airtight glass container in the refrigerator for up to 3 days.

Tip or fact: To easily remove the sides of a springform pan dampen a cloth towel with hot water and gently wrap it around the sides of the pan. The heat will loosen the bread from the pan making for a clean removal.

Shopping list

Produce
☐ blueberries
☐ raspberries, optional

Packaged
☐ maple syrup
☐ olive oil
☐ flaxseed meal

Baking Ingredients
☐ brown rice flour
☐ baking powder
☐ baking soda

Refrigerated or Frozen
☐ unsweetened almond milk

Chocolate Chai Scones

by Ashley Arpel Greenwald

| Easy | Gluten Free | 8-10 Servings | 📷 |

Dreams do come true! You and your children can have chocolate for breakfast AND IT'S HEALTHY!

Ingredients

Scones

1 c hazelnut meal
1 c blanched almond flour
1 ½ c brown rice flour
½ c cocoa powder
1 c hot water + 1 chai tea bag
½ c + 2 Tbsp maple syrup

Prebake Glaze

1 Tbsp maple syrup
½ Tbsp water
1 tsp cocoa powder

Directions

1. Preheat the oven to 350°F.
2. Gather all ingredients.
3. Boil 1 cup of water in a kettle. Place 1 Chai tea bag in the warmed pot and set aside.
4. In a medium bowl, combine hazelnut meal, almond flour, brown rice flour and cocoa powder with a whisk.
5. Add the hot tea and maple syrup to the flour mixture and whisk. The dough will be sticky and wet.
6. Transfer dough to a parchment lined cutting board and use your hands to form a ball.
7. Place another piece of parchment paper on top of the dough and use a rolling pin to roll it out slightly, creating an oval about 1.5-2 in. high.
8. Remove parchment paper and slice into 8 triangle wedges with either a pizza cutter or sharp knife. Place wedges on a parchment lined baking sheet using a spatula.
9. Mix all prebake glaze ingredients together in a small bowl. Dip your pinky in the mixture and lightly spread over the top of each scone.
10. Place scones in the oven and bake for 25 minutes.
11. When the scones are done, remove them from the oven.
12. Enjoy with a glass of unsweetened almond milk.

Bountiful Breakfast

Nutrition Per Serving 350 calories, 16g total fat, 1.5g sat fat, 10mg sodium, 49g carbohydrates, 6g fiber, 18g sugar, 8g protein

Storage: Store in an airtight glass container in the refrigerator for up to 2 days. But why do you have leftovers? CHOCOLATE!

Tip or fact: Using a ⅓ measuring cup, scoop out dough and place on a silicone or parchment lined baking sheet. This version creates a circular scone as opposed to triangles.

Shopping list

Packaged
☐ chai tea bag
☐ maple syrup

Baking Ingredients
☐ hazelnut meal
☐ blanched almond flour
☐ brown rice flour
☐ cocoa powder

Chocolate Zucchini Muffins
by Ashley Arpel Greenwald

Easy | **Gluten Free** | **8 Servings**

I'm sorry ... Did you not want me to give you a reason to start your day off with chocolate?

Ingredients

1 Tbsp chia seeds
4 Tbsp oat milk, unsweetened
2 medium ripe bananas
¼ c coconut oil
¼ c zucchini spirals
¼ c maple syrup
1 tsp almond extract
2 c almond meal, blanched
1 tsp baking powder
1 tsp ground cinnamon
¼ c cacao nibs, optional

Directions

1. Preheat the oven to 350°F.
2. Gather all ingredients.
3. Place chia seeds and oat milk in a small bowl. Set aside and let soak for 10 minutes.
4. Place both bananas and coconut oil in the bowl of a food processor or blender. Process until pureed. Add zucchini and process for another 10-15 seconds. The zucchini will not fully puree, only break apart. This is good.
5. Pour banana and zucchini mixture into a large mixing bowl and add maple syrup and almond extract. Mix using a whisk.
6. Add all dry ingredients and mix thoroughly.
7. Line a muffin tin with 8 liners and fill each liner with batter. Use a ⅓ measuring cup to fill.
8. Sprinkle extra cacao nibs on top of each muffin for fun and place in oven.
9. Bake for 40 minutes. The top of each muffin will be a bit browned and crispy when done.
10. Remove from oven and let sit for 10 minutes before serving warm.
11. Top with strawberry or raspberry preserves.

Nutrition Per Serving 320 calories, 24g total fat, 8g sat fat, 15mg sodium, 23g carbohydrates, 6g fiber, 11g sugar, 7g protein

Shopping list

Produce
☐ 2 medium ripe bananas

Packaged
☐ coconut oil
☐ chia seeds
☐ cacao nibs, optional
☐ maple syrup
☐ zucchini noodles

Baking Ingredients
☐ almond extract
☐ blanched almond meal
☐ baking powder

Refrigerated or Frozen
☐ unsweetened oat milk

Seasonings and Spices
☐ ground cinnamon

Storage: Store in an airtight glass container for up to 2 days.

Ingredient Swap: Swap almond extract for vanilla extract.

Tip or fact: The difference between blanched and unblanched almond meal is that blanched almonds have had their skin removed whereas unblanched almonds have not.

Classic Cornbread

by Ashley Arpel Greenwald

Easy | **Gluten Free** | **7-8 Servings**

Jyl told me she LOVED cornbread, so I knew I had to write a cornbread recipe for her!!

Ingredients

2 Tbsp flaxseed meal
1 c unsweetened almond milk
1 c cornmeal
1 c oat flour (ground oats)
¼ c coconut sugar
1 Tbsp baking powder
⅓ c coconut oil, melted
¼ c pure maple syrup

Directions

1. Preheat the oven to 400°F.
2. Gather all ingredients.
3. Place flaxseed meal and almond milk in a medium mixing bowl. Gently mix and set aside for at least 5 minutes.
4. Pour cornmeal, oat flour, coconut sugar and baking powder into a large mixing bowl. Mix using a whisk. Set aside.
5. Place coconut oil in a small microwavable bowl and melt in the microwave for 30 seconds. Pour into flaxseed and almond milk mixture. Add maple syrup and mix.
6. Pour wet mixture into dry mixture and whisk thoroughly.
7. Pour entire mixture into a 9 in. springform pan and place in oven. Bake for 35-40 minutes, or until caramel brown.
8. Let cool for at least 30-35 minutes before slicing. If you slice before bread has cooled, it will be very crumbly.
9. Delicious warm or room temperature!

Bountiful Breakfast

Nutrition Per Serving 210 calories, 10g total fat, 7g sat fat, 30mg sodium, 28g carbohydrates, 2g fiber, 9g sugar, 3g protein

Storage: Store in an airtight glass container at room temperature for up to 4 days.

Ingredient Swap: Swap almond milk for plant-based milk of choice.

Tip or fact: Cornbread isn't just a hearty breakfast! It can also be served with beans, soup and so much more.

Shopping list

Packaged
□ ground flaxseed
□ cornmeal
□ coconut oil
□ maple syrup

Baking Ingredients
□ oat flour
□ coconut sugar
□ baking powder

Refrigerated or Frozen
□ almond milk

Cocoa-Raspberry Pancakes by Kayli Dice

Medium | **6-8 Servings**

These sweet, chocolatey, fluffy pancakes make the perfect brunch.

Ingredients

1 ¼ c whole wheat flour
1 tsp baking powder
¼ tsp baking soda
2 Tbsp cocoa powder
¼ tsp salt
½-¾ c water
¾ c nondairy milk
½ tsp vanilla extract
2 c frozen raspberries
maple syrup, optional
almond butter, optional

Directions

1. Gather all ingredients.
2. Preheat a non-stick griddle or skillet over medium heat.
3. Warm raspberries in a saucepan on the stove or in the microwave. Gently smash with a fork to create a sauce-like texture. Add a little date sugar to sweeten if desired.
4. In a small mixing bowl, combine flour, baking powder, baking soda, cocoa powder, and salt. Set aside.
5. In a medium mixing bowl, combine water, milk, vanilla, and date sugar or maple sugar.
1. Add dry ingredients to the wet ingredients. Stir just until all dry bits of flour disappear. Tip: The thicker the batter, the fluffier the pancake.
6. Pour ¼ cup of batter onto preheated pan. When edges firm up and bubble near the center begin to pop, flip.
7. Cook for a few minutes on the second side. Repeat.
8. Serve pancakes topped with almond butter and raspberry sauce.
9. Drizzle with extra maple syrup if desired.

Nutrition Per Serving 190 calories, 2g total fat, 0g sat fat, 250mg sodium, 39g carbohydrates, 10g fiber, 5g sugar, 7g protein

Ingredient Swap: Customize them by leaving out the cocoa powder and swapping in other fruits like bananas, blueberries, or diced apples.

Tip or fact: Store your cocoa in a dry, cool and airtight glass container in your pantry. Keep it away from other spices and other strong-smelling ingredients. It will keep for up to a year, but loses flavor over time.

Shopping list

Packaged
- almond butter
- maple syrup

Baking Ingredients
- whole wheat flour
- baking powder
- baking soda
- cocoa powder

Refrigerated or Frozen
- nondairy milk (almond milk or soymilk)
- frozen raspberries

Seasonings and Spices
- salt

Earl Grey Scones

by Ashley Arpel Greenwald

| Easy | Gluten Free | 8 Servings |

Warm, comforting and usually topped with something sweet, scones are the perfect breakfast date!

Ingredients

Scones

½ c hazelnut meal
1 c blanched almond flour
1 ½ c brown rice flour
¾ c hot water + 1 earl grey tea bag
½ c maple syrup

Prebake Glaze

1 Tbsp maple syrup
½ Tbsp water

Directions

1. Preheat the oven to 350°F.
2. Gather all ingredients.
3. Boil 1 cup of water in a kettle. Place 1 earl grey tea bag in the warmed pot and set aside.
4. In a medium bowl combine hazelnut meal, almond flour and brown rice flour. Use a whisk.
5. Add the hot tea and maple syrup to the flour mixture and whisk.
6. The dough will be sticky and wet. Transfer dough to a parchment lined cutting board and use your hands to form a ball.
7. Place another piece of parchment paper on top of the dough and use a rolling pin to roll it out slightly, creating an oval about 1.5-2 in. high.
8. Remove parchment paper and slice into 8 triangle wedges with either a pizza cutter or sharp knife. Place wedges on a parchment lined baking sheet using a spatula.
9. Mix all pre-bake glaze ingredients together in a small bowl. Dip your pinky in the mixture and lightly spread over the top of each scone.
10. Place scones in the oven and bake for 25 minutes.
11. When the scones are done, remove them from the oven.
12. Top with strawberry preserves and enjoy warm ... curled up by the fire with a good book. Just me?

Bountiful Breakfast

Nutrition Per Serving 290 calories, 12g total fat, 1g sat fat, 10mg sodium, 42g carbohydrates, 4g fiber, 15g sugar, 6g protein

Storage: Store in an airtight glass container in the refrigerator for up to 2 days.

Tip or fact: Using a ⅓ measuring cup, scoop out dough and place on a silicone or parchment lined baking sheet. This version creates a circular scone as opposed to triangles.

Shopping list

Packaged
- [ ] earl grey tea bag
- [ ] maple syrup

Baking Ingredients
- [ ] hazelnut meal
- [ ] blanched almond flour
- [ ] brown rice flour

Easy Breakfast Cookies

by Ashley Arpel Greenwald

| Easy | Kid Friendly | Gluten Free | 10 Servings |

What a tasty way to start your day!

Ingredients

1 ½ c medjool dates, pitted
1 ½ c whole rolled oats
¾ c tahini

Directions

1. Preheat the oven to 350°F.
2. Gather all ingredients.
3. In the bowl of a food processor or blender, process oats until floured. Pour into a medium sized bowl and set aside.
4. In the same food processor or blender, process the pitted dates until very smooth. Transfer to oat flour bowl and add tahini. Combine using your hands, creating a thick dough.
5. Roll pieces of the dough into little balls and place on a parchment lined cookie sheet. Press down on each ball with the palm of your hand, creating a thick and round cookie.
6. Place in the oven and bake for 8 minutes.
7. Eat immediately.

Nutrition Per Serving 220 calories, 11g total fat, 1.5g sat fat, 10mg sodium, 28g carbohydrates, 3g fiber, 14g sugar, 5g protein

Storage: Store in an airtight glass container in the refrigerator for up to 3 days.

Tip or fact: Add 1 tablespoon cinnamon and ¼ cup raisins for a sweet morning burst!

Shopping list

Packaged
☐ medjool dates, pitted
☐ tahini

Baking Ingredients
☐ whole rolled oats

English Breakfast Poppyseed Scones
by Ashley Arpel Greenwald

Easy | **Gluten Free** | **8 Servings**

The combination of two glorious breakfast essentials – tea and scones!

Ingredients

Scones
½ c hazelnut meal
1 c blanched almond flour
1 ½ c brown rice flour
¾ c hot water + 1 English breakfast tea bag
½ c maple syrup
1 Tbsp lemon juice
2 Tbsp poppyseed

Prebake Glaze
1 Tbsp maple syrup
½ Tbsp water
1 tsp lemon juice

Directions

1. Preheat the oven to 350°F.
2. Gather all ingredients.
3. Boil 1 cup of water in a kettle. Place 1 English breakfast tea bag in the warmed pot and set aside.
4. In a medium bowl combine hazelnut meal, almond flour, brown rice flour and poppyseeds. Use a whisk.
5. Add the hot tea, maple syrup and lemon juice to the flour mixture and whisk.
6. The dough will be sticky and wet. Transfer dough to a parchment lined cutting board and use your hands to form a ball.
7. Place another piece of parchment paper on top of the dough and use a rolling pin to roll it out slightly, creating an oval about 1.5-2 in. high.
8. Remove parchment paper and slice into 8 triangle wedges with either a pizza cutter or sharp knife. Place wedges on a parchment lined baking sheet using a spatula.
9. Mix all pre-bake glaze ingredients together in a small bowl. Dip your pinky in the mixture and lightly spread over the top of each scone.
10. Place scones in the oven and bake for 25 minutes.
11. When the scones are done, remove them from the oven. Enjoy warm.

Bountiful Breakfast

Nutrition Per Serving 300 calories, 13g total fat, 1g sat fat, 10mg sodium, 43g carbohydrates, 4g fiber, 15g sugar, 7g protein

Storage: Store in an airtight glass container in the refrigerator for up to 2 days.

Tip or fact: Using a ⅓ measuring cup, scoop out dough and place on a parchment lined baking sheet. This version creates a circular scone as opposed to triangles.

Shopping list

Produce
☐ 1 lemon

Packaged
☐ English breakfast tea bag
☐ maple syrup

Baking Ingredients
☐ hazelnut meal
☐ blanched almond flour
☐ brown rice flour

Seasonings and Spices
☐ poppyseeds

Gingerbread Granola

by Kelley Williamson

Easy | **Gluten Free** | **4 Servings**

Spicy but heartwarming granola.

Ingredients

⅓ c orange juice
⅓ c unsweetened applesauce
2 Tbsp molasses
⅓ c coconut flakes
2 c rolled oats
½ c pecans, chopped
1 Tbsp buckwheat flour
1 tsp ground ginger
1 tsp cinnamon
½ tsp sea salt

Directions

1. Preheat the oven to 350°F.
2. Gather all ingredients.
3. Line a baking sheet with parchment paper.
4. Add all ingredients to a bowl and mix well. Then spread onto the baking sheet and spread out.
5. Place the baking sheet in the oven and bake for about 20 minutes until things become slightly crispy
6. Remove from the oven and let cool.

Nutrition Per Serving 360 calories, 16g total fat, 4.5g sat fat, 300mg sodium, 46g carbohydrates, 8g fiber, 13g sugar, 9g protein

Storage: Store in a glass dish with a lid on the countertop or refrigerator.

Ingredient Swap: Swap out the nuts for different nuts. Swap out the flour with garbanzo bean or any type of gluten free flour.

Tip or fact: Enjoy this on everything. Make peanut butter toast and then add this on top. Add to your chia seed pudding or anywhere where you want a little crunch.

Shopping list

Packaged
☐ unsweetened applesauce
☐ molasses
☐ pecans

Baking Ingredients
☐ coconut flakes
☐ rolled oats
☐ buckwheat flour

Seasonings and Spices
☐ ground ginger
☐ cinnamon
☐ sea salt

Oatmeal Raisin Bars

by Kelley Williamson

Easy | **12 Servings**

Delicious oatmeal and raisin bars which will remind you of what your grandmother used to make for you.

Ingredients

½ c unsweetened applesauce
½ c brown sugar
½ c coconut sugar
2 flax eggs (Recipe p. 9)
1 ½ c whole wheat flour
1 tsp baking soda
1 tsp cinnamon
½ tsp sea salt
3 c rolled oats
1 c raisins

Directions

1. Preheat the oven to 350°F.
2. Gather all ingredients.
3. In a large bowl, add in the applesauce, sugars and flax eggs and mix. Then add in the flours and the spices and mix well.
4. Add in the oats and raisins last and fold in but don't overmix.
5. Spoon into a 13x9 glass baking dish (not greased) and smooth the top.
6. Bake for 20 to 25 minutes or until it becomes a nice golden brown and a knife comes out clean.
7. Let cool and then cut into bars and enjoy.

Nutrition Per Serving 270 calories, 3g total fat, 0.5g sat fat, 210mg sodium, 58g carbohydrates, 5g fiber, 26g sugar, 6g protein

Storage: Store in an airtight glass container.

Ingredient Swap: Gluten free flour for the whole wheat flour. Add nuts or any other flavors.

Tip or fact: Make these for your breakfast or snacks. Also a great energy bar for the mid-day blues.

Bountiful Breakfast

Shopping list

Packaged
☐ unsweetened applesauce
☐ flax seeds
☐ raisins

Baking Ingredients
☐ brown sugar
☐ coconut flakes
☐ whole wheat flour
☐ baking soda
☐ rolled oats

Seasonings and Spices
☐ cinnamon
☐ sea salt

Overnight Tropical Blend Muesli by Jyl Steinback

| Easy | Kid Friendly | 6 Servings |

Start out with a hearty tropical twist to your morning.

Ingredients

2 c quick cooking rolled oats
¾ c unsweetened dried apricots, diced
1 c water
¾ c orange juice
¼ c almonds, chopped
¼ c dates, chopped
¼ c coconut flakes

Directions

1. Gather all ingredients.
2. Combine all ingredients in medium bowl and mix well.
3. Cover and refrigerate overnight.
4. Mix lightly before serving.

Nutrition Per Serving 240 calories, 6g total fat, 2g sat fat, 0mg sodium, 40g carbohydrates, 5g fiber, 17g sugar, 7g protein

Storage: Store in an airtight glass container.

Tip or fact: The fiber in oats helps reduce cholesterol and is good for your heart.

Shopping list

Packaged
☐ quick cooking whole grain oats
☐ unsweetened dried apricots

Baking Ingredients
☐ coconut flakes

Refrigerated or Frozen
☐ orange juice

Planterrifick Pancakes

by Ashley Arpel Greenwald

Easy | **Kid Friendly** | **4 Servings** 📷

If breakfast is the most important meal of the day, then why not make it nutritious and fulfilling?

Ingredients

1 c pureed sweet potato
2 c spelt flour
½ c oat milk
½ tsp ground cinnamon
4 Tbsp pure maple syrup
¼ tsp ground nutmeg
1 tsp lemon juice
¼ tsp ground cloves
1 tsp baking powder
½ tsp baking soda

Directions

1. Gather all ingredients.
2. In a large bowl whisk all dry ingredients together. Set aside.
3. Whisk all wet ingredients together in a medium sized bowl.
4. Pour wet mixture into dry mixture and whisk thoroughly. Batter should be thick and smooth, free of clumps.
5. Heat a large nonstick skillet on medium for 3 minutes.
6. Reduce heat slightly, between low and medium.
7. Fill a measuring cup to ½ mark and pour pancake batter onto skillet. Use a spoon to scoop out excess batter from measuring cup as the mixture is very thick and might not pour out easily. Tip: The thicker the batter, the fluffier the pancake.
8. When the top of the pancake begins to dry out, flip. Remove from heat when fully cooked and continue process until all batter is used.
9. Make sure to cook pancakes all the way through. When cooked, these pancakes hold a golden-brown color and extra fluffy center.
10. Top with blueberries or fruit of choice or maple syrup. Serve immediately.

Bountiful Breakfast

Nutrition Per Serving 350 calories, 2.5g total fat, 0g sat fat, 190mg sodium, 71g carbohydrates, 10g fiber, 16g sugar, 10g protein

Ingredient Swap: If maintaining a gluten free lifestyle, swap spelt flour for amaranth flour.

Tip or fact: Spelt is a variety of wheat that is high in fiber and commonly found in baked goods.

Shopping list

Produce
☐ 1 lemon

Packaged
☐ pure maple syrup
☐ 1 can pureed sweet potatoes

Baking Ingredients
☐ spelt flour
☐ baking powder
☐ baking soda

Refrigerated or Frozen
☐ unsweetened oat milk

Seasonings and Spices
☐ ground cinnamon
☐ ground nutmeg
☐ ground cloves

Sweet Potato Breakfast Bowl by Ashley Arpel Greenwald

Easy | **Kid Friendly** | **Gluten Free** | **2 Servings**

A fast, delicious and nutritious breakfast your kids will even want on weekends!

Ingredients

1 large sweet potato
1 ripe banana
½ c strawberries, sliced
¼ c blueberries
4 Tbsp creamy peanut butter
¼ c almonds, sliced
⅛ tsp ground cinnamon

Directions

1. Gather all ingredients.
2. Cut sweet potato in half, long ways, so that it is still attached on one side and resembles a heart or two ovals touching.
3. Place the sweet potato in the microwave and cook for 8 minutes.
4. While the sweet potato is cooking, slice the banana and strawberries. Set aside.
5. When the sweet potato is done cooking, remove from microwave and let it cool down for 30 seconds.
6. Layer the banana and strawberry slices inside the open sweet potato.
7. Top with blueberries and sliced almonds.
8. Using a spoon, drizzle peanut butter on top of the fruit, creating a zig-zag design. If peanut butter is too thick, microwave for 15 seconds before drizzling.
9. Sprinkle cinnamon and serve immediately.

Nutrition Per Serving 390 calories, 23g total fat, 4g sat fat, 170mg sodium, 42g carbohydrates, 6g fiber, 18g sugar, 12g protein

Ingredient Swap: Add frozen grapes for more crunch and sweetness.

Tip or fact: Sweet potatoes are high in fiber and rich in beta-carotene; the antioxidant responsible for the bright orange color of sweet potatoes and a nutrient found to help maintain healthy skin.

Shopping list

Produce
☐ 1 large sweet potato
☐ 1 ripe banana
☐ strawberries
☐ blueberries

Packaged
☐ creamy peanut butter

Baking Ingredients
☐ sliced almonds

Seasonings and Spices
☐ ground cinnamon

Tofu Scramble With Oil-Free Hash Browns
by Kayli Dice

Medium | **Gluten Free** | **4 Servings**

Crispy hash browns paired with egg-like tofu scramble makes the perfect savory breakfast.

Ingredients

1 block firm tofu
1 Tbsp soy sauce
1 Tbsp nutritional yeast
1 tsp turmeric powder
Black pepper, to taste
½ tsp chili powder
½ tsp cumin
½ tsp garlic powder
½ tsp onion powder
4 c baby spinach
4 potatoes
1 c salsa
1 avocado
Hot sauce, optional

Directions

1. Preheat oven to 400°F.
2. Gather all ingredients.
3. Slice open avocado, remove pit, and scoop out flesh. Cut flesh in to slices.
4. Rinse potato. Using a food processor with a grater attachment or a hand-held grater, grate potato into hash brown shreds.
5. Line a baking sheet with parchment paper.
6. Spread potato shreds on to prepared baking sheet, making sure not to pile them too high.
7. Sprinkle with onion powder, garlic powder, and pepper.
8. Bake for 10-15 minutes until the underside of the potatoes gets brown and crispy.
9. Flip potatoes and bake for another 5 minutes to crisp and brown the second side.
10. Drain and press tofu between two layers of paper towels or dish towels to remove as much water as possible.
11. Crumble the tofu with your hands into a small bowl. Add soy sauce, nutritional yeast, turmeric, chili powder, cumin, and black pepper and lightly stir until the tofu is evenly covered.
12. Heat a skillet over medium heat and add tofu mixture. Cook, stirring frequently, until the tofu is heated through and as dry as you like it. It will lose quite a bit of water.
13. Just before the tofu is done, add spinach. When spinach is wilted, remove from heat.
14. Serve tofu scramble alongside hash browns, topped salsa, avocado, and hot sauce.

Bountiful Breakfast

Shopping list

Produce
☐ baby spinach
☐ 4 potatoes
☐ 1 avocado

Packaged
☐ soy sauce
☐ nutritional yeast
☐ hot sauce, optional

Refrigerated or Frozen
☐ 1 block firm tofu
☐ salsa

Seasonings and Spices
☐ turmeric powder
☐ black pepper
☐ chili powder
☐ cumin
☐ garlic powder
☐ onion powder

Nutrition Per Serving 340 calories, 12g total fat, 1.5g sat fat, 270mg sodium, 44g carbohydrates, 10g fiber, 5g sugar, 17g protein

Ingredient Swap: Don't want to grate potatoes? Buy them pre-shredded in the frozen section of the grocery store. Just be sure they don't contain added oil or salt!

Tip or fact: Tofu is a great way to get protein. ½ cup tofu = 10g of protein, similar to 2 medium eggs = 11g protein.

Parsley

Thyme

Anise

Bay Leaf

Joyful
Juices and
Smoothies

Basic Celery Juice

by Laura Salyer

Easy | **Gluten Free** | **1-2 Servings**

A simple, healthy juice perfect for daily use.

Ingredients

2 bunches organic celery, chopped

Directions

1. Chop the tops and ends off the bunches of celery and wash well.
2. Chop them into approximately 2-inch sticks and slowly feed them through a juicer.
3. If using a blender and nut-milk bag or cheesecloth, simply add the washed and chopped celery to a high-speed blender. Blend until completely smooth. Place a clean cheesecloth or nut milk bag (I prefer DDMY's All Purpose Nut Milk Bag from Amazon) in a large bowl and pour the blended celery through the bag. Carefully squeeze the celery juice through the bag, wringing out as much liquid as possible.
4. Transfer to a glass and serve chilled.

Nutrition Per Serving 25 calories, 0g total fat, 0g sat fat, 130mg sodium, 5g carbohydrates, 3g fiber, 2g sugar, 1g protein

Storage: Best served immediately, but you may store leftovers in an airtight glass container in the refrigerator for up to 24 hours.

Tip or fact: It is best to drink celery juice first thing in the morning on an empty stomach. Start small with 2-4 oz. and build up to 16 oz. a day.

Shopping list

Produce
☐ 2 bunches organic celery

Beetilicious

by Kiana Varner

Easy | Gluten Free | 2 Servings

A beet juice that is great for blood regulation and for hydration.

Ingredients

1 beet
2 c watermelon, cubed
1 medium green apple
1 medium celery stalk

Directions

1. Gather all fruits and vegetables and wash thoroughly.
2. Cut all ingredients into small pieces. About 1 inch in size
3. Place ingredients into juicer and juice.
4. Pour into glass and enjoy.

Nutrition Per Serving 100 calories, 0g total fat, 0g sat fat, 50mg sodium, 27g carbohydrates, 4g fiber, 20g sugar, 2g protein

Storage: Store in a covered glass cup or container and place in refrigerator. Store up to 3 days.

Tip or fact: Did you know that the life expectancy of an apple tree is up to 100 years.

Joyful Juice

Shopping list

Produce
- ☐ 1 beet
- ☐ 1 small watermelon
- ☐ 1 medium green apple
- ☐ 1 medium celery stalk
- ☐ cinnamon

Beetroot Smoothie with Blueberries by Neeme Liivlaid

Easy | **Gluten Free** | **2 Servings**

I love unconventional smoothies and this beetroot smoothie with blueberries is no exception. A healthy way to start the day.

Ingredients

1 small organic beet
1 ripe banana
2 medium apples
1 bunch romaine lettuce
1 tsp cinnamon
1 small piece ginger root
2 Tbsp ground flax seeds
2 Tbsp hemp seeds, hulled or ground
1 Tbsp sunflower seeds
½ c blueberries
water, desired consistency
½ tsp agar-agar

Directions

1. Gather all ingredients and wash the fruits and vegetables thoroughly.
2. Peel the beetroot and cut into smaller chunks.
3. Blend all ingredients in a blender.
4. Add water if necessary. Blend to desired consistency.
5. Enjoy!

Nutrition Per Serving 320 calories, 10g total fat, 1g sat fat, 50mg sodium, 58g carbohydrates, 14g fiber, 34g sugar, 9g protein

Ingredient Swap: You can use ½ teaspoon of ground ginger in place of fresh ginger.

Tip or fact: If some of these ingredients are new to you or you do not particularly like an ingredient, leave it out the first time and come back to it. Some of these ingredients may grow on your over time.

Shopping list

Produce
□ 1 small organic beet
□ 1 ripe banana
□ 2 medium apples
□ 1 bunch romaine lettuce
□ fresh ginger

Packaged
□ ground flax seeds
□ hemp seeds, hulled or ground
□ sunflower seeds
□ agar-agar

Seasonings and Spices
□ cinnamon

Brighten Up
by Kiana Varner

Easy | Gluten Free | 2 Servings

A delicious and fun way to add beta-carotene to your diet.

Ingredients
2 medium carrots
1 medium sweet potato
1 c pineapple chunks
¼ in. ginger root

Directions
1. Gather all fruits and vegetables and wash thoroughly.
2. Cut up all ingredients into small pieces. About 1 inch in size.
3. Place cut up ingredients into juicer and juice.
4. Strain if needed.
5. Pour into a glass and enjoy.

Nutrition Per Serving 120 calories, 0g total fat, 0g sat fat, 80mg sodium, 30g carbohydrates, 5g fiber, 14g sugar, 2g protein

Storage: Store in a covered glass cup or container and place in refrigerator. Store up to 3 days.

Tip or fact: Did you know February is National Sweet Potato month?

Joyful Juice

Shopping list

Produce
☐ 2 medium carrots
☐ 1 medium sweet potato
☐ 1 small pineapple
☐ ginger root

Celery Cocktail

by Laura Salyer

Easy | **Gluten Free** | **1-2 Servings**

A fruity take on your average celery juice.

Ingredients

5 stalks celery
1 small lime, juiced
3 kiwis, peeled
1 ½ medium Honeycrisp apples, sliced
1 medium peach, pitted

Directions

1. Gather all fruits and vegetables and wash thoroughly.
2. Slowly add the washed celery, peeled lime, peeled kiwis, pitted peach, and apple slices to a juicer.
3. Pour into a bottle or glass jar and serve over ice or chilled with a wedge of lime.

Nutrition Per Serving 120 calories, 0g total fat, 0g sat fat, 80mg sodium, 30g carbohydrates, 5g fiber, 14g sugar, 2g protein

Storage: The lime juice in this recipe helps to keep this drink tasting delicious even when refrigerated. Although best served fresh, feel free to refrigerate this juice in an airtight glass container for up to 48 hours.

Ingredient Swap: Feel free to use any type of apples you like; however, I usually prefer the tangy sweetness of a Honeycrisp, or similar breeds like Opal, SweeTango, or Gala.

Tip or fact: Celery juice is a popular drink of choice for health-conscious individuals, but this recipe takes it a step further by combining your regular celery drink with the fruity, fresh flavors of peach, kiwi, apple, and lime. It is the perfect refreshing, yet still healthy, drink for those hot summer days!

Shopping list

Produce
☐ 5 stalks celery
☐ 1 small lime
☐ 3 kiwis
☐ 2 medium Honeycrisp apples
☐ 1 medium peach

Coconut Mango Mojito

by Laura Salyer

Easy | **Gluten Free** | **1-2 Servings**

A tropical juice twist on a classic cocktail.

Ingredients

1 large mango, pitted & peeled
1 c pineapple chunks
1 small key lime, peeled
½ c fresh Thai coconut water
1-2 sprigs mint

Directions

1. Gather all fruits and vegetables and wash thoroughly.
2. Crack open the coconut and pour the water into a measuring cup. Reserve approximately 2 tablespoons for muddling.
3. Combine the pitted and peeled mango, peeled and cored pineapple, and peeled lime in a juicer.
4. Using a muddler or a spoon and a small bowl, muddle a few mint leaves in the reserved coconut water.
5. Stir the coconut water, fruit juices, and muddled mint mixture together well.
6. Serve chilled over ice with a sprig of mint.

Nutrition Per Serving 220 calories, 7g total fat, 6g sat fat, 10mg sodium, 43g carbohydrates, 7g fiber, 32g sugar, 2g protein

Joyful Juice

Storage: Although best served fresh, feel free to refrigerate this juice in an airtight glass container and place in refrigerator for up to 48 hours.

Ingredient Swap: If you cannot find a young Thai coconut, a mature brown coconut will do in its place. Also, I find that key limes add a more intense flavor than regular limes, but feel free to substitute one for the other if you so desire.

Tip or fact: Cracking open a coconut is much easier than it looks. For a young Thai coconut, set the coconut on its flat bottom, then carefully chop off as much of the fibrous white outer layer from the pointed top. Underneath, you will find a hard shell; once you've uncovered a decent amount of the shell, use the blunt end of a knife to crack it open. Make strong, careful smacks to the shell, rotating the coconut as you go, until you are able to pry off part of the shell and pour out the water. If using a mature brown coconut, simply jab the pointed end of a knife sharpener into two of the three holes on the top, then pour the water into a glass or measuring cup.

Shopping list

Produce
☐ 1 large mango
☐ 1 small pineapple
☐ 1 small key lime
☐ 1 small coconut
☐ mint

Gazpacho Juice

by Laura Salyer

Easy | Gluten Free | 1-2 Servings

A fresh, healthy drink made with a multitude of fruits and veggies.

Ingredients

1 medium green bell pepper
1 medium tomato
1 small lime
1 c watermelon, sliced
⅓ English cucumber
2 large carrots

Directions

1. Gather all fruits and vegetables and wash thoroughly.
2. Peel and chop all fruits and vegetables into 2-inch chunks.
3. Soak the carrots for at least 10 minutes to maximize juice production.
4. Slowly add the bell pepper and tomato slices, peeled lime, carrot sticks, cucumber slices, and watermelon to a juicer.
5. Serve chilled with a sprig of parsley and a wedge of lime.

Nutrition Per Serving 90 calories, 0.5g total fat, 0g sat fat, 55mg sodium, 21g carbohydrates, 4g fiber, 12g sugar, 3g protein

Storage: The tomato in this recipe can quickly lose its flavor when stored in the refrigerator, so I highly suggest enjoying this juice immediately.

Ingredient Swap: I prefer to use English cucumbers to regular ones almost all the time, but especially when juicing. Unlike other cucumbers, they generally have a wax-free skin, limited amount of or smaller sized seeds, and they are less bitter.

Tip or fact: This juice is positively packed with vitamin C that can help boost your immune system. Drink it in the morning to get your day started off on the right foot!

Shopping list

Produce
☐ 1 medium green bell pepper
☐ 1 medium tomato
☐ 1 small lime
☐ 1 small watermelon
☐ 1 English cucumber
☐ 2 large carrots

Glow

by Kiana Varner

Easy | Gluten Free | 2 Servings

A fresh, healthy drink made with a multitude of fruits and veggies.

Ingredients

2 small carrots
1 beet
1 Honeycrisp apple
¼ lemon
1 cucumber

Directions

1. Gather all fruits and vegetables and wash thoroughly.
2. Cut up all ingredients into small pieces. About 1 inch in size.
3. Place cut up ingredients into juicer and juice.
4. Pour into glass and enjoy.

Nutrition Per Serving 100 calories, 0g total fat, 0g sat fat, 60mg sodium, 26g carbohydrates, 5g fiber, 17g sugar, 2g protein

Storage: Store in airtight glass container and place in refrigerator for up to 3 days.

Ingredient Swap: For a sweeter apple, you can switch out the Honeycrisp apple to a fuji apple or any red apple to your liking.

Tip or fact: Did you know that the whole beet is actually edible. Though many people use the root of the beet, the leaves and stem of the vegetable are also edible and an excellent source of vitamin K and A.

Joyful Juice

Shopping list

Produce
☐ 2 small carrots
☐ 1 beet
☐ 1 Honeycrisp apple
☐ 1 lemon
☐ 1 cucumber

Grapefruit-Orange Smoothie by Neeme Liivlaid

| Easy | Gluten Free | 2 Servings |

We love this smoothie when citrus fruits are in season. Most citrus fruits ripen to their sweetest and juiciest during the North American winter.

Ingredients

1 banana
1 Tbsp ground chia seeds
¾ cup + 2 Tbsp additive-free plant milk
¼ avocado
1 carrot
½ orange
½ pink grapefruit
¼ tsp ground ginger
¼ tsp cinnamon

Directions

1. Gather all ingredients and wash the fruits and vegetables thoroughly.
2. Chop the carrots into disks.
3. Peel the citrus fruits, banana and avocado.
4. Throw all ingredients into blender and process until desired consistency.
5. Enjoy!

Nutrition Per Serving 280 calories, 13g total fat, 2g sat fat, 75mg sodium, 40g carbohydrates, 11g fiber, 16g sugar, 7g protein

Tip or fact: I like to add a Brazil nut per serving for daily selenium. Use any plant milk you prefer! My favorite combo is half soy milk and half oat milk

Shopping list

Produce
☐ 1 banana
☐ 1 avocado
☐ 1 carrot
☐ 1 orange
☐ 1 pink grapefruit

Packaged
☐ ground chia seeds
☐ additive-free plant milk

Seasonings and Salt
☐ ground ginger
☐ cinnamon

Green Escape

by Kiana Varner

Easy | **Gluten Free** | **2 Servings**

A green juice high in fiber and great for digestion.

Ingredients

1 medium cucumber
1 c spinach
1 c pineapple chunks
¼ lemon, juiced
¼ in. ginger root

Directions

1. Gather all fruits and vegetables and wash thoroughly.
2. Cut up all ingredients into small pieces. About 1 inch in size.
3. Place cut up ingredients into juicer and juice.
4. Pour into glass and enjoy.

Nutrition Per Serving 70 calories, 0g total fat, 0g sat fat, 15mg sodium, 17g carbohydrates, 2g fiber, 11g sugar, 2g protein

Storage: Store in airtight glass container and place in refrigerator for up to 3 days.

Tip or fact: Did you know that March 26th is National Spinach day?

Joyful Juice

Shopping list

Produce
☐ 1 medium cucumber
☐ 1 bunch spinach
☐ 1 pineapple
☐ 1 lemon
☐ ¼ in. ginger root

Green Victory

by Kiana Varner

Easy | Gluten Free | 2 Servings

A green juice that is packed with vitamins without the heavy earthy taste.

Ingredients

1 medium cucumber
1 medium Honeycrisp apple
1 celery stalk
4-5 leaves collard greens
1 c pineapple chunks

Directions

1. Gather all fruits and vegetables and wash thoroughly.
2. Cut up all fruits and vegetables into small pieces.
3. Place in juicer (or blender) and juice
4. Strain if needed.
5. Pour into a cup and enjoy.

Nutrition Per Serving 120 calories, 0.5g total fat, 0g sat fat, 25mg sodium, 30g carbohydrates, 5g fiber, 20g sugar, 2g protein

Storage: Store in airtight glass container and place in refrigerator for up to 3 days.

Ingredient Swap: You can switch out the Honeycrisp apple for any other red apple. Also, you can switch out the collard greens for swiss chard or kale.

Shopping list

Produce
☐ 1 medium cucumber
☐ 1 medium Honeycrisp apple
☐ 1 celery stalk
☐ 4-5 leaves collard greens
☐ 1 pineapple

Lite Green

by Kiana Varner

Easy | Gluten Free | 2 Servings

A green juice that is refreshing and great for cholesterol control.

Ingredients

1 celery stalk
1 cucumber
1 green pear
¼ lime
¼ in. ginger root
2 handfuls spinach

Directions

1. Gather all fruits and vegetables and wash thoroughly.
2. Cut up all ingredients into small pieces. About 1 inch in size.
3. Place cut up ingredients into juicer and juice.
4. Pour into glass and enjoy.

Nutrition Per Serving 100 calories, 0.5g total fat, 0g sat fat, 65mg sodium, 23g carbohydrates, 7g fiber, 13g sugar, 3g protein

Storage: Store in airtight glass container and place in refrigerator for up to 3 days.

Tip or fact: Did you know during the ancient times in Rome, ginger was so expensive that 1 pound was equal to the price of a whole sheep?

Joyful Juice

Shopping list

Produce
☐ 1 celery stalk
☐ 1 cucumber
☐ 1 green pear
☐ 1 lime
☐ ¼ in. ginger root
☐ 1 bunch spinach

Mango Cacao Smoothie
by Carolina Maturana

Easy | **Gluten Free** | **1-2 Servings**

Mango and chocolate are the perfect combination of essential nutrition while satisfying your sweet tooth. Enjoy any time of day!

Ingredients
- 2 mangos
- 4 medijool dates, pitted
- 4 Tbsp cacao nibs
- 1 tsp chia seeds
- 1 c coconut milk or plant-based milk
- 1 c ice

Directions
1. Gather all ingredients and wash the fruits and vegetables thoroughly.
2. Peel and cut mangoes into chunks and add to blender together with chia seeds, dates and plant-based milk.
3. Add cacao nibs and ice, blend until desired consistency.
4. Pour into glass and enjoy.

Nutrition Per Serving 450 calories, 17g total fat, 11g sat fat, 45mg sodium, 74g carbohydrates, 13g fiber, 57g sugar, 3g protein. **With Almond Milk:** 390 calories, 12g total fat, 6g sat fat, 100mg sodium, 69g carbohydrates, 13g fiber, 54g sugar, 4g protein

Storage: Store in airtight glass container and place in refrigerator for up to 3 days.

Ingredient Swap: You can substitute freshly squeezed orange juice instead of coconut or any plant-based milk if you would like a low-fat version of this smoothie.

Tip or fact: To reduce calories and saturated fat, select soy, oat or almond milk over coconut milk.

Shopping list

Produce
- ☐ 2 mangos

Packaged
- ☐ medijool dates
- ☐ cacao nibs
- ☐ chia seeds

Refrigerated or Frozen
- ☐ coconut milk or plant-based milk

Mango-Turmeric Smoothie
by Neeme Liivlaid

Easy | Gluten Free | 3 Servings 📷

Bring this smoothie into your daily routine when you need a boost of antioxidants to support your immune system!

Ingredients

1 small ripe banana
½ avocado
1 big carrot, shredded
1 mango
½-1 tsp turmeric
2 Tbsp ginger root, chopped
1 ½ Tbsp lemon juice
½ c unsweetened plant-based milk or water
2 Tbsp ground flax seeds
dash black pepper

Directions

1. Gather all ingredients and wash the fruits and vegetables thoroughly.
2. Put harder and more fibrous ingredients (carrot and ginger root) in the bottom of blender to allow them to get well incorporated.
3. Add all the remaining ingredients and start blending using a spoon to press the mixture down. Be careful not to stick your spoon too deep while blending. It's the safest to stop blending while using the spoon.
4. Blend the smoothie to your liking (we like it a bit chunky) and pour into small bowls or glasses, top with whatever you prefer (wild berries or even parsley) and get chewing!

Nutrition Per Serving 190 calories, 7g total fat, 1g sat fat, 55mg sodium, 33g carbohydrates, 7g fiber, 21g sugar, 4g protein

Joyful Juice

Tip or fact: Mangos are the most popular fruit in the world which were first grown in India over 5,000 years ago.

Shopping list

Produce
☐ 1 small ripe banana
☐ 1 avocado
☐ 1 big carrot
☐ 1 mango
☐ ginger root
☐ lemon juice

Packaged
☐ ground flax seeds

Refrigerated or Frozen
☐ unsweetened plant-based milk, optional

Seasonings and Spices
☐ black pepper
☐ turmeric

Pink Drink
by Laura Salyer

Easy | **Gluten Free** | **1-2 Servings**

A gorgeous pink juice packed with fresh fruity flavors.

Ingredients
½ c pineapple, sliced
1 large mango, pitted & peeled
1 large beet, roughly chopped
½ c cranberries
1 c strawberries, destemmed

Directions
1. Gather all fruits and vegetables and wash thoroughly.
2. Combine the pineapple slices, peeled and pitted mango, beet chunks, cranberries, and destemmed strawberries in a juicer.
3. Serve chilled with a skewer of alternating fresh cranberries and pineapple pieces.

Nutrition Per Serving 170 calories, 1g total fat, 0g sat fat, 35mg sodium, 43g carbohydrates, 7g fiber, 34g sugar, 3g protein

Storage: This juice may be stored in an airtight glass container for up to 48 hours.

Ingredient Swap: If you cannot find fresh cranberries, feel free to use frozen. Simply thaw them before use. Frozen fruit in the package can be thawed in the refrigerator, under running water, or in a microwave oven immediately before use. If using a microwave, turn the package several times for even thawing. In a refrigerator, allow 4-6 hours for thawing a 1 pound package of frozen fruit. Allow 30 minutes to 1 hour for thawing under running cool

water.

Tip or fact: If you have not tried beets in a juice before, do not be intimidated! The combination of strong tangy and fruity flavors from the berries, pineapple, and mango overpower the earthy flavor of the beet, but the beautiful pink color from the beet will still shine through.

Shopping list

Produce
☐ 1 pineapple
☐ 1 large mango
☐ 1 large beet
☐ cranberries
☐ strawberries

Refresh

by Kiana Varner

Easy | Gluten Free | 2 Servings

This juice is great for hydration, especially on a hot, sunny day.

Ingredients

2 c watermelon, cubed
2 mint leaves
½ medium cucumber
2 handfuls spinach

Directions

1. Gather all fruits and vegetables and wash thoroughly.
2. Cut up all ingredients into small pieces. About 1 inch in size.
3. Place cut up ingredients into juicer and juice.
4. Strain if needed.
5. Pour into glass and enjoy.

Nutrition Per Serving 70 calories, 0g total fat, 0g sat fat, 45mg sodium, 16g carbohydrates, 2g fiber, 11g sugar, 3g protein

Storage: Store in airtight glass container and place in refrigerator for up to 3 days.

Tip or fact: Mint has been thought to support digestion, soothe an upset stomach and sometimes even provide headache relief. Try this and see how you feel!

Joyful Juice

Shopping list

Produce
☐ 1 small watermelon
☐ mint leaves
☐ 1 medium cucumber
☐ spinach

Strawberry Lime Smoothie
by Carolina Maturana

Easy | **Gluten Free** | **4 Servings**

This juice is great for hydration, especially on a hot, sunny day.

Ingredients

3 c frozen organic, unsweetened strawberries
4 limes, juiced
3 c cold water
⅓ c date syrup
1 ½ Tbsp chia seeds

Directions

1. Gather all ingredients and wash the fruits and vegetables thoroughly.
2. Juice the limes and add all ingredients to the blender
3. Add more date syrup if you prefer a sweeter smoothie.
4. Pour into a glass and enjoy.

Nutrition Per Serving 140 calories, 1.5g total fat, 0g sat fat, 5mg sodium, 34g carbohydrates, 4g fiber, 27g sugar, 1g protein

Storage: Can be stored in the fridge for 3-4 days in airtight glass container or bottle.

Tip or fact: 1 tablespoon of chia seeds has 5g fiber. Nearly 40% of chia seeds (by weight) consists of fiber. Be sure to add fiber slowly to your diet for comfort and best results for your body.

Shopping list

Produce
☐ 4 lime

Packaged
☐ date syrup
☐ chia seeds

Refrigerated or Frozen
☐ frozen organic, unsweetened strawberries

Sunrise

by Kiana Varner

Easy | Gluten Free | 2 Servings

A great spin on orange juice by adding the fiber and minerals of pineapple and sweet potato.

Ingredients

1 orange
1 c pineapple chunks
1 sweet potato

Directions

1. Gather all fruits and vegetables and wash thoroughly.
2. Cut up all ingredients into small pieces. About 1 inch in size.
3. Place cut up ingredients into juicer and juice.
4. Strain if needed.
5. Pour into glass and enjoy.

Nutrition Per Serving 130 calories, 0g total fat, 0g sat fat, 35mg sodium, 32g carbohydrates, 5g fiber, 17g sugar, 2g protein

Storage: Store in airtight glass container and place in refrigerator for up to 3 days.

Tip or fact: Did you know that after washing and drying the top part of the pineapple, you can then plant it in soil and a new pineapple will grow.

Joyful Juice

Shopping list

Produce
☐ 1 orange
☐ 1 pineapple
☐ 1 sweet potato

Sweet Boost

by Kiana Varner

Easy | **Gluten Free** | **2 Servings**

A sweet twist on a beet juice that is great for a boost of energy.

Ingredients

1 Honeycrisp apple
1 small beet
1 small green pear
¼ lime
¼ in. ginger root

Directions

1. Gather all fruits and vegetables and wash thoroughly.
2. Cut up all ingredients into small pieces. About 1 inch in size.
3. Place cut up ingredients into juicer and juice.
4. Strain if needed.
5. Pour into glass and enjoy.

Nutrition Per Serving 130 calories, 0.5g total fat, 0g sat fat, 35mg sodium, 32g carbohydrates, 8g fiber, 22g sugar, 2g protein

Storage: Store in airtight glass container and place in refrigerator for up to 3 days.

Ingredient Swap: You can switch the Honeycrisp apple for any other red apples.

Tip or fact: Did you know the most expensive pear in the world is the Buddha shaped pear. It goes for $9.00 each?

Shopping list

Produce
☐ 1 Honeycrisp apple
☐ 1 small beet
☐ 1 small green pear
☐ 1 lime
☐ ¼ in. ginger root

Sweet Green

by Kiana Varner

Easy | Gluten Free | 2 Servings

A sweet green juice that is not only great for hydration but also for your daily recommended greens intake.

Ingredients

¼ lime
2 green apples
5 c spinach
½ medium cucumber

Directions

1. Gather all fruits and vegetables and wash thoroughly.
2. Cut up all ingredients into small pieces. About 1 inch in size.
3. Place cut up ingredients into juicer and juice.
4. Strain if needed.
5. Pour into glass and enjoy.

Nutrition Per Serving 140 calories, 0g total fat, 0g sat fat, 110mg sodium, 34g carbohydrates, 8g fiber, 20g sugar, 4g protein

Storage: Store in airtight glass container and place in refrigerator for up to 3 days.

Tip or fact: Did you know that India is the largest grower of limes in the world?

Joyful Juice

Shopping list

Produce
☐ 1 lime
☐ 2 green apples
☐ spinach
☐ 1 medium cucumber

Upgrade
by Kiana Varner

Easy | Gluten Free | 2 Servings

A rainbow of color all blended together in a glass for a nutritious boost.

Ingredients
2 medium green apples
1 small beet
2 medium carrots
1 medium celery stalk
1 medium cucumber

Directions
1. Gather all fruits and vegetables and wash thoroughly.
2. Cut up all ingredients into small pieces. About 1 inch in size.
3. Place cut up ingredients into juicer and juice.
4. Strain if needed.
5. Pour into glass and enjoy.

Nutrition Per Serving 170 calories, 1g total fat, 0g sat fat, 100mg sodium, 42g carbohydrates, 9g fiber, 28g sugar, 3g protein

Storage: Store in airtight glass container and place in refrigerator for up to 3 days.

Tip or fact: Did you know cucumbers contain many of the vitamins you need in a day such as vitamin B1, folic acid, vitamin C, calcium, and many more?

Shopping list

Produce
- 1 lime
- 2 green apples
- spinach
- 1 medium cucumber

Parsley

Thyme

Anise

Bay Leaf

Arugula

Scrumptious Salads

Arugula Apple Beet Salad

by Diane Smith

Easy | Gluten Free | 4 Servings

Beautiful beets and crunchy walnuts top this arugula salad mixed with spinach in a light vinaigrette.

Ingredients

1 bag arugula
2-3 roasted beets, rough chopped
1 apple, chopped
⅓ c chopped walnuts
3 Tbsp white wine, champagne or
   apple cider vinegar
1 tsp prepared yellow mustard
1 tsp maple syrup
2 Tbsp water

Directions

1. Gather all ingredients.
2. If roasting the beets at home, preheat oven to 375°F.
3. Trim beet tops to about 1/2 of beets and save for another meal. Rinse any dirt or debris from the beets.
4. Put beets on a large piece of aluminum foil. (Optional: drizzle with olive oil, salt and pepper.) Fold foil over the beets and place in an oven-proof container.
5. Roast for 30 minutes or until beets are tender. Cool and remove skins.
6. Put the salad ingredients a large salad bowl.
7. Whisk dressing ingredients in small bowl.
8. Pour over salad and toss.

Nutrition Per Serving 123 calories, 7g total fat, 1g sat fat, 65mg sodium, 15g carbohydrates, 3g fiber, 10g sugar, 3g protein

Tip or fact: Using roasted beets from the market without anything but beets makes this recipe super quick.

Shopping list

Produce
☐ 1 bag arugula
☐ 2-3 roasted beets
☐ 1 apple

Packaged
☐ chopped walnuts
☐ white wine, champagne or
   apple cider vinegar
☐ prepared yellow mustard
☐ maple syrup

Berry Delicious Coleslaw
by Jyl Steinback

Easy | **Kid Friendly** | **Gluten Free** | **6 Servings**

This coleslaw is for you, if you're looking for a fresh salad that is super quick and easy to throw together.

Ingredients

⅓ c cashew sour cream (recipe p. 5)

¾ tsp crushed mustard seeds

2 Tbsp apple cider vinegar or lemon juice

2 Tbsp tamari or low-sodium soy sauce

20 oz. shredded cabbage for coleslaw

⅓ c fresh cranberries

Directions

1. Gather all ingredients.
2. Combine cashew sour cream, tamari (or soy sauce), mustard seeds and vinegar (or lemon juice) in a small bowl. Mix until blended.
3. Combine cabbage and cranberries in a large bowl.
4. Pour dressing over top and toss until coated.
5. Cover and refrigerate until ready to serve.

Nutrition Per Serving 50 calories, 2g total fat, 0g sat fat, 210mg sodium, 7g carbohydrates, 3g fiber, 1g sugar, 2g protein

Storage: Store in a sealed glass container in fridge for up to 4 days.

Ingredient Swap: Use fresh cabbage head instead of pre-packaged version – grate or chop it and use 2 cups per serving, i.e. 12 cups in total. You can also use dried or frozen cranberries in place of fresh cranberries.

Tip or fact: One cup of shredded raw cabbage contains 190% of the recommended daily amount of vitamin C. Cabbage is an excellent source of vitamin K. 1 cup (150 grams) of shredded, boiled cabbage contains 91% of the recommended daily amount of vitamin K.

Salads

Shopping list

Produce
- ☐ 2 10 oz. pkgs shredded cabbage for coleslaw
- ☐ fresh cranberries
- ☐ 1 lemon, optional

Packaged
- ☐ raw cashews
- ☐ low sodium soy sauce, optional
- ☐ apple cider vinegar, optional
- ☐ tamari, optional

Seasonings and Spices
- ☐ mustard seeds

Black Bean Salad

by Jyl Steinback

Easy | Gluten Free | 6 Servings

The magic of lemon juice adds sunshine to the flavors in this simple but delicious dish.

Ingredients

3 15.5 oz. cans low sodium black beans, rinsed and drained

3 c red and green bell peppers, chopped

2 c tomatoes, chopped

1 c green onions, sliced

¼ c lemon juice

Directions

1. Gather all ingredients.
2. Combine beans, peppers, tomatoes and green onions in a large bowl. Mix well.
3. Pour lemon juice over top and mix well.
4. Cover and refrigerate several hours before serving.

Nutrition Per Serving 230 calories, 1g total fat, 0g sat fat, 300mg sodium, 44g carbohydrates, 17g fiber, 6g sugar, 14g protein

Ingredient Swap: Try dry black beans to reduce the sodium of this recipe. Preparation instructions are on p. 6.

Tip or fact: Per serving, this recipe provides more fiber than most Americans get in a day.

Shopping list

Produce
☐ 2 green bell peppers
☐ 2 red bell peppers
☐ 2 medium tomatoes
☐ 1 bunch green onions
☐ 3 lemons

Packaged
☐ 3 15.5 oz. cans low sodium black beans

Colorful Coleslaw

by Jyl Steinback

| Easy | Kid Friendly | Gluten Free | 4 Servings |

This easy vitamin-packed coleslaw is not only delicious but loaded with lots of plant nutritious colorful veggies.

Ingredients

4 c shredded cabbage mix
1 c carrot, shredded
1 large red bell pepper, sliced thin
1 large yellow bell pepper, sliced thin
2 tsp onion powder
2 Tbsp Westbrae Natural Stone-ground Mustard
4 Tbsp apple cider vinegar or lemon juice
4 tsp low-sodium soy sauce
2 tsp date sugar, optional
black pepper, to taste

Directions

1. Gather all ingredients.
2. In a large bowl, combine cabbage, carrot, peppers, and onion powder and toss to mix.
3. In a small bowl, combine mustard, vinegar or lemon juice, soy sauce, and date sugar. Stir until all ingredients are blended.
4. Pour mixture over veggies and toss well.
5. Add black pepper to taste.
6. Refrigerate 1 to 2 hours before serving.

Nutrition Per Serving 60 calories, 0g total fat, 0g sat fat, 380mg sodium, 14g carbohydrates, 3g fiber, 4g sugar, 3g protein

Storage: Store in a sealed glass container in fridge for up to 4 days.

Ingredient Swap: Use fresh cabbage head instead of pre-packaged version – grate or chop it and use 1 cup per serving, i.e. 4 cups in total. Any bell pepper works great, i.e. red, yellow, green, orange. If you don't have suitable mustard, use 1 tsp crushed mustard seeds instead.

Tip or fact: When it comes to drying peppers, as we have all seen large bunches hanging from shops, front porches, or patios. In pepper growing regions, such as New Mexico, these drying pepper chains—called chile ristras—are thought to bring good luck and good health as well as good nutrition.

Salads

Shopping list

Produce
☐ 1 lb. shredded cabbage
☐ 1 large carrots
☐ 1 red bell pepper
☐ 1 yellow bell pepper
☐ 1 lemon, optional

Packaged
☐ Westbrae Natural Stoneground Mustard
☐ apple cider vinegar, optional
☐ low sodium soy sauce

Baking Ingredients
☐ date sugar

Seasonings and Spices
☐ onion powder
☐ black pepper

Delicious Fruit Salad

by Jyl Steinback

Easy | **Kid Friendly** | **Gluten Free** | **4 Servings**

My dad's favorite nighttime snack.

Ingredients

½ c purple grapes
½ c green grapes
1 orange
1 apple
1 banana
½ c raisins
½ c raspberries
½ c strawberry
½ c blackberries
½ kiwi
½ c sliced almonds
½ c chocolate syrup, optional

Directions

1. Gather all ingredients.
2. Cut-up apples, bananas, strawberries and kiwi.
3. Peel and section the orange.
4. Mix all of the fruit together.
5. Sprinkle sliced almonds on top.
6. Optional: Drizzle with chocolate syrup
7. Refrigerate until ready to eat.

Nutrition Per Serving Without Chocolate Syrup:
240 calories, 6g total fat, 0.5g sat fat, 0mg sodium, 47g carbohydrates, 8g fiber, 32g sugar, 5g protein.
With Chocolate Syrup: 350 calories, 7g total fat, 0.5g sat fat, 35mg sodium, 72g carbohydrates, 8g fiber, 51g sugar, 6g protein

Ingredient Swap: Any of your favorite fruits.

Tip or fact: This salad conveniently packs your colors for the day to increase the variety of vitamins, minerals and phytonutrients in every bite.

Shopping list

Produce
☐ purple grapes
☐ green grapes
☐ 1 medium orange
☐ 1 medium apple
☐ 1 medium banana
☐ raspberries
☐ strawberries
☐ blackberries
☐ 1 small kiwi

Packaged
☐ raisins
☐ sliced almonds
☐ chocolate syrup, optional

Fabulous and Fun Veggie Salad by Jyl Steinback

Easy | Gluten Free | 4 Servings

My favorite salad – it includes everything colorful in my kitchen.

Ingredients

1 bunch kale, chopped
1 bunch romaine, chopped
1 c cherry tomatoes, halved
1 large avocado, sliced
½ red onion, chopped, optional
½ c mushrooms, sliced
1 c bean sprouts
½ c bell peppers, chopped, optional
¼ c nuts and seeds

Directions

1. Gather all ingredients.
2. Prepare all veggies and mix together.
3. If using onion and mushroom, you can choose to sauté them first in water or vegetable broth for more flavor.
4. Sprinkle with a handful of nuts and seeds.
5. Refrigerate until ready to eat.

Nutrition Per Serving 190 calories, 13g total fat, 1.5g sat fat, 15mg sodium, 15g carbohydrates, 7g fiber, 5g sugar, 6g protein

Ingredient Swap: Any of your favorite veggies.

Tip or fact: A rainbow of color in your salad bowl makes for a variety of essential nutrients for you! Feel free to mix it up with whatever veggies you have in the kitchen.

Salads

Shopping list

Produce
☐ 1 bunch kale
☐ 1 bunch romaine
☐ cherry tomatoes
☐ 1 large avocado
☐ 1 red onion, optional
☐ mushrooms
☐ bean sprouts
☐ 2 bell peppers, optional

Packaged
☐ sesame seeds
☐ almond slivers
☐ pumpkin spicy edamame

Gazpacho Salad
by Jyl Steinback

Easy | **Gluten Free** | **4 Servings**

All the flavors of summer wrapped up in this rice salad. A perfect dish for your picnic or potluck.

Ingredients

½ c brown rice
2 c tomatoes, seeded and diced
1 c cucumber, seeded and diced
⅔ c green pepper, seeded and diced
¼ c onion, chopped
1 Tbsp + 2 tsp red wine vinegar
2-3 tsp garlic, minced
romaine or red-leaf lettuce

Directions

1. Gather all ingredients.
2. Cook the rice according to package directions.
3. In a blender, combine 1 cup of the tomatoes, 1/2 cup cucumber, 1/3 cup green pepper, 2 tablespoons onion, minced garlic and red-wine vinegar to make the dressing.
4. In a large bowl, combine the rice with the dressing, and toss until thoroughly blended.
5. Add the remaining tomatoes, cucumber, green pepper and onion, and toss until just combined.
6. Refrigerate up to 4 hours.
7. Line platter with lettuce and arrange salad on top.

Nutrition Per Serving: 130 calories, 1.5g total fat, 0g sat fat, 10mg sodium, 25g carbohydrates, 3g fiber, 4g sugar, 3g protein

Ingredient Swap: Swap in quinoa for brown rice.

Tip or fact: Want to support your heart health? Eat whole grains, like the brown rice, in this recipe.

Shopping list

Produce
☐ 2 tomatoes
☐ 1 cucumber
☐ 1 green bell pepper
☐ 1 white onion
☐ 2 cloves garlic
☐ 1 bunch romaine lettuce

Packaged
☐ brown rice
☐ red wine vinegar

Loaded Tender Kale Salad
With Orange Balsamic Dressing by Jyl Steinback

Easy | **Kid Friendly** | **Gluten Free** | **4 Servings**

A deliciously tangy dressing to top this colorful kale salad.

Ingredients

Salad
6 c kale, chopped
1 medium apple, peeled and chopped
1 large avocado, pitted and cubed
1 c carrots, julienned
1 c cucumber, chopped
⅓ c onion, sliced
1 c green pepper, diced
2 c canned mandarin oranges, juice drained
1 c cherry tomatoes
1 tsp lemon juice

Dressing
1 lemon, remaining juice
⅓ c balsamic vinegar
½ c orange juice
1 tsp Dijon mustard
½ tsp fresh ginger

Directions

1. Gather all ingredients.
2. Wash the kale and shake off excess water. Remove the leaves from the stem and tear into bite-sized pieces.
3. Juice lemon. drizzle 1 teaspoon of lemon juice on the kale. Reserve the rest of the lemon juice for the dressing.
4. Wash your hands and massage the kale until it reaches the consistency you like – al dente or softer (1-3 minutes). Set aside.
5. Dice the bell pepper. Slice the onion. Chop the apple and cucumber. Julienne the carrots. You can leave the cherry tomatoes whole or slice them in half.
6. Cube the avocado and drizzle with a little lemon juice. Set the avocado aside.
7. Add dressing ingredients to blender and blend until smooth. Set aside.
8. Add all the vegetables (except the avocado) and 1-2 teaspoons of balsamic vinegar dressing to the kale.
9. Mix with tongs.
10. Taste and adjust seasonings.
11. Plate the salad and top with avocado. Serve!

Salads

Nutrition Per Serving 190 calories, 6g total fat, 1g sat fat, 55mg sodium, 34g carbohydrates, 7g fiber, 18g sugar, 4g protein

Tip or fact: Until the end of the Middle Ages, kale was one of the most common green vegetables in all of Europe.

Shopping list

Produce
☐ 1 medium apple
☐ 1 large avocado
☐ 2 large carrots
☐ 1 green bell pepper
☐ 1 medium cucumber
☐ 1 bunch kale
☐ 1 medium yellow onion
☐ cherry tomatoes
☐ 1 large lemon
☐ 1 in. fresh ginger

Packaged
☐ balsamic vinegar
☐ Dijon mustard
☐ 1 can mandarin oranges

Refrigerated or Frozen
☐ orange juice

Pad Thai Zoodle Salad

by Laura Salyer

Medium | **4-6 Servings**

Colorful, fun, zesty salad topped with tofu.

Ingredients

Salad
2 oz. rice noodles
1 Tbsp toasted sesame oil
3 carrots, spiralized or julienned
2 large zucchinis, spiralized or julienned
2 large squash, spiralized or julienned
2 large beets, spiralized or julienned
2 large English cucumbers, spiralized or julienned
12 oz. tofu, cubed
1 red bell pepper, julienned
½ c cilantro, diced

Dressing
½ c warm water
3 Tbsp apple cider vinegar
½ Tbsp toasted sesame oil
3 Tbsp low sodium tamari
1 lime, juiced
½ c cilantro
1 jalapeño, cored and seeded
2 Tbsp organic peanut butter
3 Tbsp hemp seeds
1 tsp cayenne pepper
black pepper, to taste, optional

Directions

1. Gather all ingredients.
2. Pour boiling water over rice noodles and let sit for 5 minutes, then drain, rinse and set aside.
3. Meanwhile, add dressing ingredients to blender and blend until smooth. Set aside.
4. Drain and press tofu between two dish towels to remove as much water as possible. Cut into ½ inch cubes.
5. Heat 1 tablespoon sesame oil in a skillet, and season with pepper.
6. Add tofu cubes and sear over medium heat until all sides are golden-browned and crispy.
7. Spiralize all vegetables.
8. Toss rice noodles and spiralized veggies in a large salad bowl with the dressing.
9. Add the tofu and finish the bowls with fresh cilantro leaves, extra lime wedges, or any additional desired toppings.

Nutrition Per Serving: 180 calories, 6g total fat, 1g sat fat, 75mg sodium, 26g carbohydrates, 5g fiber, 11g sugar, 10g protein. **Dressing** 80 calories, 6g total fat, 1g sat fat, 310mg sodium, 4g carbohydrates, 0g fiber, 1g sugar, 4g protein

Storage: As with most raw vegetable dishes and salads, the spiralized   lose their crispness shortly after preparation. It is best to serve this dish immediately.

Ingredient Swap: If allergic to peanuts, you may want to try substituting vegenaise or another creamy ingredient to serve as the base for the dressing. Also, if you have an aversion to cilantro, beets, or any of the vegetables in this recipe, feel free to get creative!

Shopping list

Produce
☐ 3 carrots
☐ 2 large zucchinis
☐ 2 large squash
☐ 2 large beets
☐ 2 large cucumbers
☐ 1 red bell pepper
☐ 1 bunch cilantro
☐ 2 limes
☐ 1 jalapeño

Packaged
☐ sesame oil
☐ apple cider vinegar
☐ low sodium soy sauce
☐ organic peanut butter
☐ hemp seeds

Refrigerated or Frozen
☐ 12 oz. tofu

Seasonings and Spices
☐ cayenne pepper
☐ black pepper, optional

Protein Salad
by Neil Popp

Easy | **2 Servings**

This salad gives you less calories, and more gains!

Ingredients
¼ c unsalted pumpkin seeds
¼ c unsalted pistachios
¼ c unsweetened dried cranberries
2 c fresh baby spinach
1 avocado, sliced
½ c edamame, shelled
1 Tbsp balsamic vinegar

Directions
1. Gather all ingredients.
2. Crush pistachios and pumpkin seeds in a bowl.
3. Add half of the dried cranberries to the bowl.
4. Rinse spinach thoroughly and combine with all dry ingredients in a bowl.
5. Slice avocado and fan slices over bowl.
6. Add edamame on top, along with the remaining cranberries and balsamic vinegar.

Nutrition Per Serving 450 calories, 30g total fat, 4.5g sat fat, 45mg sodium, 37g carbohydrates, 13g fiber, 18g sugar, 15g protein

Storage: Store in airtight glass container and refrigerate for 3-7 days.

Tip or fact: Spinach is an extremely nutrient-rich vegetable. It packs high amounts of carotenoids, vitamin C, vitamin K, folic acid, iron, and calcium.

Salads

Shopping list

Produce
☐ 1 avocado
☐ 1 bag baby spinach

Packaged
☐ balsamic vinegar
☐ unsalted pumpkin seeds
☐ unsalted pistachios
☐ unsweetened dried cranberries

Refrigerated or Frozen
☐ 1 bag frozen edamame

Quinoa Salad with Roasted Peppers
by Jyl Steinback

| Easy | Gluten Free | 10 Servings |

Whether you serve this up immediately warm or save it for the next day and serve it up cold, this salad is an amazing complement to any meal.

Ingredients

2 Tbsp low sodium vegetable broth
2 c quinoa, rinsed and drained
2 c fresh orange juice
2 c water
kosher salt
1 large red bell pepper
1 large yellow bell pepper
½ c pine nuts
¼ c red wine vinegar
1 medium cucumber, peeled and finely diced
1 large tomato, seeded and finely diced
¼ c basil, finely chopped
freshly ground black pepper

Directions

1. Gather all ingredients.
2. In a medium saucepan, heat the 2 tablespoon of vegetable stock. Add the quinoa and cook over moderately high heat, stirring, until lightly browned, about 4 minutes.
3. Add the orange juice, water and a generous pinch of salt and bring to a boil. Cover and cook over low heat until the liquid is absorbed, about 15 minutes.
4. Fluff the quinoa with a fork and spread on a baking sheet to cool.
5. Meanwhile, roast the red and yellow peppers directly over a gas flame or under the broiler, turning occasionally, until charred all over.
6. Transfer the peppers to a bowl, cover and let steam for 10 minutes. Peel and seed them and cut into ¼ inch dice.
7. In a medium skillet, toast the pine nuts over moderate heat, stirring occasionally, until golden and fragrant, about 5 minutes. Transfer the pine nuts to a plate to cool.
8. In a large bowl, add ¼ cup red wine vinegar. Add the quinoa, peppers, pine nuts, cucumber, tomato, basil and mint and toss well, breaking up any lumps of quinoa.

Nutrition Per Serving: 210 calories, 7g total fat, 0.5g sat fat, 10mg sodium, 31g carbohydrates, 3g fiber, 7g sugar, 7g protein

Tip or fact: This is a great recipe to make a day before.

Shopping list

Produce
☐ 1 large red bell pepper
☐ 1 medium cucumber
☐ 1 large tomato
☐ 1 bunch basil
☐ 1 large yellow bell pepper

Packaged
☐ vegetable stock
☐ quinoa
☐ pine nuts
☐ red wine vinegar

Refrigerated or Frozen
☐ orange juice

Seasonings and Spices
☐ kosher salt
☐ black peppercorns

Salad with Roasted Veggies by Nele Livlaiid

Medium | 2 Servings

Roasted veggies are deliciously juicy while the Tahini-Chickpea Dressing adds this perfect richness to your lunch or dinner bowl.

Ingredients

2 medium eggplants
1 summer squash
1 big carrot
1 small fennel
2 c shredded red cabbage
⅛ tsp Himalayan salt
⅛ tsp black pepper
⅛ tsp thyme
⅛ tsp rosemary
⅛ tsp oregano
lettuce or mixed greens

Directions

1. Preheat oven to 350°F.
2. Gather all ingredients.
3. Cut your eggplants and summer squash into thicker slices. Slice the carrot and fennel as well and place them on a baking sheet lined with parchment paper. Sprinkle some Himalayan salt onto eggplants and let sit for 15-30 minutes until you see water drops on their surface.
4. Sprinkle all veggies with some dried rosemary, thyme, oregano and black pepper and bake for 35-40 minutes until you see that the eggplants are well wilted.
5. While the veggies are roasting, prepare Tahini-Chickpea Dressing (recipe p. 12).
6. Combine your salads by placing lettuce and raw cabbage into the bowl and topping it with roasted veggies.
7. Top the salad with dressing.

Nutrition Per Serving 130 calories, 1g total fat, 0g sat fat, 140mg sodium, 30g carbohydrates, 13g fiber, 14g sugar, 7g protein

Salads

Tip or fact: You may easily add more veggies and lettuce to your portion – as much as you can stuff! It's not mandatory to sprinkle the veggies with herbs before baking, but it does give them a nice note. Red cabbage can be substituted with white cabbage or even sauerkraut or kimchi. Go wild and add some fresh herbs like basil for example. Finally, alfalfa sprouts would also be an excellent addition to this vegan salad.

Shopping list

Produce
☐ 1 large red bell pepper
☐ 1 medium cucumber
☐ 1 large tomato
☐ 1 bunch basil
☐ 1 large yellow bell pepper

Packaged
☐ 2 eggplants
☐ 1 summer squash
☐ 1 large carrot
☐ 1 fennel bulb
☐ shredded red cabbage
☐ 1 bag mixed greens

Seasonings and Spices
☐ Himalayan salt
☐ black pepper
☐ thyme
☐ rosemary
☐ oregano

Spicy Quinoa Salad
by Jyl Steinback

| Medium | Gluten Free | 6 Servings |

I love quinoa in my salads. It fills me up and so delicious!

Ingredients

- 1 c dry quinoa
- 3 c water
- 2 c cucumber, diced
- 1 small red onion, finely minced, optional
- 2 c tomatoes, finely diced
- 1-2 jalapeños, seeded and finely chopped
- ½ c cilantro, chopped
- 2 Tbsp fresh lime juice
- 1 Tbsp red wine vinegar or sherry vinegar
- 3 Tbsp extra virgin olive oil
- 1 avocado, sliced

Directions

1. Gather all ingredients.
2. Place the quinoa in a bowl, and cover with cold water. Let sit for five minutes.
3. Drain through a strainer, and rinse until the water runs clear.
4. Bring 3 cups of water to a boil in a medium saucepan.
5. Add the quinoa to water and bring back to a boil. Then reduce the heat to low.
6. Cover and simmer 15 minutes or until the quinoa is tender and translucent. Each grain should have a little thread.
7. Drain off the water in the pan through a strainer and return the quinoa to the pan.
8. Cover the pan with a clean dishtowel, replace the lid and allow to sit for 10 minutes.
9. If making for the freezer, uncover and allow to cool to room temperature. Place in a glass or reusable storage container and label.
10. Meanwhile, place the finely diced cucumber in a colander, and sprinkle with salt. Toss and allow to sit for 15 minutes.
11. Rinse the cucumber with cold water and drain on paper towels.
12. If using the onion, place in a bowl and cover with cold water. Let sit for five minutes, then drain, rinse with cold water and drain on paper towels.
13. Combine the tomatoes, cilantro, vinegar, lime juice and olive oil in a bowl.
14. Add the cucumber, onion, quinoa and cilantro.
15. Toss together, and taste and adjust seasonings.
16. Serve garnished with sliced avocado and cilantro sprigs.

Shopping list

Produce
- ☐ 2 cucumbers
- ☐ 1 small red onion
- ☐ 2 tomatoes
- ☐ 1-2 jalapeños
- ☐ 1 bunch cilantro
- ☐ 1 lime
- ☐ 1 avocado

Packaged
- ☐ quinoa
- ☐ red wine vinegar or sherry vinegar
- ☐ extra virgin olive oil

Nutrition Per Serving: 240 calories, 14g total fat, 2g sat fat, 10mg sodium, 27g carbohydrates, 5g fiber, 4g sugar, 6g protein

Tip or fact: Quinoa is highly nutritious and the most complete protein of any grain. Ideal for a vegetarian or vegan diet!

Summer Salad with Miso-Lime Dressing by Kayli Dice

Easy | **Gluten Free** | **1 Serving**

This salad tastes like summer. It's cool, crunchy, spicy, and sweet – a beautiful celebration of the abundant and powerful colors and flavors of the season.

Ingredients

1 beet, trimmed
1 carrot
1 c arugula
1 c mixed greens
1 Tbsp cashews
¼ avocado
½ tomato
¼ cucumber
¼ red onion
1 tsp white miso
1 tsp tahini
lime cayenne, to taste
pinch ginger powder
black pepper, to taste

Directions

1. Gather all ingredients and rinse all produce.
2. Trim beet root.
3. Using a food processor with a grater attachment or a hand held grater, shred beet root and carrot.
4. Chop cucumber and tomato into small pieces.
5. Peel and thinly slice onion.
6. Peel and mince garlic.
7. Slice open avocado, remove pit, scoop out flesh, and cut into slices.
8. In a bowl, add mixed greens and arugula, shredded beet root and carrot, cucumber, and tomato.
9. Roughly chop cashews and sprinkle on top.
10. To make dressing, whisk together miso, tahini, lime juice, cayenne, ginger powder, and black pepper.
11. Add a splash of water to thin if needed.
12. Drizzle over salad and top with sliced avocado.

Salads

Nutrition Per Serving 270 calories, 15g total fat, 2g sat fat, 250mg sodium, 34g carbohydrates, 11g fiber, 14g sugar, 8g protein

Tip or fact: Arugula is known as the "Garden Rocket" because it grows at rapid speed. Leaves are ready for the harvest 40 days after sowing of seed.

Shopping list

Produce
☐ 1 beet
☐ 1 carrot
☐ arugula
☐ mixed greens
☐ 1 avocado
☐ 1 tomato
☐ 1 cucumber
☐ 1red onion

Packaged
☐ cashews
☐ tahini
☐ white miso

Seasonings and Spices
☐ lime cayenne
☐ ginger powder
☐ black pepper

Summer Veggie and Tahini Salad
by Laura Salyer

| Easy | Gluten Free | 3-4 Serving |

A fresh and flavorful salad filled with tons of healthy veggies.

Ingredients

Salad
- 6 c mixed lettuce greens or spring mix
- 1 orange bell pepper, diced finely
- 1 large English cucumber, chopped
- 3 large carrots, peeled and chopped
- 1 c corn kernels
- 1 c sugar snap peas, roughly chopped
- 5 spring onions, sliced
- 1-2 ripe avocados, pitted and sliced
- ½ c cherry tomatoes, sliced

Dressing
- ¼ c tahini
- 2 Tbsp fresh lemon juice
- 1 Tbsp apple cider vinegar
- 2 cloves garlic, minced
- 1 Tbsp pure maple syrup
- pepper, to taste
- ¼ c warm water, to thin the dressing

Directions

1. Gather all ingredients and rinse all produce.
2. Combine all ingredients for the salad dressing (except water) in a food processor or blender.
3. Process until smooth, adding 1 tablespoon of warm water to the mixture until the desired consistency is reached (I generally like very thin dressing, so I add all of the water and sometimes more).
4. Set aside or refrigerate until ready to use. If refrigerating, you may need to add more warm water and mix well to refresh dressing immediately before serving.
5. In a large bowl, lay down the lettuce and pour approximately half of the dressing over top. Mix well with salad tongs.
6. Add bell pepper, cucumber, carrot, corn, snap peas, spring onion, and tomato slices.
7. Pour remaining dressing over the vegetables and mix gently.
8. Add avocado slices on the top.
9. Serve immediately.

Nutrition Per Serving Dressing: 110 calories, 8g total fat, 1g sat fat, 5mg sodium, 8g carbohydrates, 1g fiber, 3g sugar, 3g protein. **Salad** 270 calories, 16g total fat, 2g sat fat, 105mg sodium, 31g carbohydrates, 13g fiber, 9g sugar, 7g protein

Storage: The dressing may be stored in an airtight glass container for up to 3 days, however the salad itself should be consumed immediately to avoid wilting.

Ingredient Swap: English cucumbers are less bitter and have fewer seeds, but you can use any type of cucumber in this salad.

Tip or fact: Tahini is a condiment made from toasted and ground hulled sesame seeds. It normally has a consistency similar to peanut butter or other nut butters, and it is one of the main ingredients in hummus, baba ghanoush, and halva.

Shopping list

Produce
- ☐ spring mix
- ☐ 1 orange bell pepper
- ☐ 1 large English cucumber
- ☐ 3 large carrots,
- ☐ 1 ear of corn
- ☐ sugar snap peas
- ☐ 5 spring onions
- ☐ 1-2 ripe avocados
- ☐ cherry tomatoes

Packaged
- ☐ tahini
- ☐ apple cider vinegar
- ☐ pure maple syrup

Seasonings and Spices
- ☐ black pepper

Super Fruity Salad

by Laura Salyer

| Easy | Gluten Free | 3-4 Serving |

A festive rainbow of fresh fruits and greens.

Ingredients

Salad

- 3-4 mandarin oranges, peeled and sectioned
- 10 strawberries, quartered
- ½ c pineapple, chopped into thin wedges
- ½ c blueberries
- 1 c pecans, toasted
- 1 English cucumber, peeled and diced
- 3 large carrots, peeled and chopped
- 3 stalks celery, thinly sliced
- 1 ½ heads iceberg lettuce, coarsely chopped
- 4 c spinach

Dressing

- 1 c fresh strawberries, de-stemmed
- ½ bunch spring onions
- ¼ c balsamic vinegar
- ¼ c unsweetened applesauce
- ½ c water
- 1 Tbsp pure maple syrup
- ½ lemon, juiced
- ¼ tsp salt
- ⅛ tsp black pepper

Directions

1. Gather all ingredients and rinse all produce.
2. Combine dressing ingredients in a food processor and process until smooth. Set aside or transfer to storage container.
3. Wash and cut all salad fruits and vegetables as directed.
4. Place chopped lettuce in a large serving bowl, then pour approximately ¼ of the dressing onto lettuce and mix well.
5. Top lettuce with fruits and veggies, preferably in a rainbow or symmetrical pattern for an enticing appearance.
6. Top salad with a mild drizzle of dressing and serve.

Nutrition Per Serving Dressing 50 calories, 0g total fat, 0g sat fat, 150mg sodium, 12g carbohydrates, 1g fiber, 9g sugar, 1g protein. **Salad** 370 calories, 22g total fat, 2g sat fat, 135mg sodium, 29g carbohydrates, 12g fiber, 23g sugar, 9g protein

Storage: Any extra dressing may be stored in an airtight glass container for up to a week after serving, however the salad itself will wilt quickly, so enjoy it immediately.

Ingredient Swap: Feel free to substitute any salad dressing you prefer.

Salads

Shopping list

Produce

- ☐ strawberries
- ☐ 1 bunch spring onion
- ☐ 1 lemon
- ☐ 3-4 mandarin oranges
- ☐ 1 pineapple
- ☐ blueberries
- ☐ 1 English cucumber
- ☐ 3 large carrots
- ☐ 3 stalks celery
- ☐ 2 heads iceberg lettuce
- ☐ spinach

Packaged

- ☐ balsamic vinegar
- ☐ unsweetened apple sauce
- ☐ pure maple syrup
- ☐ pecans

Seasonings and Spices

- ☐ salt
- ☐ black pepper

Tip or fact: If you prefer an even sweeter treat, you might try candying the pecans. Heat your oven to 325°F, combine the cup of pecans, ½ teaspoon ground cinnamon, 3 tablespoons pure maple syrup, and 1 tablespoon coconut sugar in a small bowl, mixing to coat. Line a baking sheet with parchment and pour the pecans onto the sheet. Spread evenly and bake for 15 minutes. Flip the pecans and bake for 6-10 more minutes. Allow to cool for about 30 minutes and enjoy (in the salad or just by themselves!).

Wild Rice Salad

by Jyl Steinback

Easy | **Gluten Free** | **4 Serving**

Serve over some leafy greens with a grilled mushroom sandwich for a satisfying summertime meal.

Ingredients

2 c cooked wild rice
2 Tbsp green onion, chopped
½ c corn kernels
½ c red bell pepper, diced
⅛ tsp garlic powder
⅛ tsp pepper
2 Tbsp white wine vinegar
2 Tbsp lemon juice
2 tsp Dijon mustard
2 tsp horseradish

Directions

1. Gather all ingredients.
2. Combine rice, green onions, corn, and red pepper in a medium bowl.
3. Sprinkle with garlic powder and pepper and toss lightly.
4. In a small bowl make the dressing.
5. Combine vinegar, lemon juice, mustard, and horseradish. Mix until blended smooth.
6. Just before serving, pour dressing over rice salad and toss until coated.

Nutrition Per Serving 110 calories, 0.5g total fat, 0g sat fat, 85mg sodium, 23g carbohydrates, 2g fiber, 3g sugar, 4g protein

Tip or fact: Wild rice is not actually rice. In fact, wild rice is the grain of four different species of grasses. You can also find it labeled as water oats, Canad rice or Indian rice. Store in a cool, dry place.

Shopping list

Produce
☐ 2 green onions
☐ 1 red bell pepper
☐ 2 lemons

Packaged
☐ white wine vinegar
☐ Dijon mustard
☐ horseradish

Refrigerated and Frozen
☐ 1 bag frozen corn kernels

Seasonings and Spices
☐ garlic powder
☐ black pepper

Parsley

Thyme

Anise

Bay Leaf

Arugula

Mint

Savory Soups, Bowls & Stews

Avocado Shell Bowls
by Aspen Sims

Easy | Gluten Free | 5 Servings

Who knew delicious food could be so healthy? Great blend of Hispanic flavors, great for a fun, beautiful, filling snack.

Ingredients

2-3 radishes, finely chopped
½ c cilantro, finely chopped
2 bell peppers, any color, diced
1 pineapple, diced
1 small red onion, thinly sliced
1 head Frisee
¼ tsp red wine vinegar
½ tsp salt
¼ tsp black pepper
2 c cooked black beans (recipe p. 6).
4 large avocados

Directions

1. Gather all ingredients.
2. Slice and finely chop radishes and cilantro.
3. Medium dice bell peppers and pineapple.
4. Thinly slice red onion.
5. Mix all into a bowl and add salt and pepper.
6. Cut frisee into bite size pieces, and season separately with red wine vinegar, salt, and pepper.
7. Add black beans.
8. Slice avocado in half and gently remove from shell. Discard the pit and chop the avocado flesh.
9. Place bowl mix into avocado shells, and top with avocado.

Nutrition Per Serving 470 calories, 24g total fat, 3.5g sat fat, 270mg sodium, 61g carbohydrates, 24g fiber, 21g sugar, 12g protein

Tip or fact: Prepare avocados last to avoid browning. Use a spoon to remove the avocado flesh from the shell.

Shopping list

Produce
- 2-3 radishes
- 1 bunch cilantro
- 2 bell peppers
- 1 pineapple
- 1 small red onion
- 1 head of Frisee
- 4 large avocados

Packaged
- red wine vinegar
- dried black beans

Seasonings and Spices
- salt
- black pepper

Beefless Stew

by Diane Smith

Medium | Gluten Free | 6 Servings

This delicious, creamy beefless stew is a healthier take on the original traditional comfort dish. So hearty and satisfying you'll want to savor each bite.

Ingredients

1 large yellow onion, sliced
6 cloves garlic, minced
3 large stalks celery, cubed
3 large carrots, cubed
16 oz. mushrooms, cubed
2 lbs potatoes, cubed
2 c frozen peas thawed
3 oz. tomato paste mixed with a
little water to thin
1 Tbsp Italian herbs
1 Tbsp fresh rosemary, chopped
½ tsp smoked paprika
2 c low-sodium vegetable broth
½ c water or more as needed
sea salt, to taste
pepper, to taste

Directions

1. Gather all ingredients.
2. Dice celery, carrots and mushrooms into ¾ inch chunks. If the potatoes aren't organic, peel them before chopping them into 1 inch chunks.
3. Sauté the onion, celery, and carrots in a large soup pot with about 1/4 cup of water until they start to soften.
4. Add in the minced garlic and mushroom and sauté for a few minutes more.
5. Add the vegetable broth, potatoes, tomato paste, herbs, smoked paprika, salt, and pepper.
6. Cook covered over medium heat until the potatoes and carrots are tender about 20-15 minutes. Add up to a ½ cup of water or more as needed if the stew is too thick.
7. Take about 1 ½ cups of the broth with a some of the vegetables and blend in a blender until smooth.
8. Return the blended sauce to the pot and stir to combine.
9. Add in the thawed peas and heat through for about 5 minutes.
10. Serve with a crusty bread and a salad for a complete meal.

Soups & Stews

Nutrition Per Serving 240 calories, 1g total fat, 0g sat fat, 140mg sodium, 52g carbohydrates, 9g fiber, 10g sugar, 9g protein

Tip or fact: A great way to create gravy in a dish is to combine a bit of the broth with some of the cooked vegetables which are then blended and added back to the dish.

Shopping list

Produce
☐ 1 large yellow onion
☐ 6 cloves garlic
☐ 3 large stalks celery
☐ 3 large carrots
☐ mushrooms
☐ 2 lbs potatoes
☐ fresh rosemary

Packaged
☐ low sodium vegetable broth
☐ 6 oz. can tomato paste

Refrigerated and Frozen
☐ frozen peas

Seasonings and Spices
☐ Italian herbs
☐ smoked paprika
☐ salt
☐ black pepper

Black Bean and Lentil Soup
by Jyl Steinback

Easy | **Gluten Free** | **4 Servings**

This is a go-to soup that satisfies every time.

Ingredients

8 oz. dry black beans
3 c water
1 large carrot, chopped
½ c celery, chopped
½ c red onion, chopped
1 ½ tsp garlic, minced
¾ c green bell pepper, chopped
¼ c dry lentils, rinsed and drained
14.5 oz. can petite-cut diced tomatoes with jalapeños, do not drain
1 Tbsp + 1 tsp chili powder
¼ tsp dried oregano
¼ tsp pepper
1 ½ Tbsp red wine vinegar
¼ c uncooked brown rice

Directions

1. Gather all ingredients.
2. Place beans in large soup pot. Cover with water and bring to a boil.
3. Boil 10 minutes.
4. Cover pot, remove from heat, and let stand 1 hour.
5. Drain beans and rinse.
6. Combine beans and 3 cups water in slow cooker. Cover and cook on high heat for 3 hours.
7. Add remaining ingredients except rice and mix well. Cover and cook on low heat for 2-3 hours.
8. Add rice and cook 20-30 minutes.
9. Puree half of soup in food processor or blender until smooth. Return to slow cooker and mix well.

Nutrition Per Serving 330 calories, 1.5g total fat, 0g sat fat, 100mg sodium, 63g carbohydrates, 14g fiber, 7g sugar, 18g protein

Tip or fact: Did you know that beans contain proteins called lectins that helps defend the plant in nature, even from humans? Lectins are inactivated when a bean is cooked, which is traditionally how we eat beans. Instructions for cooking dry beans can be found on p. 6.

Shopping list

Produce
□ 1 carrot
□ celery
□ 1 red onion
□ 1 green bell pepper
□ 2 garlic cloves

Packaged
□ 14.5 oz. can petite-cut diced tomatoes with jalapeños
□ red wine vinegar
□ brown rice
□ lentils
□ black beans

Seasonings and Spices
□ chili powder
□ dried oregano
□ black pepper

Brown Lentil Stew with Green Peas and Corn
by Nele Liivlaid

Easy | **Gluten Free** | **4 Servings**

Perfectly quick and filling main dish to add to your salad bowls! Lentils and peas make it so hearty and creamy.

Ingredients

7 oz. dry brown lentils
1 small onion
2 cloves garlic
2 tsp turmeric
1 tsp cumin seeds, toasted and crushed
1 tsp mustard seeds, toasted and crushed
½ c frozen corn
1 c frozen green peas
1 c carrot, coarsely grated
4 Tbsp coconut milk/cream
black pepper, to taste

Directions

1. Gather all ingredients.
2. Start by soaking lentils for 6-8 hours. Rinse, drain and set aside.
3. Prepare the spices – toast cumin seeds (30 seconds to 1 minute) and mustard seeds (2-5 minutes) on a dry pan, let cool and crush using mortar and pestle. Or make a bigger batch and grind in a spice grinder.
4. Crush garlic cloves, finely dice onion and grate carrots.
5. Heat up a few tablespoons of water in a skillet or large pan. After that, add onions and sauté them covered for 2-3 minutes stirring every now and then. Add water whenever necessary.
6. Add turmeric, soaked lentils, frozen peas and corn. Give everything a good stir. Add enough water to cover the ingredients. Mix well and cover with lid.
7. Bring to boil, then reduce the heat and simmer covered for 10-15 minutes or until the lentils are tender.
8. Mix in crushed garlic and toasted and crushed cumin and mustard seeds. Bring to boil and turn off the heat.
9. Add coconut milk/cream. Mix until it's well incorporated.
10. Let cool a bit before you add black pepper to taste.
11. Garnish with fresh herbs – onion greens, parsley or coriander.

Soups & Stews

Nutrition Per Serving 440 calories, 2.5g total fat, 0g sat fat, 250mg sodium, 82g carbohydrates, 22g fiber, 11g sugar, 27g protein

Shopping list

Produce
☐ 1 small onion
☐ 2 cloves garlic
☐ 1 carrot

Packaged
☐ dry brown lentils

Refrigerated and Frozen
☐ frozen corn
☐ frozen green peas
☐ coconut milk/cream

Seasonings and Spices
☐ black pepper
☐ turmeric
☐ cumin seeds
☐ mustard seeds

Ingredient Swap: In place of coconut milk or cream you can use cashew sour cream (recipe p. 5). In place of frozen peas and carrots, you can used canned. If you used canned, add with the toasted cumin and mustard seeds.

Tip or fact: Any lentils would work well – unhulled red lentils, black lentils, or any variety of green lentils.

Chickpea Noodle Soup

by Kayli Dice

Easy | **4 Servings**

There's nothing cozier than this Chickpea Noodle Soup. It's like a warm blanket for your belly. Make a huge pot on Sunday and heat it up for dinner all week long.

Ingredients

1 onion, diced
1 garlic clove, minced
4 carrots, diced
6 celery stalks, diced
8 c water
4 oz. whole wheat shell pasta
2 Tbsp white miso paste
¼ c nutritional yeast
15 oz. can chickpeas
2 handfuls baby spinach
black pepper

Directions

1. Gather all ingredients.
2. Heat soup pot over medium and add a few tablespoons of water. Add onion, garlic, carrots, and celery. Water sauté until veggies soften – about 5 minutes.
3. Add water and bring to a boil. Once boiling, add pasta.
4. When pasta is almost cooked, stir in miso paste, nutritional yeast, and chickpeas.
5. When pasta is tender, turn off heat and fold in spinach leaves until wilted.
6. Season with pepper.

Nutrition Per Serving 350 calories, 4.5g total fat, 0.5g sat fat, 340mg sodium, 64g carbohydrates, 15g fiber, 11g sugar, 18g protein

Ingredient Swap: Any whole wheat pasta shape will work in this recipe.

Tip or fact: Miso paste is usually found refrigerated near the tofu.

Shopping list

Produce
☐ 1 onion
☐ 1 garlic clove
☐ 4 carrots
☐ 6 celery stalks
☐ 2 handfuls baby spinach

Packaged
☐ nutritional yeast
☐ whole wheat shell pasta
☐ 15 oz. can low sodium chickpeas

Refrigerated and Frozen
☐ white miso paste

Seasonings and Spices
☐ black pepper

Chickpea Red Bean Stew

by Nele Liivlaid

Easy | **Gluten Free** | **4 Servings**

Here's a perfect dish if there's no time to soak those lentils! Make a hearty and creamy chickpea-red bean stew with Indian flavors.

Ingredients

1 small yellow onion, minced
2 medium garlic cloves, minced
1 large celery stalk, diced
1 large carrot, diced
1 medium potato, diced
1 tsp turmeric
1 ½ tsp crushed cumin seeds
1 ½ tsp crushed mustard seeds
¾ + ⅛ c sweet corn, rinsed and drained
8.5 oz chickpeas, rinsed and drained
8.5 oz red beans, rinsed and drained
2 Tbsp coconut milk
¾ tsp Himalayan salt
black pepper, to taster

Directions

1. Gather all ingredients.
2. Prepare the spices. Toast cumin seeds (from 30 seconds to 1 minute until your nose just gets a whiff of smoke and fragrance) and mustard seeds (2-5 minutes until fragrant and lightly browned, removing from heat when the seeds start to pop) on a dry pan.
3. Let the spices cool and crush using mortar and pestle or make a bigger batch and grind in a spice grinder.
4. Heat up a few tablespoons of water in a skillet or large pan. Add onions and sauté them covered for 2-3 minutes stirring every now and then. Add water whenever necessary.
5. Add the carrots, celery, potato cubes and turmeric; give everything a good stir and sauté until the veggies are tender, about 8 minutes. Add extra water if necessary.
6. When the veggies are cooked, add chickpeas, beans and corn. If the stew is too dry, add a bit of water. Then, bring to boil and turn off the heat. For a more mushy result, take potato masher or fork and mash the stew until it has thickened to desired consistency.
7. Add the toasted spices. Season with black pepper, Himalayan salt and fresh herbs like coriander, parsley and/or onion greens.

Soups & Stews

Nutrition Per Serving 210 calories, 4g total fat, 2g sat fat, 540mg sodium, 37g carbohydrate, 9g fiber, 7g sugar, 9g protein

Ingredient Swap: Any beans would work well in this stew – black beans, navy beans, pinto beans etc. In place of coconut milk, you can use cashew sour cream (recipe p. 5).

Shopping list

Produce
- [ ] 1 small yellow onion
- [ ] 2 medium garlic cloves
- [ ] 1 large celery stalk
- [ ] 1 large carrot
- [ ] 1 medium potato
- [ ] sweet cor

Packaged
- [ ] chickpeas
- [ ] red beans

Refrigerated or Frozen
- [ ] coconut milk

Seasonings and Spices
- [ ] turmeric
- [ ] crushed cumin seeds
- [ ] crushed mustard seeds
- [ ] Himalayan salt
- [ ] black pepper

Chunky and Creamy Tomato Soup by Caryn Dugan

Easy | **Gluten Free** | **4 Servings**

This thick, chunky and oh, so creamy tomato soup has a lot of little secrets, but one of them is the use of San Marzano tomatoes.

Ingredients

1 large yellow onion, diced
1 ½ c celery, diced
2 tsp smoky paprika
½ tsp dried thyme
½ tsp dried basil
½ tsp ground pepper
½ tsp sea salt
3 c low sodium vegetable broth
40 oz. whole San Marzano tomatoes
15 oz. low sodium cannellini beans, drained and rinsed
1 c sun-dried tomatoes, diced
½ c cashews
1 c water

Directions

1. Gather all ingredients.
2. To a pre-heated soup pot, add in the onion and celery. Bring the heat down to medium-high and continually stir. If there is some sticking, add a little water to de-glaze.
3. When the onion begins to caramelize, add in the spices. Continue to stir.
4. Add in the broth.
5. Add in the tomatoes one by one and squeeze them in your hand as you drop them into the pot.
6. Add ½ cup of the beans and the sun-dried tomatoes.
7. Stir and allow to simmer for about 20 minutes.
8. To a blender add the remaining cup of beans, the cashews and water. Begin by drizzling the water in as you want a really thick cream-like consistency.
9. Pour this into the tomato soup and either transfer one-half of the soup in batches to a blender or use an immersion blender to make a nice creamy soup that still has some chunkiness.
10. Garnish with croutons if you like.

Nutrition Per Serving 290 calories, 9g total fat, 1g sat fat, 280mg sodium, 43g carbohydrates, 14g fiber, 16g sugar, 13g protein

Storage: Soup stays in refrigerator 2-3 days, frozen for one month.

Tip or fact: Cashews grow on trees and are actually attached to the bottom of a "cashew apple" or cashew fruit. The fruit flesh is edible and most commonly the juice of the fruit is used to make an astringent fruit drink in Brazil or distilled to make feni in Indian.

Shopping list

Produce
☐ 1 large yellow onion
☐ 2 celery stalks

Packaged
☐ unsalted cashews
☐ low sodium vegetable broth
☐ 2 20oz cans San Marzano tomatoes
☐ 15 oz can low sodium cannellini beans
☐ sun-dried tomatoes

Seasonings and Spices
☐ smoky paprika
☐ dried thyme
☐ dried basil
☐ ground pepper
☐ sea salt

Cinna-Melberry Summer Soup
by Jyl Steinback

Easy | **Gluten Free** | **4 Servings**

Soup for dessert! Yup! It won't disappoint!

Ingredients

4 c cantaloupe, cubed
1 c orange juice
1 tsp lime juice
¾ tsp cinnamon
¼ c fresh blueberries

Directions

1. Gather all ingredients.
2. Combine all ingredients except blueberries in food processor or blender. Process until smooth and creamy.
3. Pour into bowl, cover, and refrigerate several hours or overnight.
4. Garnish with fresh blueberries before serving.

Nutrition Per Serving 90 calories, 0g total fat, 0g sat fat, 25mg sodium, 21g carbohydrates, 2g fiber, 18g sugar, 2g protein

Tip or fact: Cantaloupe is an excellent source of vitamin A and C and should be stored in the refrigerator. Did you know this is the most popular melon in the United States!

Soups & Stews

Shopping list

Produce
☐ 1 cantaloupe
☐ 1 lime
☐ blueberries

Refrigerated and Frozen
☐ orange juice

Seasonings and Spices
☐ cinnamon

Cold Beet Soup

by Nele Liivlaid

Medium | **Gluten Free** | **4 Servings**

Here's a perfectly cooling 7-ingredient vegan cold beet soup for hot summer days. This chilled beet soup really arouses your taste buds and is ready in just 15 minutes.

Ingredients

14 oz. boiled beets, grated
14 oz. plain soy yogurt
1 lemon, juiced
4 Tbsp green onions, chopped
2 Tbsp fresh dill, chopped
1 long cucumber, chopped
4 small radishes, chopped
½ c beetroot cooking liquid
4 Tbsp coconut milk
black pepper, to taste
½ c water

Directions

1. Gather all ingredients.
2. Wearing gloves, finely grate beets. Alternatively, buy grated beetroot to save some time.
3. Pour yogurt into a bigger bowl and mix in grated beetroot, finely chopped cucumber, radishes, green onions and dill.
4. Thin the soup with some water if necessary.
5. Season with pepper and add some extra green onions and fresh dill as garnish before serving.

Nutrition Per Serving 150 calories, 5g total fat, 3g sat fat, 170mg sodium, 24g carbohydrates, 3g fiber, 15g sugar, 5g protein

Ingredient Swap: Instead of soy yogurt any plain plant yogurt, sour cream or kefir will do, such as cashew or almond yogurt or kefir.

Tip or fact: If you want to save some more time, use apple cider vinegar instead of lemon juice. You can go an extra mile and prepare the beetroot from scratch – boil whole beetroot until tender or cut into smaller cubes and bake in the oven at 390°F for about 20 minutes (until tender).

Shopping list

Produce
☐ 4 small radishes
☐ 14 oz. beets
☐ 1 long cucumber
☐ 1 small bunch dill
☐ 2 green onions
☐ 1 lemon

Packaged
☐ beetroot cooking liquid

Refrigerated and Frozen
☐ coconut milk
☐ plain soy yogurt

Seasonings and Spices
☐ black pepper

Creamy Pea and Broccoli Soup by Nele Liivlaid

Easy | Gluten Free | 2 Servings

This soup is a real protein bomb that doesn't lack in flavor. In a word, perfect for those looking for a lean and low-fat yet filling and satiating meal option.

Ingredients

2 c frozen green peas
1 c leek, chopped
2 small potatoes, cubed
2 large carrots, cubed
1 ¾ c broccoli florets
6 c kale, chopped
2 tsp garlic powder
⅛ tsp Himalayan salt
black pepper, to taste

Directions

1. Gather all ingredients.
2. Add frozen peas, chopped leek, carrot, potatoes and garlic powder to small pot. Add enough hot water to cover and bring to boil.
3. Simmer for 5 minutes.
4. Add chopped kale and broccoli florets to the soup.
5. Pour in more hot water as well (just enough to cover) and simmer for another 5 minutes.
6. Let the soup cool a bit and puree using regular or immersion blender.
7. Add water if necessary. Feel free to leave it chunky.
8. Season with black pepper and Himalayan salt.
9. Garnish with a tablespoon of nutritional yeast, a handful of alfalfa sprouts, a sprinkle of sesame seeds and some mint leaves, parsley or cilantro (optional). You also may add a splash of coconut milk.

Soups & Stews

Nutrition Per Serving 350 calories, 2g total fat, 0g sat fat, 360mg sodium, 73g carbohydrates, 17g fiber, 16g sugar, 17g protein

Ingredient Swap: Feel free to use onion instead of leek. Also, sweet potatoes instead of potatoes work just as fine.

Tip or fact: To prepare more servings, simply multiply with the number of people you're going to serve.

Shopping list

Produce
☐ leek
☐ 2 small potatoes
☐ 2 large carrots
☐ broccoli
☐ kale

Refrigerated and Frozen
☐ peas

Seasonings and Spices
☐ garlic powder
☐ Himalayan salt
☐ black pepper

Easy Lunch Buddha Bowl
by Nele Liivlaid

Easy | **Gluten Free** | **1 Servings**

This bowl is a real protein bomb that doesn't lack in flavor. In a word, perfect for those looking for a lean and low-fat yet filling and satiating meal option.

Ingredients

1 small celery stalk, chopped
1 portobello mushroom, chopped or sliced
¼ bigger fennel bulb, chopped or sliced
5.3 oz. green beans
½ tsp turmeric
¼ tsp garam masala, optional
¼ tsp garlic powder
½ c broccoli florets
1 c kale, chopped
½ c finely shredded red cabbage
Himalayan or black salt, to taste
black pepper, to taste
2.8 oz. chickpeas, drained and rinsed
1.2 oz. avocado slices
alfalfa sprouts

Directions

1. Gather all ingredients.
2. Place chopped or sliced mushroom, celery, fennel, green beans, turmeric, garlic powder and garam masala into a saucepan with a few tablespoons of water. Sauté for about 5 minutes, stir occasionally. You'll have more liquid as the water seeps out of the mushrooms.
3. Throw in broccoli and sauté for 2 minutes. Make sure there's enough liquid or it can burn!
4. Add the kale, which needs another 3-4 minutes.
5. Add water 1 tablespoon at a time if necessary.
6. Add shredded cabbage, turn off the heat and cover for additional 2-3 minutes to soften it a bit.
7. Season the dish with black pepper and Himalayan or black salt.
8. Combine your bowl. Pour the sautéed veggies into a salad bowl and add chickpeas, oven-baked and sliced Portobello mushroom, avocado slices and alfalfa sprouts.

Nutrition Per Serving 290 calories, 8g total fat, 1g sat fat, 460mg sodium, 48g carbohydrates, 18g fiber, 16g sugar, 15g protein

Ingredient Swap: You can easily change the veggies if you don't have them all. For example, white or Chinese cabbage instead of red cabbage, cauliflower instead of broccoli, and chard, spinach or pak choi instead of kale. If you want, you can use any mushrooms you like. Portobellos are not a must. Use any preferred spice blend or curry powder instead of turmeric and garam masala. Chickpeas can be substituted with any other legumes, i.e. beans, lentils or mung beans.

Tip or fact: To prepare more servings, simply multiply with the number of people you're going to serve. Should you have some extra time, chop up fresh garlic and use it instead of powder.

Shopping list

Produce
□ 1 celery stalk
□ 1 portobello mushroom
□ 2.6 oz fennel bulb
□ 5.3 oz green beans
□ kale
□ red cabbage
□ 1 avocado
□ alfalfa sprouts

Packaged
□ garam masala, optional
□ 2.8 oz. low sodium canned chickpeas

Seasonings and Spices
□ turmeric
□ garlic powder
□ Himalayan or black salt
□ black pepper

French Wild Rice Vegetable Soup
by Sharon Palmer

Easy | **Gluten Free** | **6 Servings**

There is nothing quite like a hearty vegetable grain soup to calm the mind, body and soul.

Ingredients

5 c vegetable broth (recipe p. 124)
14.5 oz. can diced tomatoes
2 cloves garlic, minced
½ c uncooked wild rice
1 medium carrot, sliced
1 small zucchini, sliced
1 c leek, sliced
1 tsp Herbs de Provence
⅛ tsp black pepper

Directions

1. Gather all ingredients.
2. Make the homemade vegetable broth (recipe p. 124).
3. Place all ingredients in a large pot.
4. Cover with a tight lid and bring to a boil.
5. Reduce heat to a simmer and cook for about 1 hour, until wild rice and vegetables are tender.
6. You may need to add additional water to replace water lost in evaporation. Should make a thick, hearty soup.
7. Serve immediately.

InstantPot Directions: Place all ingredients in the container of the InstantPot. Press "Bean/Chili" setting. Cook according to manufacturer's directions. Serve immediately.

Slowcooker Directions: Place all ingredients in the container of the Slowcooker. Cook on low for 4-6 hours or on high for 8-12 hours. Serve immediately.

Soups & Stews

Nutrition Per Serving 170 calories, 0.5g total fat, 0g sat fat, 125mg sodium, 35g carbohydrates, 5g fiber, 8g sugar, 7g protein

Tip or fact: You can keep wild rice forever. Keep it in a closed glass container in a cool and dry place in your kitchen. When you cook the wild rice and drain it – it will keep in the freezer for up to 6 months and in the refrigerator for a week in a sealed glass container.

Shopping list

Produce
☐ 2 cloves fresh garlic
☐ 1 medium carrot
☐ 1 small zucchini
☐ 1 small leek
☐ vegetable broth ingredients

Packaged
☐ wild rice
☐ 14.5 oz. can tomatoes

Seasonings and Spices
☐ Herbs de Provence
☐ black pepper

Green Lentil Stew with Tomatoes by Nele Liivlaid

Medium | **4 Servings**

I love this plant nutritious lentil stew with tomatoes for dinner. Together with potatoes, it becomes a comfort food the whole family will love.

Ingredients

7 oz. dry green lentils
1 small yellow onion, diced
2 medium garlic cloves, minced
1 large celery stalk, diced
1 large carrot, diced
1 medium potato, diced
1 Tbsp turmeric
2 ½ tsp crushed cumin seeds
2 ½ tsp crushed mustard seeds
1¼ c unsalted tomato puree
1 Tbsp peanut butter
1/8 tsp Himalayan salt
black pepper, to taste

Directions

1. Gather all ingredients.
2. Wash the lentils, make sure to wash them thoroughly and remove any debris.
3. Prepare the spices. Toast cumin seeds (30 seconds to 1 minute) and mustard seeds (2-5 minutes) on a dry pan, let cool and crush using mortar and pestle. Or make a bigger batch and grind in a spice grinder.
4. Heat up a few tablespoons of water in a skillet or large pan. After that, add onions and sauté them covered for 2-3 minutes stirring every now and then. Add water whenever necessary.
5. Add the carrots, celery, potato and turmeric. Give everything a good stir and sauté for another few minutes.
6. Add the turmeric. Add extra water if necessary.
7. Place lentils and enough water to cover the ingredients. Mix well and cover with lid.
8. Bring to boil, then reduce the heat and simmer covered for 15 minutes or until the lentils are tender.
9. Mix in crushed garlic and toasted/crushed cumin and mustard seeds.
10. Add tomato puree and mix well.
11. Bring to boil and simmer for another 5 minutes. You may leave the lid off, if there's plenty of liquid or add extra water if necessary.
12. When the stew is done, mix in peanut butter. Make sure it's well incorporated.
13. Garnish with fresh herbs, i.e. onion greens, parsley or coriander.

Nutrition Per Serving 300 calories, 4g total fat, 0.5g sat fat, 170mg sodium, 54g carbohydrates, 12g fiber, 8g sugar, 16g protein

Tip or fact: Try substituting regular potatoes with sweet potato that are both delicious and nutritious.

Shopping list

Produce
☐ 1 small yellow onion
☐ 2 medium garlic cloves
☐ 1 large celery stalk
☐ 1 large carrot
☐ 1 medium potato

Packaged
☐ 7 oz. dried lentils
☐ peanut butter
☐ unsalted tomato puree

Seasonings and Spices
☐ turmeric
☐ cumin seeds
☐ mustard seeds
☐ Himalayan salt
☐ black pepper

Hearty Steamed Veggie Bowl
by Neil Popp

| Easy | Kid Friendly | Gluten Free | 4 Servings |

Start the day off with a great tasting veggie bowl anyone can love!

Ingredients

1 large tomato, diced
1 c frozen corn
1 c frozen carrots and peas
1 large russet potato, washed and cube
1 c baby bella mushrooms
½ c water
1 tsp red pepper flakes
herbs, to taste

Directions

1. Gather all ingredients.
2. Wash and cube potato.
3. Add corn, potato cubes, carrots/peas, and mushrooms to a pan with water. Start on high heat until you can see water steaming, then reduce heat to half. Stir continuously but be careful not to squish potato cubes.
4. Once nearly all the water is gone, simply transfer to a bowl.
5. Add fresh tomato, and red pepper flakes.

Nutrition Per Serving 150 calories, 1g total fat, 0g sat fat, 45mg sodium, 32g carbohydrates, 5g fiber, 4g sugar, 6g protein

Storage: Store in an airtight glass container in the refrigerator for 1-4 days.

Ingredient Swap: Feel free to use fresh corn and carrots.

Tip or fact: Make this a meal by adding a 1 cup of whole grains, like quinoa or bulgur wheat.

Soups & Stews

Shopping list

Produce
☐ 1 large tomato
☐ 1 large russet potato
☐ baby bella mushrooms

Frozen and Refrigerated
☐ frozen corn
☐ frozen carrots and peas

Seasonings and Spices
☐ red pepper flakes

Homemade Vegetable Broth
by Caryn Dugan

Easy | Gluten Free | 8 Servings

This is a great broth base for soups, stews, grains, etc. as it allows you ultimate control over the ingredients you use in a recipe.

Ingredients

3-5 carrots, peeled and roughly chopped

3-4 stalks celery, washed and roughly chopped

2 white or yellow onions, roughly chopped

4-5 cloves garlic, peeled

3 bay leaves

handful dried mushrooms

Directions

1. Gather all ingredients.
2. Chop all the carrots, celery and onion. Peel the garlic cloves. Keep them whole.
3. Put all ingredients into a stock pot.
4. Pour 2 quarts of water into a large stock pot, just covering the vegetables.
5. Bring to a boil, down to a simmer and allow to cook for about 90 minutes.
6. Strain out the vegetables, cool.

Nutrition Per Serving 50 calories, 0g total fat, 0g sat fat, 50mg sodium, 12g carbohydrates, 3g fiber, 5g sugar, 2g protein

Storage: Store in the freezer.

Ingredient Swap: Unless you don't mind your broth turning purple, do not add red onion or purple cabbage to your broth.

Tip or fact: Stay away from cruciferous vegetables and adding a lot of stems from the greens as it will add a bitter flavor.

Shopping list

Produce
- [ ] 3-5 carrots
- [ ] 3-4 stalks celery
- [ ] 2 white or yellow onions
- [ ] 4-5 cloves garlic

Packaged
- [ ] dried mushrooms

Seasonings and Spices
- [ ] bay leaves

Lentil Quinoa Soup

by Carolina Maturana

Medium | **Kid Friendly** | **Gluten Free** | **4-5 Servings**

Snuggle up with a bowl of this hearty delicious soup filled with lentils, barley and veggies.

Ingredients

1 c dry lentils
¼ c dry quinoa
1 medium carrot, diced
1 large Yukon gold potato, diced
1 medium yellow or white onion, finely chopped
2 garlic cloves, minced
2 kale leaves
¼ c cilantro leaves.
1 tsp ground cumin
¼ tsp black pepper
¼ tsp chili powder
5 c warm water
1 lime, juiced
⅛ tsp pink Himalayan salt

Directions

1. Gather all ingredients.
2. Peel and dice carrots and potato. Finely chop the onion. Peel and mince garlic. Remove stems from kale and cut into thin strips. Chop cilantro leaves.
3. Rinse lentils and set aside
4. Rinse quinoa using a strainer and remove as much water as possible.
5. Heat a large soup pot to medium heat and toast quinoa for 3 minutes. Shake occasionally to prevent burning. Set quinoa aside.
6. Make sure the pot is hot enough by testing with a little water. The water should form mercury like ball on the surface. Dry sauté onions continuously stirring to prevent burning until they are translucent and have a little of a golden color.
7. Add carrots, potatoes, lentils, cumin, pepper, chili powder, salt and stir for 1-2 minutes.
8. Add garlic, cook and stir for 1 minute.
9. Add ½ cup of water and stir until most of the water has evaporated.
10. Add 5 cups of warm water, reduce heat to low, cover and cook for 10 minutes.
11. Add quinoa, stir and cover. Cook for 15 minutes.
12. Add Kale and cook for 2 minutes
13. Remove from heat and let it rest uncovered for 3-5 minutes.
14. Before serving squeeze a little of lime juice and add cilantro to garnish.

Soups & Stews

Nutrition Per Serving 240 calories, 1g total fat, 0g sat fat, 70mg sodium, 47g carbohydrates, 7g fiber, 3g sugar, 13g protein

Storage: Store in an airtight glass container in the fridge for up to 4 days.

Tip or fact: Try to choose organic produce, quinoa and lentils when possible.

Shopping list

Produce
☐ 1 medium carrot
☐ 1 large Yukon gold potato
☐ 1 medium yellow or white onion
☐ 2 garlic cloves
☐ 1 bunch kale
☐ 1 bunch cilantro
☐ 1 lime

Packaged
☐ dry lentils
☐ dry quinoa

Seasonings and Spices
☐ ground cumin
☐ black pepper
☐ chili powder
☐ pink Himalayan salt

Lentil-Tomato Soup

by Jyl Steinback

Easy | **Gluten Free** | **6 Servings**

The addition of lentils adds a protein punch to this Italian style tomato soup.

Ingredients

1 c dry lentils, rinsed and drained
1 c carrots, chopped
1 c celery, chopped
1 c onion, chopped
1 tsp garlic, minced
1 ¼ tsp dried Italian seasoning
1 bay leaf
28 oz. low sodium vegetable broth
1 ½ c water
14.5 oz. can Italian recipe stewed tomatoes with oregano and basil, do not drain

Directions

1. Gather all ingredients.
2. Combine all ingredients in slow cooker and mix lightly.
3. Cover and cook on low heat for 10-12 hours or high heat for 5-6 hours.
4. Remove bay leaf before serving.

Nutrition Per Serving 170 calories, 0.5g total fat, 0g sat fat, 135mg sodium, 32g carbohydrates, 6g fiber, 8g sugar, 10g protein

Tip or fact: There are four main categories of lentils: brown, green, red/yellow, and specialty. Brown lentils are the most common variety.

Shopping list

Produce
□ 2 carrots
□ 2 celery stalks
□ 1 medium onion
□ 2 garlic cloves

Packaged
□ 2 14 oz. cans low sodium vegetable broth
□ 14.5 oz. can Italian recipe stewed tomatoes with oregano and basil
□ dry lentils

Seasonings and Spices
□ Italian seasoning
□ bay leaf

Meatless Stew

by Jyl Steinback

Easy | **Gluten Free** | **6 Servings**

Looking for a hearty stew? Look no further. Our stew has an abundance of flavor and vegetables to fill up your belly.

Ingredients

2 lbs. potatoes, sliced
1 large onion, sliced
2 large carrots, sliced
1 green bell pepper, sliced
1 zucchini, sliced
1 c frozen corn, thawed and drained
1 c frozen peas, thawed and drained
1 c frozen cut green beans, thawed and drained
2 ½ c low sodium tomato sauce
¼ c low sodium soy sauce
2 tsp dried Italian seasoning
1 tsp dry mustard
2 tsp chili powder
½ tsp ground cinnamon
2 Tbsp dried parsley
⅛ tsp dried rosemary

Directions

1. Gather all ingredients.
2. Layer potatoes, onion, carrots, bell pepper, zucchini, corn, peas, and green beans in slow cooker.
3. Combine remaining ingredients in a medium bowl and mix well.
4. Pour tomato sauce mixture over vegetables.
5. Cover and cook on low heat for 10-12 hours or high heat for 5-6 hours.

Nutrition Per Serving 290 calories, 2.5g total fat, 0g sat fat, 510mg sodium, 60g carbohydrates, 8g fiber, 13g sugar, 10g protein

Tip or fact: Want to use fresh herbs? Triple the quantity of any fresh herb you use in place of a dried herb.

Soups & Stews

Shopping list

Produce
☐ 2 lbs. potatoes
☐ 1 large onion
☐ 2 large carrots
☐ 1 medium green bell pepper
☐ 1 medium zucchini

Packaged
☐ 2 14.5 oz. cans tomato sauce
☐ low-sodium soy sauce

Refrigerated or frozen
☐ frozen corn
☐ frozen peas
☐ frozen cut green beanslt

Seasonings and Spices
☐ dried Italian seasoning
☐ dry mustard
☐ chili powder
☐ ground cinnamon
☐ dried parsley
☐ dried rosemary

Mediterranean-Style Stew

by Jyl Steinback

Easy | **Gluten Free** | **4 Servings**

Slow cookers are one of my favorite way to prepare family meals – quick, easy and plant nutritious.

Ingredients

1 butternut squash, seeded and cubed
½ lb. eggplant, cubed
1 medium zucchini, cubed
1 medium yellow squash, cubed
10 oz. frozen okra, thawed and drained
8 oz. can low sodium tomato sauce
1 c frozen chopped onions, thawed and drained
14.5 oz. can no salt added petite-cut diced tomatoes, drained
6 baby carrots, cut into thirds
½ c low sodium vegetable broth
⅓ c raisins
1 tsp garlic, minced
¼ tsp chili powder
½ tsp ground turmeric
¼ tsp crushed red pepper
¼ tsp ground cinnamon
¼ tsp paprika

Directions

1. Gather all ingredients.
2. Combine all ingredients in slow cooker and mix well.
3. Cover and cook on low heat for 8-10 hours or high heat for 4-5 hours.

Nutrition Per Serving 160 calories, 0.5g total fat, 0g sat fat, 110mg sodium, 39g carbohydrates, 8g fiber, 21g sugar, 5g protein

Tip or fact: Turmeric is a spice used extensively in Indian and Southeast Asian cooking. It is known for its brilliant yellow color, mildly aromatic scent, and pungent, bitter flavor.

Shopping list

Produce
☐ 1 medium butternut squash
☐ ½ lb. eggplant
☐ 1 medium zucchini
☐ 1 medium yellow squash
☐ 1 package baby carrots
☐ 2 garlic cloves

Packaged
☐ 8 oz. can unsalted tomato sauce
☐ 14.5 oz can petite-cut diced tomatoes

☐ low sodium vegetable broth
☐ raisins

Refrigerated or frozen
☐ frozen okra
☐ frozen chopped onions

Seasonings and Spices
☐ chili powder
☐ ground turmeric
☐ crushed red pepper
☐ ground cinnamon
☐ paprika

Mushroom Barley Soup

by Jyl Steinback

Medium | **6 Servings**

Mushrooms and Barley come together to create a creamy soup with nutty overtones with a touch of dill to brighten things.

Ingredients

3 c water
3 c low sodium vegetable broth
1¾ c onion, chopped
1½ tsp garlic, minced
⅔ c dry barley
3 ½ c mushrooms, chopped
2 tsp dried dill weed

Directions

1. Gather all ingredients.
2. Combine water and vegetable broth in a large saucepan. Bring to a boil over high heat.
3. Add onion, garlic, and barley to pan.
4. Cover, reduce heat to low, and simmer 40 to 45 minutes.
5. Add mushrooms to soup, cover pan, and cook over low heat 15 to 20 minutes.
6. Using a slotted spoon, scoop ¾ of vegetables and barley from pan. Place in food processor or blender and process until smooth.
7. Return pureed vegetables to soup
8. Stir in dill. Bring soup to a boil over high heat.
9. Serve hot.

Nutrition Per Serving 123 calories, 0.5g total fat, 0g sat fat, 80mg sodium, 26g carbohydrates, 5g fiber, 4g sugar, 4g protein

Tip or fact: Mushrooms are 90% water.

Soups & Stews

Shopping list

Produce
☐ ¾ lb. mushrooms
☐ 2 onions
☐ garlic

Packaged
☐ 24 oz. vegetable broth
☐ dried dill weed
☐ barley

Red Lentil Stew with Root Vegetables by Sharon Palmer

Easy | **Gluten Free** | **10 Servings**

This savory soup is a bright, sunny shade of orange—the perfect way to cheer up the cloudiest of days. Its hearty flavor and texture makes it ideal.

Ingredients

6 c homemade vegetable stock (recipe p. 124)
14.5 oz diced tomatoes, in juice
1 onion, diced
2 stalks celery, chopped
2 medium carrots, chopped
4 small turnips, chopped
2 small red potatoes, chopped
2 cloves garlic, minced
2 c red lentils, dried
1 ½ tsp smoked paprika
1 ½ tsp turmeric
1 tsp ground cumin

Directions

1. Gather all ingredients.
2. Place water and tomatoes in a large pot and bring to a simmer.
3. Add vegetable stock, onion, celery, carrots, turnips, garlic, red lentils, smoked paprika, turmeric, and cumin.
4. Stir well, cover, and cook over medium heat for about 30 minutes, until vegetables are just tender.
5. May need to add additional water to replace water lost to evaporation. Should make a thick, hearty stew.

Nutrition Per Serving 220 calories, 1g total fat, 0g sat fat, 105mg sodium, 42g carbohydrates, 7g fiber, 6g sugar, 12g protein

Tip or fact: If using an InstantPot, use the bean/chili setting and cook to the manufacturer's dircetions. For a slowcooker, cook on high for 4-6 hours or on low for 8-12 hours.

Shopping list

Produce
□ 1 onion
□ 2 celery stalks
□ 2 medium carrots
□ 4 small turnips
□ 2 small red potatoes
□ 2 cloves garlic
□ vegetable stock ingredient

Packaged
□ dried red lentils
□ 14.5 oz. diced tomatoes

Seasonings and spices
□ smoked paprika
□ turmeric
□ ground cumin

Roasted Veggies Bowl

by Carolina Maturana

Easy | Kid Friendly | Gluten Free | 4 Servings

This bowl is a great way of exposing children to new flavors and textures.

Ingredients

3 medium beets
2 large yams
2 medium red bell peppers
½ red onion
8 oz. fresh Brussel sprouts
1 tsp garlic powder
3 tsp fresh thyme
1 c low sodium vegetable broth
fresh parsley, to garnish

Directions

1. Preheat oven to 425°F.
2. Gather all ingredients.
3. Place two baking trays inside the oven while preheating to obtain a crispier result.
4. Peel beets and cut into wedges. Peel and cut yams into medium size wedges. Cut red bell peppers into medium size wedges. Cut red onion into medium size wedges. Half the Brussel sprouts lengthwise.
5. Toss onions, bell peppers and Brussel sprouts with enough vegetable broth to evenly coat veggies.
6. Add a pinch of pink Himalayan salt, pepper and garlic granules, thyme and combine well. Set aside.
7. In a separate bowl, toss yam wedges with vegetable broth and seasoning.
8. Use a separate bowl to do the same with beets.
9. Carefully remove one tray from the oven. Place down parchment paper and spread yams and beets evenly.
10. Roast for 15 minutes.
11. Stir them and continue to roast for 20 more minutes or until crispy.
12. Remove the other tray. Place down parchment paper and spread the rest of the veggies evenly and roast for 10 minutes.
13. Stir them and continue to roast for 15 more minutes or until crispy.
14. You may add more vegetable stock if they seem too dry.
15. Serve on a blend of brown rice and quinoa and garnish with parsley.

Soups & Stews

Shopping list

Produce
☐ 3 medium beets
☐ 2 yams
☐ 2 red bell peppers
☐ 1 red onion
☐ 8 oz. Brussel sprouts
☐ 1 small bunch thyme
☐ 1 small bunch parsley

Packaged
☐ low sodium vegetable broth

Seasonings and Spices
☐ pink Himalayan salt
☐ garlic powder

Nutrition Per Serving 140 calories, 0.5g total fat, 0g sat fat, 180mg sodium, 31g carbohydrates, 8g fiber, 12g sugar, 5g protein

Storage: Store in the fridge for 4 days.

Ingredient Swap: If you would like to make your own vegetable broth, follow the recipe on p. 124.

Tip or fact: Working with beets can be a little messy. You can wear gloves to prevent getting your hands stained. Blending brown rice with a little of quinoa helps children and adults to get familiarized with quinoa.

Southern Stew

by Kayli Dice

Medium | **Gluten Free** | **4 Servings**

Chock full of southern flavor with a creamy sweet potato broth base. This truly is food for the soul!

Ingredients

4 c water
1 yellow onion, diced
4 celery stalks, diced
1 Tbsp cumin
1 Tbsp dried thyme
½ tsp cayenne
2 sweet potatoes, cubed
3 c cooked black-eyed peas
2 c corn kernels
2 c chard or collard greens, chopped
28 oz. can diced tomatoes
pepper, to taste

Directions

1. Gather all ingredients.
2. In a soup pot over medium heat, sauté onion and celery in water.
3. Add cumin, thyme and cayenne and sauté for one more minute.
4. Add the cubed sweet potatoes and enough water to cover (about 4 cups). Turn heat to high, cover and bring to a boil. Let simmer until sweet potatoes are tender.
5. Once tender, puree with an immersion blender or transfer to a blender to puree.
6. Return sweet potato broth to soup pot.
7. Add black-eyed peas, corn, greens, and diced tomatoes.
8. Season with pepper to taste.
9. Bring to a simmer for about 10 more minutes or until greens are softened and soup thickens. Add more water if soup gets too thick.

Nutrition Per Serving 400 calories, 2g total fat, 0g sat fat, 320mg sodium, 74g carbohydrates, 14g fiber, 13g sugar, 24g protein

Tip or fact: The name "collard" originates from the word "colewort" which is synonymous with wild cabbage.

Shopping list

Produce
☐ 1 yellow onion
☐ 4 celery stalks
☐ dried thyme
☐ 2 sweet potatoes
☐ chard or collard greens

Packaged
☐ black-eyed peas
☐ 28-oz. can diced tomatoes

Refrigerated or frozen
☐ frozen corn

Seasonings and spices
☐ cayenne
☐ pink Himalayan salt
☐ black pepper
☐ cumin

Spicy Cauliflower Soup

by Jyl Steinback

Easy | **Gluten Free** | **4 Servings**

Cauliflower is filled with lots of nutrients and fiber. A bowl of this soup is a great way to reap those wonderful benefits.

Ingredients

4 c cauliflower, chopped

29 oz. petite-cut diced tomatoes with roasted garlic and sweet onion, do not drain

14 oz. can low sodium vegetable broth

1 c onion, chopped

½ tsp garlic, minced

⅛ tsp chili powder

2 tsp curry powder

⅛ tsp black pepper

Directions

1. Gather all ingredients.
2. Combine cauliflower, undrained tomatoes, broth, onion, and minced garlic in cooker and mix well.
3. Cover and cook on low heat for 7-8 hours or high heat for 3 ½ to 4 hours.
4. Increase heat to high. Add chili powder, curry powder, and pepper.
5. Cover and cook 30-35 minutes until heated through.
6. Serve soup hot or cold.

Nutrition Per Serving 100 calories, 0.5g total fat, 0g sat fat, 350mg sodium, 19g carbohydrates, 5g fiber, 8g sugar, 5g protein

Ingredient Swap: If you would like to make your own vegetable broth, follow the recipe on p. 124.

Tip or fact: Cauliflower is now being used in place of rice. Check out the freezer section or produce department to find a bag and give it a try!

Soups & Stews

Shopping list

Produce
- 1 large cauliflower
- 1 onion
- garlic

Packaged
- 2 14.5 oz. petite-cut diced tomatoes with roasted garlic and sweet onion
- 14 oz. can low sodium vegetable broth

Seasonings and Spices
- chili powder
- curry powder
- black pepper

Spicy Sonoran Chili
by Jyl Steinback

Medium | **Kid Friendly** | **Gluten Free** | **10 Servings**

Indulge your taste with this chunky, yummy spice combo!

Ingredients

12 oz. can chili beans
12 oz. can low sodium great northern beans
12 oz. can low sodium chickpeas
12 oz. can low sodium black beans
28 oz. can unsalted diced tomatoes
6 oz. can chopped green chilis
1 c ribbon pasta
1 onion, diced.
1 tsp black pepper
1 tsp hot Mexican chili powder
1 ½ c low sodium vegetable broth

Directions

1. Gather all ingredients.
2. Dice your onion and drain/rinse all of the canned beans in a strainer.
3. Add all beans and onion to crock pot, and add chili powder and black pepper along with green chilis.
4. Add vegetable broth and turn on high.
5. Once the pot is boiling, immediately add ribbon pasta.
6. After 10 minutes, reduce heat to medium.
7. Keep on medium heat for 1 hour.
8. Reduce heat to low for another hour.
9. Serve and enjoy!

Nutrition Per Serving 190 calories, 1.5g total fat, 0g sat fat, 290mg sodium, 34g carbohydrates, 7g fiber, 5g sugar, 10g protein

Storage: Refrigerate for 2-5 days.

Ingredient Swap: If you would like to make your own vegetable broth, follow the recipe on p. 124.

Tip or fact: Beans are a timeless tradition! They have been cultivated by humans for over 6,000 years.

Shopping list

Produce
☐ 1 onion

Packaged
☐ 12 oz. can chili beans
☐ 12 oz. can low sodium great northern beans
☐ 12 oz. can low sodium chickpeas
☐ 12 oz. can low sodium black beans
☐ 28 oz. can unsalted diced tomatoes
☐ 6 oz. can chopped green chilis
☐ 1 c ribbon pasta
☐ low sodium vegetable broth

Seasonings and spices
☐ black pepper
☐ hot Mexican chili powder

Super Quinoa Bowl

by Jyl Steinback

Easy | **Gluten Free** | **4 Servings**

This is one of my all time favorite bowls. I have fallen in love with Quinoa and mixed with sweet potato and an avocado is a taste of heaven.

Ingredients

1½ c dry quinoa
3 c sweet potato, cubed
½ medium avocado, diced
3 c spinach
2 Tbsp balsamic vinegar
black pepper, to taste

Directions

1. Preheat oven to 450°F.
2. Gather all ingredients.
3. Place cubed sweet potatoes in a pot, completely cover with water and bring to a boil.
4. Once water is boiling, continue to cook for 5 more minutes.
5. Placed parboiled potatoes on baking sheet that is sprayed with non-stick spray.
6. Place in oven for about 45 minutes, or until cooked, stirring halfway.
7. Cook quinoa according to package directions.
8. Once quinoa and potatoes are cooked, steam spinach in either a pot or the microwave.
9. Once cooked, chop and mix with vinegar.
10. In a bowl, mix together quinoa, sweet potatoes and spinach.
11. Plate and top with avocado chunks.

Soups & Stews

Nutrition Per Serving 410 calories, 11g total fat, 1.5g sat fat, 370mg sodium, 67g carbohydrates, 11g fiber, 7g sugar, 12g protein

Tip or fact: This bowl is truly super for you – quinoa, sweet potato, avocado, and spinach are all super foods! Super foods are full of nutrients to keep you healthy.

Shopping list

Produce
☐ 2 sweet potatoes
☐ 1 medium avocado
☐ 1 bunch spinach

Packaged
☐ dry quinoa
☐ balsamic vinega

Seasonings and Spices
☐ black pepper

Tropical Blend Gazpacho

by Jyl Steinback

Easy | **Gluten Free** | **6 Servings**

This is a summertime must! A refreshing tropical pineapple twist on the traditional gazpacho.

Ingredients

35 oz. can crushed tomatoes undrained
16 oz. can chopped tomatoes undrained
1 c 100% pineapple juice
2 medium cucumbers, cubed
2 medium bell peppers
4 oz. green chilies, chopped
1 ½ c celery, diced
1 ½ c pineapple chunks
¾ tsp garlic powder
¼ tsp chili powder
¼ tsp pepper
½ tsp ground cumin
½ c cilantro, chopped
½ tsp Tabasco pepper sauce

Directions

1. Gather all ingredients.
2. Combine all ingredients in a large mixing bowl. Mix well.
3. Cover and refrigerate 3-6 hours.
4. Serve.

Nutrition Per Serving 160 calories, 1g total fat, 0g sat fat, 430mg sodium, 37g carbohydrates, 7g fiber, 24g sugar, 5g protein

Tip or fact: A five-year study of 48,000 men found that those eating 10 servings a week of cooked tomato products had the lowest risk of prostate cancer. Their risk was ⅓ that of men eating fewer than 2 servings a week.

Shopping list

Produce
☐ 2 medium cucumbers
☐ 2 medium bell peppers
☐ 4 oz. green chilies
☐ celery
☐ 1 pineapple
☐ 1 bunch cilantro

Packaged
☐ 35 oz. can crushed tomatoes undrained
☐ 16 oz. can chopped tomatoes undrained
☐ Tabasco pepper sauce

Refrigerated and frozen
☐ 100% pineapple juice

Seasonings and spices
☐ garlic powder
☐ chili powder
☐ pepper
☐ ground cumin

Vegetarian Minestrone

by Jyl Steinback

Easy | **Gluten Free** | **6 Servings**

I absolutely love Minestrone soup. It is full of beans, veggies, grains, herbs, and loaded with lots of whole plant nutritious foods. Beyond delicious!

Ingredients

- ¾ c frozen chopped onions, thawed and drained
- 2 medium carrots, chopped
- 1 c celery, chopped
- 1 red bell pepper, sliced
- 1 medium zucchini, cubed
- 1 tsp garlic, minced
- 28 oz. low sodium vegetable broth
- 28 oz. can crushed tomatoes, drained
- 15 oz. can low sodium red kidney beans, drained
- ¾ tsp dried basil
- ¾ tsp dried thyme
- ¼ tsp black pepper
- 1 ½ c cooked brown rice

Directions

1. Gather all ingredients.
2. Combine all ingredients except rice in slow cooker and mix well.
3. Cover and cook on low heat for 8-10 hours or high heat for 4-5 hours.
4. Add rice, stir to combine, and heat through.

Nutrition Per Serving 190 calories, 1.5g total fat, 0g sat fat, 440mg sodium, 40g carbohydrates, 9g fiber, 11g sugar, 9g protein

Ingredient Swap: If you would like to make your own vegetable broth, follow the recipe on p. 124.

Tip or fact: For added flavor, shred fresh plant-based parmesan cheese over the soup just before serving.

Soups & Stews

Shopping list

Produce
- ☐ 2 medium carrots
- ☐ celery
- ☐ 1 red bell pepper
- ☐ 1 medium zucchini
- ☐ garlic

Packaged
- ☐ 28 oz. low sodium vegetable broth
- ☐ 28 oz. can crushed tomatoes, drained
- ☐ 15 oz. can low sodium red kidney beans
- ☐ brown rice

Refrigerated and frozen
- ☐ frozen chopped onions

Seasonings and spices
- ☐ dried basil
- ☐ dried thyme
- ☐ black pepper

Zucchini Basil Bowl
by Neil Poppre

Medium | Kid Friendly | 2 Servings

The complex taste of this bowl makes it great for lunch or dinner!

Ingredients
Homemade crus:
1 large zucchini
12 oz. can pinto beans
⅓ c fresh basil
¼ c black olives, chopped
½ c spinach leaves
1 Tbsp black pepper
¼ c water

Directions
1. Preheat the oven to 355°F.
2. Gather all ingredients.
3. Cut zucchini into slices and arrange on a baking sheet.
4. Sprinkle slices with black pepper and bake for 10 minutes or until edges become crispy.
5. While the zucchini is baking, rip apart basil leaves and set them aside.
6. Rinse pinto beans in a strainer.
7. In a pan, combine pinto beans, black olives, water, and spinach leaves.
8. Cook on high until steaming occurs, then reduce to low until zucchini is done cooking.
9. Combine zucchini and beans in a bowl, then top with basil. It's that simple, enjoy!

Nutrition Per Serving 490 calories, 7g total fat, 1g sat fat, 300g sodium, 85g carbohydrates, 30g fiber, 8g sugar, 29g protein

Storage: Store in a airtight glass container in the refrigerator for 1-4 days.

Tip or fact: The flower of the zucchini plant is edible, and quite tasty!

Shopping list

Produce
☐ 1 large zucchini
☐ fresh basil
☐ black olives
☐ spinach leaves

Packaged
☐ 12 oz. can pinto beans

Seasonings and Spices
☐ black pepper

p. **7**   Indian Spice Mix

p. **12** Tahini-Chickpea Dressing

p.**29** Wonderful Tortillas

p. **41** Roasted Red
Pepper Dip

p. **19** Guacamole

p. **27** Summer Bruschetta

p. **21**   Heirloom Tomato Olive Bruschetta

Touch o' Spice
Lentil Dip

p. **48**   Spinach Dip

p. **46** Tomato Dipping Sauce

p. **38**   Pineapple Salsa

p. **65** Planterrifick Pancakes

p. **59** Earl Grey Scones

p. **62** Gingerbread Granola

p. **51** Apple Cinnamon Porridge

p. **26** Roasted Red Pepper Hummus

p. **60** Easy Breakfast Cookies

p. **54** Brown Rice Fruit Bread

p. **56** Chocolate Zucchini Muffins

p. **55** Chocolate Chai Scones

p. **86** Strawberry Lime Smoothie

p. **82** Mango Cacao Smoothie

p. **83** Mango-Turmeric Smoothie

p. **103** Salad with Roasted Veggies

p. **125**   Lentil Quinoa Soup

p. **119** Creamy Pea and Broccoli Soup

p. **122** Green Lentil Stew with Tomatoes

p. **120** Easy Lunch Buddha Bowl

p. **118** Cold Beet Soup

p. **115** — Chickpea-Red Bean Stew

p. 113

Brown Lentil Stew with Green Peas & Corn

p. 111 Beefless Stew

p. 128 Mediterranean-Style Stew

p. **213**
Portobello Burger with
Black Bean-Beet Patty

p. **204**   Baked Falafel

p. **211** Lentil Loaf

p. 207 Chickpea-Summer Squash Burger

p. **43**   Super Salsa

p. **280** Roasted Curry Cauliflower with Peas

p. **277** Polenta Fries with Marinara

p. 299 **Sticky Strawberry Donuts**

p. 298 **Shortbread Cookies**

p. 294 Insanely Delicious Cinnamon Rolls

p. 291 Cacao Chip Cookies

p. **289** Banana Soft Serve Ice Cream

p. **290** Blondie Brookies

p. **308** Chocolate Protein Balls

p. **306** Chocolate Bread

p. **317**   Ants On A Log

p. **319**   Apple Turtles

p. 323 Chocolate-Vanilla Swirl
Chia Pudding

p. 330 No Bake Whole Grain Bars

p. **338** Veggie Faces

p. **337** Sweet Cream and Fruit

p. 327 Fruit Bears

p. 326 Eye Popping Fruit Kabobs

p. **328** Healthy Popcorn Balls

p. **333**

Raw Gingerbread
Granola Apple Parfait

AMERICAN COLLEGE OF
Lifestyle Medicine

A WHOLE FOOD, PLANT-BASED PLATE
Nutrition Prescription for Treating & Reversing Chronic Disease

The American College of Lifestyle Medicine Dietary Lifestyle Position Statement for Treatment and Potential Reversal of Disease: ACLM recommends an eating plan based predominantly on a variety of minimally processed vegetables, fruits, whole grains, legumes, nuts and seeds.

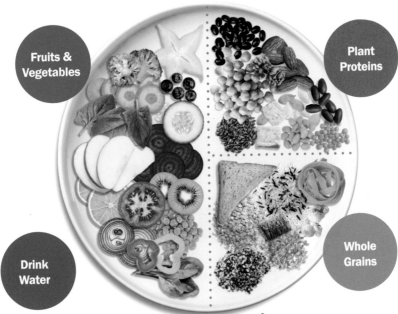

Fruits & Vegetables

Plant Proteins

Drink Water

Whole Grains

ADD HERBS & SPICES

Include a wide array of fiber-filled, nutrient-dense, and antioxidant-rich whole plant foods at every meal. Use a variety of herbs and spices to enhance flavors.

Work with a Registered Dietitian to assist in transitioning to a 100% plant-based dietary lifestyle, the health-protecting, disease-fighting prescription.

Copyright © 2019. American College of Lifestyle Medicine. All rights reserved.

lifestylemedicine.org

- **Focus on whole fruits and vegetables and eat a rainbow of color.**

Vegetables: Dark leafy greens (spinach, kale, arugula, etc.), broccoli, squash, zucchini, carrots, tomatoes, beets, peppers, mushrooms, onions, celery, cauliflower, cucumbers, white & sweet potatoes, green peas, cabbage, whole plant fats (avocados, olives), and more.

Fruits: Apples, bananas, grapes, citrus fruit, berries, peaches, pears, pineapple, kiwi, plums, watermelon, starfruit, mangoes, just to name a few.

- **Drink water for hydration.**
- **Eat a variety of plant protein.**

Legumes: Peas and beans, including kidney beans, pinto beans, white beans, black beans, lima beans, black-eyed peas, garbanzo beans (chickpeas), split peas and lentils, edamame, tofu.

Nuts and seeds: Almonds, pistachios, walnuts, pecans, nut butters, pumpkin/sunflower/chia/flax seeds, and more.

- **Choose whole grains.**

Amaranth, barley, brown rice, buckwheat, bulgur, millet, popcorn, rye, quinoa, whole oats, whole grain bread/tortillas/cereals/flours, to name a few.

Parsley

Thyme

Anise

Bay Leaf

Arugula

Mint

Sage

Best Burgers,
Loaves &
Meatballs

Baked Falafel

by Nele Liivlaid

Medium | **5-6 Servings**

Those simple falafel balls are full of flavor and have perfect consistency despite being gluten-free.

Ingredients

- 1 c dry chickpeas, cooked, drained and rinsed
- ½ c cauliflower, grated
- 1 Tbsp ground chia seeds
- 1 tsp turmeric
- 1 tsp Indian spice mix (recipe p. 7)
- ¼ tsp smoked paprika
- ½ tsp Himalayan salt (or less)
- black pepper, to taste
- 1 small onion
- 2 medium garlic cloves
- 3 Tbsp water
- handful parsley leaves

Directions

1. Preheat oven to 375°F.
2. Gather all ingredients.
3. Prepare the chickpeas.
4. Peel and roughly chop onion and garlic and grate or process raw cauliflower.
5. Next, add the chickpeas, ground chia seeds, cauliflower, spices, Himalayan salt, black pepper, onion and garlic into food processor. Process until you have fine crumbs. Scrape sides whenever necessary.
6. Add water and fresh parsley. Process again, until you have homogeneous batter, but avoid mashing it up too much.
7. Let the batter sit for 5 minutes to let chia seeds absorb water.
8. Line baking sheet with parchment paper and start shaping falafel balls with your hands. Each ball should be about 1 heaping tablespoon of mixture. You should wind up with about 16 balls.
9. Place them onto a baking sheet and bake at 375°F for 25 minutes. Add an additional 5 minutes with fan on.
10. Let cool a bit to let the flavors set.
11. Enjoy!

Nutrition Per Serving 180 calories, 3g total fat, 0g sat fat, 170mg sodium, 30g carbohydrates, 9g fiber, 6g sugar, 10g protein

Ingredient Swap: You're welcome to use any unsalted curry powder, if you don't have the time or ingredients for my dry roasted Indian spice mix.

Shopping list

Produce
- ☐ 1 head cauliflower
- ☐ 1 small onion
- ☐ 2 medium garlic cloves
- ☐ 1 bunch parsley

Packaged
- ☐ dry chickpeas
- ☐ chia seeds

Seasonings and Spices
- ☐ turmeric
- ☐ Indian spice mix
- ☐ smoked paprika
- ☐ Himalayan salt
- ☐ black pepper

Black Bean Jalapeño Burger
by Jyl Steinback

Medium | 4 Servings

Looking for a hearty stew? Look no further. Our stew has an abundance of flavor and vegetables to fill up your belly.

Ingredients

½ medium onion, diced
1 jalapeño pepper, seeded and diced
1 garlic clove, minced
28 oz. low sodium black beans, rinsed and drained
⅓ c plain dry breadcrumbs
2 tsp ground cumin
1 tsp dried oregano, crumbled
½ tsp cayenne
½ tsp chili powder
¼ c cilantro, finely chopped
4 whole wheat hamburger buns
sour cream, for topping
salsa, for topping
guacamole, for topping,
lettuce, for topping

Directions

1. Gather all ingredients.
2. Heat a non-stick pan. Add the onions and cook taking care not to brown, until soft, fragrant, and translucent, about 8 minutes.
3. Stir in the garlic, jalapeño and sauté for 2 more minutes.
4. Pour the beans, breadcrumbs, spices, and cilantro into a larger bowl. Add the onion, garlic, and jalapeño mixture. Using your hands, mash and crush the beans until paste-like.
5. Form mixture into 4 patties.
6. Spray a 12-inch heavy skillet with cooking spray and place over medium-high heat until it shimmers.
7. Cook burgers until outsides are crisp and lightly browned, turning once, about 5 minutes total.
8. Serve on buns with toppings.

Nutrition Per Serving 340 calories, 3g total fat, 1g sat fat, 570mg sodium, 62g carbohydrates, 15g fiber, 6g sugar, 18g protein

Burgers, Loaves & Meatballs

Tip or fact: To reduce the heat in this meatless burger, leave out the cayenne pepper and chili powder.

Shopping list

Produce
☐ 1 onion
☐ 1 jalapeño pepper
☐ 1 garlic clove
☐ 1 bunch cilantro
☐ 1 head lettuce, optional

Packaged
☐ plain dry breadcrumbs
☐ 4 whole wheat hamburger buns
☐ 2 14 oz. cans low sodium black beans

Refrigerated or frozen
☐ sour cream, optional
☐ salsa, optional
☐ guacamole, optional

Seasonings and Spices
☐ ground cumin
☐ dried oregano
☐ cayenne
☐ chili powder

Brown Rice Burger in Whole Wheat Pita by Jyl Steinback

Easy | **4 Servings**

All your veggies and beans and grains wrapped up in one flavorful burger.

Ingredients

2 Tbsp low sodium vegetable broth, divided
1 c mushrooms, sliced
¾ c carrots, shredded
¾ c onion, chopped
1 c zucchini, shredded
2 c quick-cooking oatmeal, uncooked
1 c dried kidney beans (recipe p.6)
1 c cooked brown rice
2 Tbsp low-sodium teriyaki sauce
½ tsp garlic powder
⅛ tsp black pepper
4 whole wheat pita pockets

Directions

1. Gather all ingredients.
2. In a large non-stick skillet, add 1 tablespoon broth to skillet and heat over medium-high heat.
3. Add mushrooms, carrots, onion, and zucchini to skillet. Cook, stirring frequently 6-7 minutes until vegetables are tender.
4. Transfer vegetables from skillet to food processor bowl. Add oatmeal, beans, rice, teriyaki sauce, garlic powder, and pepper.
5. Process mixture by pulsing 10-20 seconds until ingredients are blended.
6. Shape mixture into four patties. Cover and refrigerate 1-2 hours.
7. In a large non-stick skillet, add 1 tablespoon broth and heat over medium-high heat.
8. Add patties to skillet. Cook 3-5 minutes per side until golden brown and crisp.
9. Serve patties in whole-wheat pita pockets. Garnish with lettuce tomato, onions or your favorite salsa.

Nutrition Per Serving 450 calories, 4.5g total fat, 0.5g sat fat, 330mg sodium, 87g carbohydrates, 9g fiber, 6g sugar, 21g protein

Ingredient Swap: Feel free to use a 15 oz. can low sodium canned kidney beans; however, it will increase the sodium by 100mg If you would like to make your own vegetable broth, follow the recipe on p. 124.

Tip or fact: Brown rice is another fun superfood – it is a complex carbohydrate that contains fiber, magnesium, copper, and selenium. We love it it because it is a satiety food – a food that fills you up.

Shopping list

Produce
□ 1 package mushrooms
□ 2 carrots
□ 1 small onion
□ 1 large zucchini

Packaged
□ teriyaki sauce
□ quick-cooking oatmeal
□ brown rice
□ 4 in. whole wheat pitas
□ red kidney beans

Seasonings and Spices
□ garlic powder

Chickpea-Summer Squash Burger
by Nele Liivlaid

Medium | **4-5 Servings**

Enjoy summer heat with that light, lean and juicy veggie burger that won't leave your stomach empty!

Ingredients

16 oz. unsalted chickpeas
6 2-in. leek slices
6 two-centimetre thick leek slices
3 garlic cloves
1 tsp turmeric
handful, soaked walnuts
1 Tbsp ground flax seeds
Himalayan salt, to taste
black pepper, to taste
1 large summer squash, finely grated
1 Tbsp rice flour

Directions

1. Preheat oven to 375°F.
2. Gather all ingredients.
3. Finely grate the summer squash and place it in a big bowl.
4. If you used canned chickpeas, rinse them well. Place the chickpeas, garlic, leek, walnuts, flax seeds and turmeric with sea salt and black pepper into a food processor.
5. Process well. Scrape the sides with a spoon and process again.
6. Pour this mixture into a bowl of summer squash. Mix well with a spoon or use your hands.
7. Add rice flour and mix again. I find using my hand the most effective.
8. Depending on how much liquid you got from the summer squash, you might want to add a few tablespoons of water or plant-based milk.
9. Take a baking sheet and cover it with parchment paper. Take one heaped tablespoon of the batter at a time, form a nice patty and place it on the baking sheet.
10. Bake for 25-30 minutes.
11. The burgers will firm up as they cool down.

Burgers, Loaves & Meatballs

Nutrition Per Serving 210 calories, 11g total fat, 1g sat fat, 160mg sodium, 22g carbohydrates, 6g fiber, 5g sugar, 8g protein

Tip or fact: You may use any flour you like – corn, spelt, buckwheat, oat, and whole wheat.

Shopping list

Produce
☐ 1 large summer squash
☐ 1 leek
☐ 3 garlic cloves

Packaged
☐ ground flaxseeds
☐ raw walnuts
☐ rice flour
☐ unsalted chickpeas

Seasonings and Spices
☐ turmeric
☐ Himalayan salt
☐ black pepper

Festive Lentil Potato Nut Roast
by Jyl Steinback

Easy | **Gluten Free** | **6 Servings**

I love this version of vegan nut roast – it contains a mixture of sweet potato and potato bringing the sweetness down and adding heartiness.

Ingredients

- 3.5 oz. dry red lentils
- 3 oz. boiled unsalted chickpeas
- 1 red onion, chopped
- 12 leeks, sliced 1 cm thick
- 1 medium carrot, chopped
- ½ sweet potato
- 1 big potato
- 4 garlic cloves
- 2 pinches chili flakes
- 1 tsp smoked paprika powder
- ½ oz. miso paste
- 3 rosemary stalk leaves, chopped
- 5 sage stalk leaves, chopped
- 0.9 oz. hazelnuts
- 0.9 oz. almonds
- 2 Tbsp ground flax seeds + 4 Tbsp water
- 3 tsp dried tomato granules
- ½ Tbsp raw buckwheat flour
- black pepper, to taste
- Himalayan salt, to taste

Directions

1. Preheat oven to 375°F.
2. Gather all ingredients.
3. Wash the lentils well and boil. Set aside.
4. Process the nuts in food processor into coarse crumbs or chop them with knife. Process the chickpeas in food processor or mash with fork.
5. Mix ground flax seeds with water and set aside.
6. Chop onion, leek, carrot, sweet potato and potato into smaller cubes and throw them into a bowl.
7. Take a big pot, add 2 tablespoons of water and heat it up. Once the water starts to sizzle, bring down the heat, add chopped veggies and mix for a while. Cover with lid and mix every now and then. Sauté the veggies for a total of 8-10 minutes.
8. Peel garlic cloves and crush them through garlic press. Add to pot of veggies and mix well. Add chili flakes, paprika powder, miso paste and chopped sage and rosemary into the pot. Mix well. All this in the range of 8-10 minutes.
9. Turn off the heat and cool the veggies a bit by mixing it with spoon and let the excess water to vaporize.
10. Add into pot the boiled lentils, processed nuts and chickpeas, tomato granules and flax eggs. Mix really well. Taste and season with Himalayan salt and black pepper.
11. Finally mix in ½ tablespoon of buckwheat flour. The mixture has to be quite dry – it's still moist, but not liquid.
12. Take loaf tin (I used 23cm x 8cm x 7cm) and line it with parchment paper.
13. Transfer the loaf mixture into tin and press it down really well using spatula to make sure there are no air bubbles.
14. Bake for 50 minutes until it's golden. Remove from oven and let breathe for a couple of minutes. Then, place chopping board over the tin and flip it over. Remove the tin letting the loaf to breathe for another couple of minutes before taking off the parchment paper.
15. Let cool before slicing.

Shopping list

Produce
- ☐ 1 red onion
- ☐ 12 leeks
- ☐ 1 medium carrot
- ☐ 1 sweet potato
- ☐ 1 big potato
- ☐ 4 garlic cloves
- ☐ 3 rosemary stalks
- ☐ 5 sage stalks

Packaged
- ☐ 3.5 oz. dry red lentils
- ☐ 3 oz. boiled unsalted chickpeas
- ☐ miso paste
- ☐ 0.9 oz.

- hazelnuts
- ☐ 0.9 oz. almonds
- ☐ ground flax seeds
- ☐ dried tomato granules
- ☐ raw buckwheat flour

Seasonings and Spices
- ☐ chili flakes
- ☐ smoked paprika powder
- ☐ black pepper
- ☐ Himalayan salt

Nutrition Per Serving 340 calories, 10g total fat, 1g sat fat, 320mg sodium, 52g carbohydrates, 9g fiber, 6g sugar, 15g protein

Garbanzo Bean Veggie Burger by Jyl Steinback

Easy | 8 Servings

Garbanzo beans are my all time favorite bean. You will love this veggie burger!

Ingredients

30 oz. unsalted canned chickpeas
1 ½ c quick-cooking oats
2 cloves garlic, minced
½ tsp cumin
¼ tsp red pepper
whole wheat hamburger buns
salt, optional
pepper, optional

Directions

1. Gather all ingredients.
2. Drain the unsalted chickpeas, reserving the liquid. Rinse the chickpeas.
3. Add the chickpeas and the ½ cup of reserved liquid to a food processor or blender and process.
4. Add more reserved liquid if necessary to make a smooth paste.
5. Add garlic, cumin, red pepper, salt and pepper and process to combine well.
6. In a medium mixing bowl, combine bean paste mixture with oats. Mix well, adding additional bean liquid or oats as necessary to make a mixture that holds together well and keeps its shape.
7. Shape mixture into 8 patties about ½ inch thick.
8. Heat a non-stick skillet.
9. Over medium high heat, cook patties until golden brown on each side, about 5 minutes.
10. Serve patties on a bun with toppings and condiments.

Burgers, Loaves & Meatballs

Nutrition Per Serving 440 calories, 5g total fat, 1g sat fat, 410mg sodium, 73g carbohydrates, 6g fiber, 6g sugar, 8g protein

Ingredient Swap: To make gluten free, swap out whole wheat buns for gluten free buns.

Tip or fact: To save time, purchase your garlic already minced in the produce section of your grocery store.

Shopping list

Produce
☐ 2 cloves garlic

Packaged
☐ quick-cooking oats
☐ 30 oz. unsalted chickpeas
☐ whole wheat hamburger buns

Seasonings and Spices
☐ cumin
☐ red pepper
☐ salt, optional
☐ black pepper, optional

Juicy Beet-Chickpea Patties
by Nele Liivlaid

Easy | **6 Servings**

It just is so delicious, beets providing the juiciness and chickpeas the heartiness.

Ingredients

8.5 oz. can unsalted chickpeas, washed and drained

2 Tbsp chickpea flour, optional

2 c boiled beets, grated

parsley

black pepper, to taste

Himalayan salt, to taste

fresh oregano

Directions

1. Preheat oven to 350°F.
2. Gather all ingredients.
3. Process the chickpeas in a food processor. You could also mash them with fork, but it is more time-consuming.
4. Mix together the chickpeas, grated beets, chickpea flour and herbs/spices.
5. Form 6 patties and place them on a baking sheet lined with parchment paper.
6. Bake for 15 minutes, then give the patties a flip and bake for another 10-15 minutes.

Nutrition Per Serving 110 calories, 1.5g total fat, 0g sat fat, 210mg sodium, 19g carbohydrates, 5g fiber, 8g sugar, 5g protein

Tip or fact: If your beets are not very juicy you might not need to use chickpea flour. Chickpea flour can be substituted with other flours (brown rice, buckwheat, etc.). Use any herbs/spices you deem fit. Make Indian or Mexican version of the patties – whatever appeals you at the moment you start cooking. I did not use any extra salt as the canned chickpeas already came with it. Should yours be without salt, feel free to use some in the recipe.

Shopping list

Produce
- 2 beets
- 1 bunch parsley
- 1 bunch oregano

Packaged
- 8.5 oz. can unsalted chickpeas
- chickpea flour, optional

Seasonings and Spices
- black pepper
- Himalayan salt

Lentil Loaf

by Nele Liivlaid

Medium | 8 Servings

Here's a simple gluten-free vegan lentil loaf recipe requiring only well-known ingredients. It's hearty, holds together well and is full of flavor.

Ingredients

1½ c dry split red lentils, cook
½ c dry brown lentils, cook
1 bay leaf
2 tsp unsalted Mediterranean seasoning mix
3 c water
1 small yellow onion, minced
2 medium celery stalks, minced
1 c carrot, grated
3 garlic cloves, minced
1 Tbsp fresh rosemary leaves
1½ Tbsp fresh thyme, chopped
1 Tbsp fresh sage leaves, chopped
½ tsp smoked paprika
3 Tbsp ground chia seeds
1 c walnuts
2 Tbsp buckwheat flour
1 tsp Himalayan salt
Black pepper, to taste

Shopping list

Produce
- 1 bay leaf
- 1 small yellow onion
- 2 medium celery stalks
- 1 large carrot
- 3 garlic cloves
- fresh rosemary leaves
- fresh thyme
- fresh sage leaves

Packaged
- dry split red lentils
- dry brown lentils
- walnuts
- buckwheat flour

Seasonings and Spices
- unsalted Mediterranean seasoning mix
- smoked paprika
- ground chia seeds
- Himalayan salt
- black pepper

Directions

1. Gather all ingredients.
2. Wash the dry lentils until the water is clear and then soak for 6-8 hours. Then, rinse and drain.
3. Preheat oven to 375°F.
4. Boil the lentils with 3 cups of water, a bay leaf and 2 teaspoons of Mediterranean seasoning mix for 15 minutes or until soft. Remove bay leaf.
5. Drain the excess liquid by placing the lentils into a sieve. Use the discarded broth in other dishes (soups, stews, dressings, sauces).
6. Heat a few tablespoons of water in a skillet or large pan. Toss in chopped onions and celery. Sauté the veggies with the lid on until softened, about 3 minutes stirring every now and then. Add splashes of water whenever necessary.
7. Add shredded carrots, stir and sauté for another 3 minutes. Add splashes of water when needed. Add garlic, herbs and smoked paprika. Give it a stir and simmer for another few minutes. Set aside, covered.
8. Pour drained lentils into a large bowl. Add the veggie mix and stir well.
9. Add ground chia seeds and give it another good stir before adding chopped walnuts and buckwheat flour. Mix well until you have a nice mushy and homogeneous batter. Finally, season with Himalayan salt and black pepper.
10. Line a 9×5 inch pan with parchment paper.
11. Firmly pack the batter into loaf pan and bake for 1 hour.
12. Let the baked loaf sit for 5 minutes before lifting it onto folded kitchen paper to cool.
13. Wait at least 30 minutes before slicing.

Burgers, Loaves & Meatballs

Nutrition Per Serving 240 calories, 5g total fat, 0.5g sat fat, 210mg sodium, 37g carbohydrates, 8g fiber, 2g sugar, 14g protein

Tip or fact: Serve with plenty of greens and make yourself a really comforting bowl with mashed potatoes or a mix of potatoes, sweet potatoes and/or cauliflower to accompany the loaf. My favorite sauce for this lentil loaf is Tahini-Chickpea Dressing.

Nuts & Seeds Burger
by Laura Salyer

Easy | **Gluten Free** | **4 Servings**

Hearty, flavorful nut and seed burgers.

Ingredients

1 c brown rice, cooked
1 can low sodium cooked black beans, drained and rinsed
½ c sunflower seeds
½ c cashews
½ c walnuts
½ tsp cumin
¼ tsp chili powder
½ tsp minced or powdered garlic
½ tsp onion powder
½ tsp turmeric powder
½ c water, as needed
black pepper, to taste

Directions

1. Gather all ingredients.
2. If baking, preheat oven to 350°F degrees.
3. Cook the brown rice. Combine 1 cup of brown rice to 2 ½ cups liquid (I use water, but feel free to use vegetable broth) in a saucepan and bring to a boil, then reduce heat to a simmer and cover.
4. Simmer until the water has evaporated, about 40 to 45 minutes.
5. Remove from heat but keep pan covered and let rice cool for about 10 minutes.
6. Blend all burger ingredients except water in a food processor until well-combined and sticky.
7. If mixture is dry, add water in small amounts until you can form sturdy patties.
8. Pat out burgers into desired thickness, then pan fry until golden browned on both sides.
9. If you'd prefer to bake, line a baking sheet or two with parchment paper and bake in oven at for 20 minutes. Flip and bake for 15 more minutes.
10. Serve on whole wheat buns, in wraps or as meatballs.

Nutrition Per Serving 490 calories, 25g total fat, 3g sat fat, 55mg sodium, 49g carbohydrates, 16g fiber, 2g sugar, 20g protein

Storage: These burgers can be cooked and stored in an airtight glass container for 2-3 days, or they can be made into patties and frozen before cooking for up to several months. However, after freezing, it is best to bake these nut burger patties to keep them from breaking apart during cooking.

Ingredient Swap: The canned beans can be replaced with dry beans. Follow the recipe on p. 6.

Tip or fact: Serve with plenty of greens and make yourself a really comforting bowl with mashed potatoes or a mix of potatoes, sweet potatoes and/or cauliflower to accompany the loaf. My favorite sauce for this lentil loaf is Tahini-Chickpea Dressing.

Shopping list

Packaged
☐ sunflower seeds
☐ cashews
☐ walnuts
☐ brown rice
☐ 1 can low sodium black beans

Seasonings and Spices
☐ cumin
☐ chili powder
☐ powdered garlic
☐ onion powder
☐ ground turmeric
☐ pink Himalayan salt
☐ black pepper

Portobello Burger with Black Bean-Beet Patty by Nele Liivlaid

Hard | **Gluten Free** | **6 Servings**

Delicious yet lean and healthy vegan Portobello burger with juicy black bean-beet patty and chickpea hummus.

Ingredients

15 oz. unsalted chickpeas, washed and rinsed
pinch sea salt
2 Tbsp lemon juice
½ tsp garlic powder
1 tsp tahini or ground sesame seeds
½ tsp cumin seeds, crushed, optional
1 tsp turmeric
1 can low sodium black beans, rinsed and drained
1 medium onion, chopped
1 tsp garlic powder
½ tsp cumin seeds, crushed
handful fresh coriander, chopped
1 Tbsp raw buckwheat flour
1 Tbsp tapioca flour
1 Tbsp gluten-free jumbo oats
14 oz. grated beets
6 large portobello caps
greens, for topping

Directions

1. Preheat oven to 425°F.
2. Gather all ingredients.
3. Make the chickpea hummus. Blend the chickpeas, lemon juice, sea salt, garlic powder, tahini, cumin seeds and turmeric with an immersion blender until smooth.
4. Roast the portobello mushroom. Preheat oven to 425°F.
5. Place the mushrooms, gill side up on baking sheet lined with parchment paper and brush the gills as well as caps of mushrooms with some soy sauce.
6. Bake for 20 minutes flipping the caps halfway through.
7. lower the over to 350°F.
8. Mash rinsed and drained black beans in a bigger bowl.
9. Drain grated beets from excess liquid (drink it or use as salad dressing).
10. Add chopped onion, garlic powder, crushed cumin seeds, beets, coriander, flours, and oats to the bowl of black beans and mix well until homogeneous batter forms. It's best achieved by using your hands.
11. Form 6 patties and place them on a baking sheet lined with parchment paper.
12. Bake for 30 minutes flipping them halfway through.
13. Assemble the burger. Cut the stems off the Portobello mushrooms – eat them then or store for use in another meal.
14. Spread some hummus onto the gill-side of the mushroom.
15. Add something green – spinach, arugula, chicory or lettuce.
16. Add the black bean-beet patty.
17. Add more hummus to the top of the patty.
18. Place a thin slice of carrot over the hummus layer and more greens.
19. Spread more hummus onto the gill-side of another mushroom cap. Place it gill-side down on top of your vegan Portobello burger.

Burgers, Loaves & Meatballs

Shopping list

Produce
- 1 medium yellow onion
- grated beets
- 6 portobello mushrooms
- 2 lemons
- greens of choice

Packaged
- rolled oats
- tahini
- buckwheat flour
- tapioca flour
- 15 oz. can

- low sodium black beans
- 15 oz. can unsalted chickpeas

Seasonings and Spices
- cumin seeds
- coriander
- garlic powder
- turmeric
- sea salt
- black pepper

Nutrition Per Serving Black Bean-Beet Patties with Portobello Caps 140 calories, 1g total fat, 0g sat fat, 160mg sodium, 26g carbohydrates, 9g fiber, 8g sugar, 8g protein. **Chickpea Hummus** 80 calories, 1g total fat, 0g sat fat, 65mg sodium, 12g carbohydrates, 3g fiber, 1g sugar, 4g protein

Storage: Hummus can be store in an airtight glass container in the fridge for up to 3 days.

Quinoa Chickpea Burger

by Nele Liivlaid

Easy | 4 Servings

It is a perfect recipe to batch cook effortless weeknight meals.

Ingredients

17 oz. canned unsalted chickpeas, rinsed and drained
1.76 oz. dry white quinoa
1.76 oz. dry red quinoa
2 garlic cloves
6 leek slices, 2 cm thick
handful fresh parsley
1 tsp paprika powder
2 Tbsp (not heaped) corn flour
3 Tbsp oat milk
Himalayan salt, to taste
black pepper, to taste

Directions

1. Preheat oven to 375°F.
2. Gather all ingredients.
3. Measure the quinoas, wash thoroughly and boil for 17 minutes. Let sit covered for another two minutes. Should there be any water left in the pot, drain it.
4. While the quinoa-mix is cooking, place the chickpeas, garlic, leek, parsley and paprika powder into a food processor. If your chickpeas are unsalted, add some sea salt as well. Process well. Scrape the sides with a spoon when necessary and process again.
5. Pour this mixture into a bowl and add boiled quinoa-mix. Mix well with a spoon or use your hands.
6. Add corn flour and oat milk and mix again. I find using your hands is the most effective.
7. Take a baking sheet and cover it with parchment paper.
8. Take one tablespoon of the batter, form a nice patty and place it on the baking sheet. Repeat.
9. Bake for 15-20 minutes. They firm up as they cool down.

Nutrition Per Serving 240 calories, 4g total fat, 0g sat fat, 240mg sodium, 43g carbohydrates, 8g fiber, 6g sugar, 10g protein

Tip or fact: Substitute oat milk with any other plant-based milk or water. You can use only white or only red quinoa, if you do not have both in hand. Serve with "Cheesy" sauce from "Cheesy" Veggie Divan recipe on p. 233.

Shopping list

Produce
- 2 garlic cloves
- 1 leek
- 1 bunch parsley

Packaged
- 17 oz. canned unsalted chickpeas, rinsed and drained
- 1.76 oz. dry white quinoa
- 1.76 oz. dry red quinoa
- corn flour
- oat milk

Seasonings and Spices
- paprika powder
- black pepper
- Himalayan salt

Summertime Burger

by Caryn Dugan

Medium | **Gluten Free** | **6 Servings**

Bake it or grill it, it's up to you. This summertime burger packs some deep flavors from the mushrooms and sweet potato and the seasonings give it a kick.

Ingredients

2 ½ Tbsp ground flax
5 Tbsp water
1 c sweet potato, shredded
8 oz. mushrooms, roughly chopped
½ red onion, diced small
2 garlic cloves, minced
pinch of sea salt
14 oz. can low sodium black beans, drained and rinsed
½ c cooked chickpeas (recipe p. 6)
¼ c Italian parsley, roughly chopped
2-3 green onion stalks, roughly chopped
2 Tbsp sunflower seeds
2 Tbsp dried oregano
1 Tbsp ground cumin
½ Tbsp paprika
½ teaspoon red pepper flakes (or to taste)
½ teaspoon sea salt
½ teaspoon ground black pepper
1 avocado
1¾ c whole oat

Directions

1. Gather all ingredients.
2. Mix the flax and the water together in a small bowl and allow it to sit for 15 minutes or until it begins to become gelatinous (this will be your "egg" and act as a binder).
3. Wash, but do not peel the sweet potato. Shred it by using a hand grater or run it though a food processor using the shred blade.
4. To a large non-stick pan, add the sweet potato, red onion and mushrooms. Over medium heat and stirring often, allow the vegetables to cook down.
5. Once they begin to soften, add in the garlic and a pinch of sea salt.
6. Transfer to a food processor. Add the black beans, chickpeas, parsley, green onion, sunflower seeds, spices and flax/water mix.
7. To a blender, add one cup of the oats and grind down until it is a coarse flour.
8. Add the flour and ¼ of the whole oats to the food processor with the rest of the mixture.
9. Pulse the mixture until well mixed, but not blended or pureed.

Burgers, Loaves & Meatballs

Nutrition Per Serving 390 calories, 11g total fat, 1.5g sat fat, 360mg sodium, 59g carbohydrates, 12g fiber, 3g sugar, 17g protein

Shopping list

Produce
□ 1 small sweet potato
□ 8 oz. mushrooms
□ 1 small red onion
□ 2 garlic cloves
□ 1 bunch Italian parsley
□ 2-3 green onion stalks
□ 1 avocado

Packaged
□ ground flax
□ raw unsalted sunflower seeds

□ whole oat
□ dry chickpeas
□ 14 oz. can low sodium black beans

Seasonings and Spices
□ sea salt
□ dried oregano
□ ground cumin
□ paprika
□ red pepper flakes
□ ground black pepper

Tip or fact: Onions have been a part of the human diet for more than 7,000 years. Archaeologists have discovered traces of onions dating back to 5000 B.C., found alongside stones from figs and dates in settlements from the Bronze Age.

Sweet Potato Meatballs

by Ashley Arpel Greenwald

Medium | **Gluten Free** | **6 Servings**

Appetizer or entree, these sweet potato meatballs are packed with flavor and protein.

Ingredients

2 c cooked brown rice
1 tsp garlic, minced
½ tsp parsley flakes
1 tsp onion powder
1½ tsp chili powder
15.5 oz. can low sodium black beans, drained
¾ c sweet potato, pureed
1 Tbsp nutritional yeast
1 c tapioca flour

Directions

1. Preheat oven to 400°F.
2. Gather all ingredients.
3. Open can of black beans and drain out all liquid.
4. Place beans in a large mixing bowl and add sweet potato puree and nutritional yeast.
5. Pour cooked rice into mixture and mix.
6. Finally, add tapioca flour ⅓ cup at a time, mixing in between each.
7. Refrigerate for 20 minutes to set mixture.
8. After 20 minutes, remove mixture from refrigerator. Scoop mixture into the palm of your hands and roll into individual balls.
9. Place meatballs on a parchment lined baking sheet and bake for 20 minutes.
10. Serve immediately or refrigerate and eat for lunch the next day! Best serve with our Sweet Potato Sauce. Recipe p. 45.
11. If making burgers, DO NOT place mixture in refrigerator to set. Use a ⅓ cup measuring cup to scoop out mixture onto silicone lined baking sheet and bake for 20 minutes.

Nutrition Per Serving 300 calories, 1.5g total fat, 0g sat fat, 180mg sodium, 63g carbohydrates, 8g fiber, 3g sugar, 8g protein

Storage: Store cooked patties or meatballs in an airtight glass container in the refrigerator for up to 2 days.

Ingredient Swap: In place of brown rice, you can use quinoa. You can also use all-purpose flour in place of tapioca flour. This will make the recipe no longer gluten free.

Tip or fact: Nutritional yeast is a condiment, not a supplement. It is used as an alternative to dairy cheese.

Shopping list

Produce
☐ 1 garlic clove

Packaged
☐ brown rice
☐ nutritional yeast
☐ tapioca flour
☐ 15.5 oz. can low sodium black beans

Seasonings and Spices
☐ dried parsley
☐ onion powder
☐ chili powder

Parsley

Thyme

Anise

Bay Leaf

Arugula

Mint

Sage

Vanilla

Wraps, Pizzas & Sandwiches

Black Bean and Vegetable Pocket by Jyl Steinback

Medium | **Gluten Free** | **4 Servings**

If you are craving Mexican flavors but are limited on time, this quick, flavorful pocket of goodness is just the ticket.

Ingredients

6 c broccoli florets, steamed

11 oz. can Mexicorn or whole kernel corn

15 oz. can black beans, rinsed and drained

1½ c unsalted tomato paste

1 c fresh cilantro, chopped

1 c fresh chives, chopped

dash Tabasco sauce

5 large whole grain pita pocket breads, cut in half

cashew sour cream, optional

Directions

1. Gather all ingredients.
2. Cut bigger broccoli florets into quarters and medium ones into half. Measure 6 cups and steam for 4-5 minutes (should remain a bit crunchy).
3. While the broccoli is steaming, combine corn, beans, tomato paste, Tabasco sauce and chopped herbs in a large bowl.
4. Add steamed broccoli and give it a final stir.
5. Fill pita pockets with broccoli, corn, and bean mixture.
6. Garnish with cashew sour cream (recipe p. 5), if desired. Serve immediately.

Nutrition Per Serving 309 calories, 1.5g total fat, 0g sat fat, 1376mg sodium, 63g carbohydrates, 10g fiber, 13g sugar, 16g protein

Storage: Should you have some filling left over, store in airtight glass container in fridge for up to 4 days.

Ingredient Swap: Instead of store-bought pita bread, try the gluten-free tortillas (recipe p. 29). Use 2 per serving! If you don't like cilantro, sub it with parsley. Tabasco can be substituted with Himalayan salt and chili pepper flakes or crushed black pepper.

Tip or fact: One of the greatest versatile aspects of sandwiches is that they can be served hot or cold.

Shopping list

Produce
□ 6 broccoli crowns
□ 1 bunch cilantro
□ 1 bunch chives

Packaged
□ 11 oz. can Mexicorn or whole kernel corn
□ 15 oz. can black beans, rinsed and drained
□ unsalted tomato paste
□ Tabasco sauce
□ 5 whole grain pita pocket breads

Cucumber Chickpea Sandwich
by Jyl Steinback

Easy | **4 Servings**

Umeboshi (pickled Plum) adds an exotic flare to this otherwise unassuming salad.

Ingredients
2 Tbsp umeboshi vinegar
1 tsp whole grain mustard
1 medium tomato
2 Tbsp scallions, chopped
2 c lettuce
1 c cucumber, chopped
1 c chickpeas
1 c celery, chopped
8 slices whole wheat bread
ground pepper

Directions
1. Gather all ingredients.
2. Place chickpeas in the bowl of a food processor and pulse two or three times to roughly chop.
3. Add mustard, scallions, celery, vinegar and cucumber. Pulse until shredded.
4. Toast each slice of bread, add lettuce, tomato and dollop with cucumber chickpea spread.
5. Add fresh ground pepper and enjoy!

Nutrition Per Serving 232 calories, 3g total fat, 0.5g sat fat, 407mg sodium, 39g carbohydrates, 9g fiber, 11g sugar, 12g protein

Tip or fact: Chickpeas high fiber content prevents blood sugar levels from rising too rapidly after a meal, making these beans an especially good choice for individuals with diabetes, insulin resistance or hypoglycemia.

Wraps, Pizzas & Sandwiches

Shopping list

Produce
☐ 1 medium tomato
☐ scallions
☐ 1 head lettuce
☐ 1 cucumber
☐ 1 bunch celery

Packaged
☐ umeboshi vinegar
☐ whole wheat bread
☐ chickpeas

Seasonings and Spices
☐ whole grain mustard
☐ ground pepper

Golden-Wedge Lettuce Wraps by Jyl Steinback

Medium | 3 Servings

This easy to make wrap is a simply delicious complement to any meal.

Ingredients

1 Tbsp dried rosemary
2 lbs Yukon gold potatoes
1 large head lettuce
1 large tomato, diced

Directions

1. Preheat oven to 350°F.
2. Gather all ingredients.
3. Cut potatoes into wedges, then arrange on a pan and bake for 10-15 minutes or until they begin to brown.
4. Separate all lettuce leaves and rinse well.
5. Dice tomato.
6. Combine a pinch of tomatoes with a few potato wedges in a lettuce leaf, add rosemary, and roll it into a wrap.
7. Line up 3 on a plate and serve!

Nutrition Per Serving 270 calories, 0.5g total fat, 0g sat fat, 125mg sodium, 66g carbohydrates, 10g fiber, 9g sugar, 8g protein

Storage: Store in an airtight glass container for 1-2 days in the fridge.

Tip or fact: You may have heard to eat more dark leafy greens because it is better for you (which is true), but keep in mind that iceberg lettuce is still a great way to get plant nutrition for very few calories. It is also a perfect fit for this dish!

Shopping list

Produce
☐ 2 lbs Yukon gold potatoes
☐ 1 large head lettuce
☐ 1 large tomato

Seasonings and Spices
☐ dried rosemary

Inside Out Burrito

by Jyl Steinback

Medium | **Gluten Free** | **4 Servings**

Green goodness all wrapped up inside this tasty veggie burrito.

Ingredients

1 bunch asparagus
1 medium yellow onion, sliced
1 medium head cabbage
3 jalapeños, thick slices
1 medium red onion, julienned
⅛ tsp chili flakes
⅛ tsp salt
⅛ tsp black pepper
½ Tbsp garlic powder
½ c date sugar
1 c water
3 limes, juiced
2 ½ Tbsp water

Directions

1. Preheat oven to 350°F.
2. Gather all ingredients.
3. Take asparagus and remove bottom stump, cut into threes on a bias. Put into a bowl of ice water.
4. Bring a pot of water to a boil. Put asparagus in boiling water for 20 seconds then remove and put back into the ice water.
5. Drain asparagus and season with chili flakes, garlic powder, and black pepper.
6. Take date sugar and 1 cup of water, cook until dissolved and syrupy.
7. Thickly sliced jalapeños and put into boiling water for 20 minutes, drain, and repeat 3 times.
8. Remove jalapeños and put into syrup and cook for another 10 minutes, remove from heat and store accordingly.
9. Put your lime juice and water into a pot bring it to a simmer, and pour over your julienned red onions hold at room temperature until color begins to change.
10. Slice large onion. Remove the top and bottom pieces.
11. Char each side of the onion slices in your skillet with 2 tablespoons of water.
12. Once charred, add water to the skillet so it covers the bottom of the pan.
13. Cover the skillet with foil and let the onions steam for 5 minutes in the oven.
14. Cut your cabbage or lettuce at the bottom and remove leaves big enough to put in ingredients for your inside out burrito.

Wraps, Pizzas & Sandwiches

Shopping list

Produce
- 1 bunch asparagus
- 1 medium yellow onion
- 1 medium head cabbage
- 3 jalapeños
- 1 medium red onion
- 3 limes

Packaged
- date sugar

Seasonings and Spices
- chili flakes
- salt
- black pepper
- garlic powder

Nutrition Per Serving 190 calories, 1g total fat, 0.5g sat fat, 120mg sodium, 44g carbohydrates, 8g fiber, 28g sugar, 5g protein

Tip or fact: When the weather is right, asparagus grows very fast at about 1 inch per hour.

Mango Pizza with Black Beans & Squash by Jyl Steinback

Easy | 6 Servings

Pizza time with sweet and savory ingredients.

Ingredients

¾ c black beans, rinsed
3 large whole wheat pita bread
¼ c cilantro
½ c mango, sliced
½ c mushroom, sliced
1 medium green onion
¾ c salsa
½ c squash, sliced
1 c tofu, blended smooth

Directions

1. Preheat oven to 325°F.
2. Gather all ingredients.
3. Place pita on baking sheet and spread salsa onto it, leaving a 1-inch border on all sides.
4. Cube the tofu into ½ inch cubes. Blend the tofu until smooth in blender.
5. Pour the blended tofu onto the crust.
6. Add the zucchini, mango, mushrooms and beans.
7. Bake 12-15 minutes.
8. Top with green onions and cilantro prior to serving.

Nutrition Per Serving 131 calories, 2g total fat, 0g sat fat, 358mg sodium, 23g carbohydrates, 7g fiber, 2g sugar, 7g protein

Tip or fact: Women are twice as likely as men to order vegetables on their pizza.

Shopping list

Produce
☐ 1 bunch cilantro
☐ 1 mango
☐ mushrooms
☐ 1 medium green onion
☐ 1 squash

Packaged
☐ salsa
☐ tofu
☐ 3 large whole wheat pita bread
☐ black beans

Mexican Vegetable Pizza
by Jyl Steinback

Easy | **4 Servings**

From now on Mexican pizza nights will contribute to health! Enjoy your spicy pizza with friends without any harmful side effects!

Ingredients

1 thin New York pizza crust
10 Tbsp tomato paste
1⅓ c grated cashew cheese
4 Tbsp oil-free/sugar-free chunky-style salsa
1 large green bell pepper, cut into thin strips
4 Tbsp green onion, chopped
4 Tbsp fresh cilantro, chopped

Directions

1. Preheat oven to 400°F.
2. Gather all ingredients.
3. Prepare thin NY pizza crust.
4. Spread 2½ tablespoons of tomato paste onto each pizza crust.
5. Cover pizza crusts with bell pepper strips. Around ¼ of a bell pepper per pizza.
6. Sprinkle 1/3 cup of cashew cheese on crust.
7. Top with salsa.
8. Bake for 13-15 minutes.
9. When the pizzas are out of oven, garnish with fresh green onion and cilantro.

Nutrition Per Serving 190 calories, 6g total fat, 0.5g sat fat, 400mg sodium, 28g carbohydrates, 3g fiber, 7g sugar, 4g protein

Ingredient Swaps: In place of cashew cheese you can use chopped tofu or marinated tempeh. If you don't like cilantro, you can use parsley more green onions or chives.

Tip or fact: To save time, bake 2 pizzas at a time. While the first 2 are in oven, roll out and top the other two.

Wraps, Pizzas & Sandwiches

Shopping list

Produce
☐ 1 large green bell pepper
☐ 1 bunch green onion
☐ 1 bunch cilantro

Packaged
☐ tomato paste
☐ oil-free/sugar-free chunky-style salsa

Refrigerated or frozen
☐ thin New York pizza crust
☐ cashew cheese

Open-Faced Black Bean Quesadilla by Jyl Steinback

Easy | **4 Servings**

Makes for a quick and easy Mexican-style lunch.

Ingredients

15 oz. can black beans, rinsed
½ c low-fat shredded pepper jack cheese
½ c prepared fresh salsa
8 in. whole-wheat tortillas
¼ c cilantro, chopped
1 ripe avocado, diced

Directions

1. Gather all ingredients.
2. Combine beans, cheese and ¼ cup salsa in a medium bowl.
3. Place tortillas on a work surface.
4. Spread ½ cup filling on each tortilla.
5. Using the cooking spray, spray a large non-stick skillet over medium heat.
6. Add a quesadilla and cook for about 3 minutes, or until cheese is melted.
7. Repeat with the cooking spray and quesadillas.
8. Top all quesadillas with cilantro and serve with avocado and the remaining salsa.

Nutrition Per Serving 470 calories, 18g total fat, 6g sat fat, 680mg sodium, 66g carbohydrates, 15g fiber, 2g sugar, 16g protein

Tip or fact: For a healthy after school snack, serve this easy open-face black bean quesadilla.

Shopping list

Produce
☐ cilantro
☐ avocado

Packaged
☐ 15 oz. can black beans, rinsed
☐ fresh salsa
☐ 4 whole-wheat tortillas

Refrigerated or frozen
☐ low-fat shredded pepper jack cheese

Plant Art
by Jyl Steinback

Easy | **Kid Friendly** | **4 Servings**

Kids can be as creative as they want.

Ingredients
8 whole wheat slices of bread
¼ c peanut butter
1 c broccoli florets
8 celery sticks, cut into 2 in.
1 c spinach leaves
1 c carrots, shredded

Directions
1. Gather all ingredients.
2. Toast whole wheat bread.
3. Place one toasted bread in the middle of a small plate.
4. Lightly spread bread with peanut butter.
5. Create a plant in a garden design using shredded carrot for roots, celery sticks for stems, spinach for leaves, and broccoli for flowers.

Nutrition Per Serving 170 calories, 6g total fat, 1g sat fat, 170mg sodium, 24g carbohydrates, 1g fiber, 5g sugar, 2g protein

Storage: refrigerate until ready to eat.

Ingredient Swaps: Swap in any of your favorite veggies.

Tip or fact: Use this snack to teach kids that when you are eating a fruit or veggie you are eating a part of a plant.

Wraps, Pizzas & Sandwiches

Shopping list

Produce
☐ 1 head broccoli
☐ 1 bunch celery
☐ 1 bunch spinach
☐ 1 large carrot

Packaged
☐ whole wheat bread
☐ peanut butter

Rice and Black Bean Burritos by Jyl Steinback

Easy | 6 Servings

Perfect grab and go meal! Make extras for the freezer!

Ingredients

3 ½ c boiled beans
¾ c super salsa (recipe p. 43)
⅓ c tomatoes, chopped
¼ c green chilies, chopped
1 ½ c cooked brown rice
6 8 in. whole wheat tortillas
6 Tbsp shredded vegan cheese

Directions

1. Gather all ingredients.
2. Heat nonstick skillet over medium-low heat.
3. Add beans, salsa, tomatoes and chiles to skillet and cook until heated through over medium-low heat
4. Add rice and mix well.
5. Divide filling among tortillas. Top with cheese.
6. Roll tortillas up burrito style and place seam-side down on plate.
7. You can serve with additional salsa (recipe p. 43), cashew sour cream (recipe p. 5) and chopped green onions.

Nutrition Per Serving 430 calories, 8g total fat, 3g sat fat, 540mg sodium, 75g carbohydrates, 14g fiber, 2g sugar, 18g protein

Tip or fact: This can be an easy and quick solution. Freeze burritos and place in individual containers for future use. To reheat, place in a microwave-safe dish and heat on high 1 to 2 minutes per burrito.

Shopping list

Produce
☐ 1 large tomato

Packaged
☐ brown rice
☐ dry beans
☐ 1 small can chopped chilies
☐ 6 8 in. whole wheat tortillas

Refrigerated and Frozen
☐ shredded vegan cheese

Sweet Treat Pizza
by Laura Salyer

Easy | **2-4 Servings**

A delicious, sweet take on classic pizza.

Ingredients

Homemade crust:
1 tsp active yeast
½ c warm water
1 Tbsp unbleached white flour
1 ¼ c unbleached white flour
¼ tsp salt
1 tsp walnut or coconut oil

Pizza Topping:
dairy-free chocolate hazelnut spread
1 banana, sliced
1 c strawberries, sliced
2 mandarin oranges, peeled and sectioned
2 kiwis, peeled and sliced
½ c shredded, unsweetened coconut, optional
½ tsp cinnamon, optional

Directions

1. Preheat the oven to 435°F.
2. Gather all ingredients.
3. Making the dough. In a bowl, mix warm water, yeast and 1 tbsp flour. Let it sit for a few minutes to activate.
4. Add 1 cup flour and ¼ tsp salt and mix. Add another 3 tbsp flour and mix. Knead for a few seconds just until a soft and slightly sticky dough forms. Add another tablespoon of flour if needed to handle.
5. Gather dough into a ball and let sit for 15 minutes in a warm place.
6. Brush ½ tsp oil over dough. Gather the dough into a ball and place on parchment lined sheet.
7. Use flour to spread dough into a 14-inch size circle, or to desired thickness.
8. Bake pizza for 16-18 minutes or until nicely golden on the edges.
9. Topping the pizza. Cover the slightly cooled pizza with your spread of choice, leaving about an inch uncovered around the outside.
10. Arrange sliced bananas, strawberries, kiwi, mandarin slices, shredded coconut, and any other toppings you want in a pretty pattern, then top with a sprinkle of cinnamon if desired.
11. Slice and serve!

Wraps, Pizzas & Sandwiches

Nutrition Per Serving 320 calories, 13g total fat, 11g sat fat, 90mg sodium, 48g carbohydrates, 4g fiber, 23g sugar, 6g protein

Storage: As fruit will brown if left uneaten, it is best to enjoy this sweet pizza immediately. If serving later, you may want to toss fruit slices in lemon juice before using to keep from browning so soon.

Ingredient Swap: In place of dairy-free chocolate hazelnut spread, you can use your favorite jam, jelly, nut butter, coconut whipped cream, or dairy-free cream cheese. Also, you may want to use a plant-based crust or ready-to-use dough from the store. Simply prepare it according to the directions, then top with dessert pizza ingredients!

Tip or fact: Feel free to get creative with the toppings! Use your favorite combination of sauces (like strawberry preserves, coconut cream, or plant-based Nutella) along with flavorful fruits and spices.

Shopping list

Produce
☐ 1 banana
☐ 1 package strawberries
☐ 2 mandarin oranges
☐ 2 kiwis

☐ active yeast
☐ unbleached white flour
☐ unbleached white flour
☐ walnut or coconut oil
☐ unsweetened coconut

Seasonings and Spices
☐ salt
☐ cinnamon

Thin NY Pizza Crust

by Laura Salyer

Easy | **Kid Friendly** | **4 Servings**

This simple pizza crust is for you, if you need a really quick recipe that doesn't mess with yeast and extra ingredients.

Ingredients

1¾ c whole grain flour
⅓ + ¼ c water
½ tsp Himalayan salt

Directions

1. Preheat the oven to 400°F.
2. Gather all ingredients.
3. Mix together the flour and sea salt.
4. Add water and mix until soft dough forms.
5. Take a round cutting board and line it with parchment paper. Flour the parchment paper.
6. Using a spoon or spatula, place ¼ of the batter in the middle of the floured surface.
7. Sprinkle some flour on the dough ball and flour your hands as well. Start shaping the batter with your hands into a 6.3 inch shell. If your hands start to stick, flour them again or sprinkle more flour onto the batter. If you like, you can use floured rolling pin to get smoother result.
8. Add your desired toppings and bake at for 12-15 minutes.

Nutrition Per Serving 190 calories, 0g total fat, 0g sat fat, 190mg sodium, 40g carbohydrates, 2g fiber, 0g sugar, 4g protein

Storage: Best eaten fresh.

Ingredient Swap: Use any whole grain flours you like – wheat, spelt, buckwheat, oat, or teff.

Tip or fact: If you use gluten-free flour (buckwheat, oat or teff), add 2 teaspoons of psyllium powder and an extra tablespoon of water to the recipe. It's always better to use scale when measuring flours as you could pack it tight or loose making a huge difference to the outcome! For this recipe you want 7.4 oz of flour.

Shopping list

Packaged
☐ whole grain flour

Seasonings and Spices
☐ Himalayan salt

Tofu & Mixed Vegetable Lettuce Wraps by Jyl Steinback

| Medium | Gluten Free | 4 Servings |

Have fun with this colorful wrap with a blend of veggie goodness.

Ingredients

2 c black beans
1 c carrots, grated
1 c celery, chopped
2 cloves garlic, chopped
4 large iceberg lettuce leaves
2 c mushrooms, diced
1 c onion, chopped
½ c firm tofu
¼ c mixed nuts, dry roasted with no salt added
½ tsp basil
½ tsp ginger
½ lemon, juiced

Directions

1. Gather all ingredients.
2. Slice and dice the vegetables and mince the garlic.
3. Heat a wok or frying pan over medium heat and spray with nonstick cooking spray.
4. Sauté the onions, celery, carrots and garlic until the onions are translucent, about 5 minutes.
5. Add the basil, and juice from the lemon.
6. Add the mushrooms and cook for 1-2 minutes.
7. Add the beans and cook until everything is warm. Add a little white wine or water if the pan gets too dry.
8. Spoon 1/4 of the bean mixture into each of the lettuce leaves and serve.

Nutrition Per Serving 220 calories, 6g total fat, 1g sat fat, 50mg sodium, 32g carbohydrates, 11g fiber, 5g sugar, 14g protein

Tip or fact: For each 100 calorie serving, tofu contains 11 grams of protein.

Wraps, Pizzas & Sandwiches

Shopping list

Produce
☐ 1 large carrot
☐ 1 bunch celery
☐ 2 cloves garlic
☐ 4 large iceberg lettuce leaves
☐ mushrooms
☐ 1 onion
☐ basil
☐ ginger
☐ 1 lemon

Packaged
☐ black beans
☐ tofu
☐ mixed nuts, dry roasted

Vegetarian Pizza

by Jyl Steinback

Easy | **Kid Friendly** | **4 Servings**

Never miss a pizza night again because you think it'd contribute to weight gain – this veggie pizza is a healthy balanced meal, especially when eaten with a salad.

Ingredients

Homemade crus:

1 Thin NY Pizza Crust (recipe p. 228)
10 Tbsp tomato paste
15 oz. can unsalted beans, rinse and drain
2 tsp onion powder
1 tsp chili powder
½ tsp ground cumin or curry powder
½ c fat-free unsalted salsa
¼ tsp Himalayan salt
1 ⅓ c grated cashew cheese or tofu in oil-free marinade
½ c frozen corn kernels, thawed and drained
fresh greens, optional

Directions

1. Preheat the oven to 400°F.
2. Gather all ingredients.
3. Prepare thin NY pizza crust (recipe p. 228).
4. Spread 2½ tablespoons of tomato paste onto each pizza crust.
5. In a medium mixing bowl, combine beans, onion powder, chili powder, cumin, salt and salsa. Divide into 4 parts and top your pizzas.
6. Top with corn. 1/8 cup per pizza.
7. Sprinkle cheese or crumbled/chopped tofu on crust – 1/3 cup per pizza – and bake for 13-15 minutes.
8. When the pizzas are out of oven, garnish with fresh chopped herbs/greens (chives, onion greens, cilantro parsley) or arugula.

Nutrition Per Serving 280 calories, 3.5g total fat, 3g sat fat, 450mg sodium, 51g carbohydrates, 11g fiber, 6g sugar, 14g protein

Storage: Best eaten fresh.

Ingredient Swap: If you're not into spicy foods or need to feed kids, leave the chili powder out. Should your salsa contain salt, don't use any additional salt in the recipe.

Tip or fact: For extra cheesy flavor, sprinkle some vegan Parmesan (cashews or other nuts combined with nutritional yeast and salt) on top of the pizza. To save time, bake 2 pizzas at a time. While the first 2 are in oven, roll out and top the other two.

Shopping list

Produce
☐ fresh greens, optional

Packaged
☐ tomato paste
☐ 15 oz. can unsalted beans
☐ fat-free unsalted salsa

Refrigerated or Frozen
☐ grated cashew cheese or tofu in oil-free marinade
☐ frozen corn kernels

Seasonings and Spices
☐ onion powder
☐ chili powder
☐ ground cumin or curry powder
☐ Himalayan salt

Parsley

Thyme

Anise

Bay Leaf

Arugula

Mint

Sage

Vanilla

Outstanding
One Pot &
One-Dish
Meals

Terragon

Big Bold Chili
by Caryn Dugan

Medium | **8-10 Servings**

Packed full of BIG BOLD flavor, this recipe will be an instant family favorite! Top with chopped onion and a dollop of cashew sour cream (p. 5) to make it extra special!

Ingredients

- 1 large sweet onion, diced
- 3 cloves garlic, minced
- ½ small jalapeño, deseeded and diced
- 2 large carrots, large diced
- 2 cups mushrooms, chopped
- 1 green bell pepper, large dice
- ⅛-¼ tsp cayenne, optional
- ½ tsp dried oregano
- 1 tsp smoke paprika
- 1 tsp ground cumin
- 2 Tbsp chili powder
- 1 c kidney beans, cooked
- 1 c black beans, cooked
- 1 zucchini or large yellow squash, chopped
- 1 roasted red pepper, de-seeded, chopped
- 4 c whole Roman tomatoes, peeled
- 1 date, pitted
- 5 Tbsp tomato puree
- ¾ c bulgur wheat
- 3 c vegetable broth (recipe p. 124)
- ½ lemon, juiced

Directions

1. Gather all ingredients.
2. In a large pot boil water. Prepare an ice bath by filling a large bowl with ¼ cold water and ¼ ice.
3. Wash the tomatoes and make an x on the bottom with a sharp knife and then carefully place them in the pot for no more than 1 minute.
4. Scoop them out with a slotted spoon and plunge into the ice bath and then pull them out. You can now easily peel back the skins with a knife or your fingers.
5. Place peeled tomatoes in a bowl and place to the side.
6. Add the onion to a large pot or Dutch oven (SLOW COOKER) over high heat. Stir until you begin to see caramelization (browning) on the onions, and then add the garlic.
7. Stir for another minute and add in the jalapeño, carrots, mushrooms, green bell pepper and spices. Cook for about 4-5 minutes until the mushrooms begin to release their juices.
8. Add in the beans, squash, roasted red pepper, tomatoes, date paste, and tomato paste. Stir well.
9. Add in the bulgur wheat and broth. Stir and cover for about 20 minutes.
10. Right before serving stir in juice of ½ lemon to brighten. Garnish with cashew sour cream, cilantro, nacho chips or corn bread.

Nutrition Per Serving 340 calories, 2.5g total fat, 0g sat fat, 280mg sodium, 70g carbohydrates, 20g fiber, 15g sugar, 17g protein

Shopping list

Produce
- ☐ 1 large sweet onion
- ☐ 3 cloves garlic
- ☐ 1 small jalapeño
- ☐ 2 large carrots
- ☐ 1 package mushrooms
- ☐ 1 green bell pepper
- ☐ 1 zucchini or large yellow squash
- ☐ 1 roasted red pepper
- ☐ 1 lemon

Packaged
- ☐ 28 oz. whole Roman tomatoes
- ☐ 1 pitted date
- ☐ bulgur wheat
- ☐ vegetable broth
- ☐ kidney beans
- ☐ black beans
- ☐ tomato puree

Seasonings and Spices
- ☐ cayenne
- ☐ dried oregano
- ☐ smoke paprika
- ☐ ground cumin
- ☐ chili powder

Tip or fact: Serve in a bowl topped with cilantro and cashew sour cream, over roasted sweet potato, blend and serve as a dip

Cheesy Veggie Divan
by Caryn Dugan

Easy | **Gluten Free** | **6-8 Servings**

This "cheezy" sauce is made with super, good-for-you cannellini beans and red roasted peppers. Great for a crowd or a weeknight meal.

Ingredients

1 head broccoli, cut into bite-sized pieces

½ head cauliflower, cut into bite-sized pieces

4 carrots, sliced into bite-sized pieces

1 large onion, chopped

15 oz. can white cannellini beans, drained and rinsed

½ c roasted red peppers home-made

⅓ c nutritional yeast

4 Tbsp fresh lemon juice

2 Tbsp tahini

1 tsp yellow mustard

½ tsp garlic powder

½ tsp onion powder

1½ c vegetable broth (recipe p. 124)

Directions

1. Preheat oven to 350°F.
2. Gather all ingredients.
3. Steam the veggies in a large frying pan over boiling water or in a steamer basket until crisp tender.
4. Place into your prepared baking pan.
5. Prepare the cheese sauce by placing the beans, roasted red peppers, nutritional yeast, lemon juice, tahini, mustard, and spices in a blender.
6. Blend until very smooth adding a little vegetable broth to thin and make it easier to remove.
7. Scrap the cheese sauce from the blender into a large pan over medium heat. Reuse your steaming pan if that works. Add the veggie broth.
8. Mix carefully with a whisk until the sauce is smooth and liquid is incorporated together with the cheese sauce. Let heat through.
9. Pour the sauce over the veggies and move them around a little to make sure the sauce covers them. Cover with foil and bake for 30 minutes or until heated through.
10. Serve with your choice of grain.

*One Pot &
One-Dish
Meals*

Nutrition Per Serving 180 calories, 4g total fat, 0.5g sat fat, 240mg sodium, 29g carbohydrates, 9g fiber, 8g sugar, 11g protein

Tip or fact: Roasted and fresh red peppers or even cooked carrots can be used for the "cheese" sauce instead for the "cheese" sauce in this recipe.

Shopping list

Produce
- ☐ 1 head broccoli
- ☐ 1 head cauliflower
- ☐ 4 carrots
- ☐ 1 large onion
- ☐ 1 lemon
- ☐ 1 red pepper

Packaged
- ☐ 15 oz. can white cannellini beans
- ☐ nutritional yeast
- ☐ tahini
- ☐ yellow mustard

Seasonings and Spices
- ☐ garlic powder
- ☐ onion powder

Comfy Broccoli Chickpea Casserole
by Caryn Dugan

Easy | **6 Servings**

In a delicious cheesy sauce, this hearty broccoli and chickpea casserole is the perfect one-dish meal covering all your family's nutritional needs.

Ingredients

Casserole:
- 1½ c brown rice, soaked in hot water for 1 hour
- 1 head broccoli, cut to bite sized pieces
- 14 oz. can cooked chickpeas, drained and rinsed
- 1 Tbsp dried oregano
- fresh ground pepper

Brown Sauce:
- 2½ c unsweetened almond milk
- ½ c old fashioned oats
- ⅓ c nutritional yeast
- ⅓ c raw, unsalted cashews
- 1 Tbsp arrowroot powder
- ½ Tbsp smoked paprika
- 1 tsp mustard powder
- 1 tsp onion powder
- ½ tsp garlic powder
- ½ tsp turmeric powder
- pinch salt

Shopping list

Produce
- ☐ 1 head broccoli

Packaged
- ☐ brown rice
- ☐ 14 oz. can cooked chickpeas
- ☐ old fashioned oats
- ☐ nutritional yeast
- ☐ raw, unsalted cashews

Refrigerated or Frozen
- ☐ unsweetened almond milk

Seasonings and Spices
- ☐ dried oregano
- ☐ ground pepper
- ☐ arrowroot powder
- ☐ smoked paprika
- ☐ mustard powder
- ☐ onion powder
- ☐ garlic powder
- ☐ turmeric powder
- ☐ salt

Directions

1. Soak the rice in hot water for 1 hour.
2. Preheat oven to 400°F.
3. Gather all ingredients.
4. Steam the broccoli for 4-5 minutes, until barely fork tender, transfer to a mixing bowl.
5. To a high-speed blender add the sauce ingredients and blend until creamy, about 3 minutes. If you don't have a high-speed blender, soak the cashews for 2-3 hours, drain and use.
6. Transfer to a sauce pan and over medium-high heat, stir continually for 7-8 minutes, or until it thickens up a bit. You are looking for the sauce to become creamy.
7. Add the sauce to the broccoli bowl along with the chickpeas, drained rice, oregano and a few twists of freshly ground pepper.
8. Add the mixture to an 8 x 8 baking dish, cover and cook for 30 minutes. Uncover and cook for a remaining 8-10 minutes, or until crusty on top.

Nutrition Per Serving 360 calories, 8g total fat, 1g sat fat, 230mg sodium, 59g carbohydrates, 8g fiber, 3g sugar, 13g protein

Tip or fact: Arrowroot powder is a white, flavorless powder form that is used to thicken sauces, soups and other foods.

Corn Casserole
by Jyl Steinback

Easy | **Gluten Free** | **8 Servings**

A sweet corn crowd pleasing side for any occasion.

Ingredients
8 c water
3 c whole grain cornmeal
16 oz. can tomato sauce, reduced sodium
6 c frozen whole kernel corn, thawed and drained
1 c onion, chopped
¾ c canned chopped green chiles
8 oz. canned chopped black olives, drained

Directions
1. Preheat oven to 350°F.
2. Gather all ingredients.
3. Pour water into Dutch oven and bring to a boil over high heat.
4. Add cornmeal and cook, stirring occasionally, until mixture becomes consistency of mush. Remove from the heat.
5. Heat non-stick skillet on medium. pour tomato sauce into skillet.
6. Add corn, onion, chiles and olives. Cook, stirring frequently, until onion is softened and transparent.
7. In a 9 x 13 inch baking dish, layer half the cornmeal mixture on bottom of dish.
8. Top with vegetable mixture and then remaining cornmeal mix.
9. Bake for 45-60 minutes

Nutrition Per Serving 350 calories, 6g total fat, 0g sat fat, 210mg sodium, 72g carbohydrates, 12g fiber, 4g sugar, 8g protein

One Pot &
One-Dish
Meals

Storage: Place the glass covered baking dish in the freezer. If frozen, bake for 2 hours.

Tip or fact: Tomatoes are a natural source of lycopene, and the more a tomato is cooked, the more bioavailable lycopene becomes to the body. Lycopene is being studied for its potential to help reduce the risk of several cancers.

Shopping list

Produce
☐ 1 onion

Packaged
☐ whole grain cornmeal
☐ 16 oz. can tomato sauce, reduced sodium
☐ 1 can chopped green chiles
☐ 8 oz. can chopped black olives, drained

Refrigerated or Frozen
☐ 1 package frozen whole kernel corn

Instant Pot Chickpea Curry by Sharon Palmer

Easy | **Gluten Free** | **8 Servings**

This 100% plant-based curry pays tribute to the vibrantly flavored, Indian classic comfort food, Chana Masala.

Ingredients

1 onion, diced
1 small green chili, finely diced
1 Tbsp fresh ginger, grated
4 cloves garlic, minced
1 Tbsp ground cumin
2 tsp ground coriander
½ tsp ground mustard
1 tsp ground turmeric
½ tsp black pepper
14 oz. can diced tomatoes, with liquid
14 oz. can reduced sodium tomato sauce
½ c fresh cilantro, finely chopped
30 oz. canned chickpeas, rinsed, drained
2 tsp garam masala
1 Tbsp lemon juice
4 c cooked gluten-free whole grains

Shopping list

Produce
☐ 1 onion, diced
☐ 1 small green chili
☐ fresh ginger
☐ 4 cloves garlic
☐ 1 bunch fresh cilantro
☐ 1 lemon

Packaged
☐ 14 oz. can diced tomatoes
☐ 14 oz. can reduced sodium tomato sauce
☐ 30 oz. canned chickpeas, rinsed, drained
☐ garam masala
☐ gluten-free whole grains (brown rice, quinoa, etc.)

Seasonings and Spices
☐ ground cumin
☐ ground coriander
☐ ground mustard
☐ ground turmeric
☐ black pepper

Directions

1. Gather all ingredients.
2. Fill the container of an Instant Pot with all of the ingredients (except the cooked whole grains) and stir well with mixing spoon.
3. Close the lid, and push the "bean/chili" setting (which is 30 minutes on high pressure) according to manufacturer instructions.
4. When Instant Pot cooking cycle is complete, release the pressure according to the manufacturer instructions.
5. Serve chickpea curry over cooked whole grains (serve these warm).

Nutrition Per Serving 220 calories, 3g total fat, 0g sat fat, 160mg sodium, 39g carbohydrates, 6g fiber, 6g sugar, 7g protein

Tip or fact: You can pull double duty and cook the whole grains in the Instant Pot by placing the uncooked grains in a glass bowl with the recommended amount of water on the tray that comes with your Instant Pot. The tray allows the grains to cook—elevated above the curry—in a separate container. When the cooking cycle is done, you will find the grains cooked in one container, and the curry cooked on the bottom. You may have to drain off extra liquid in the grains before serving them.

One Pot Thai Coconut Curry Tofu by Diane Smith

Easy | **Gluten Free** | **6 Servings**

Who doesn't love curry and tofu made in one pot? This recipe is light and oh so divine. Don't be surprised if you end of making it a few times a month.

Ingredients

12-14 oz. container firm organic tofu, drained and cut into 1" squares

1 c uncooked brown rice or quinoa

1 large onion, coarsely chopped

¼ c water

5 c green beans, cut into thirds

2 medium red peppers, seeded and coarsely chopped

15 oz. can low-sodium kidney beans, drained and rinsed

13.5 oz. can light coconut milk

1 tsp ginger, grated

2 tsp curry powder

pinch sea salt

Directions

1. Gather all ingredients.
2. Over medium-low heat, cook the tofu in a dry skillet and press lightly with a spatula to allow water to evaporate. The tofu will turn a golden yellow color. Flip to cook the other side.
3. Remove from the pan and reserve for later.
4. Heat ¼ cup water in the pan and sauté the onion until translucent.
5. Add the green beans and red pepper and another ¼ cup of water and continue to cook until soft-crisp.
6. Add the kidney beans, grated ginger, curry powder (or 1 tablespoon red curry paste) and salt to the vegetables.
7. Add the tofu back in along with the coconut milk and stir. Thin with a little water or veggie stock, if needed.
8. Continue to cook until the sauce thickens.
9. Serve over prepared brown rice or quinoa.

Nutrition Per Serving 230 calories, 7g total fat, 3g sat fat, 170mg sodium, 33g carbohydrates, 8g fiber, 9g sugar, 11g protein

One Pot & One-Dish Meals

Tip or fact: Because we're striving to eat a lot of vegetables, you can always add more to this recipe and/or substitute a different vegetable for the beans which are not traditional for a Thai dish. Cauliflower would be delicious.

Shopping list

Produce
- ☐ 1 large onion
- ☐ green beans
- ☐ 2 medium red peppers
- ☐ ginger

Packaged
- ☐ 12-14 oz. container firm organic tofu
- ☐ brown rice or quinoa
- ☐ 15 oz. can low-sodium kidney beans
- ☐ 13.5 oz. can light coconut milk

Seasonings and Spices
- ☐ curry powder
- ☐ sea salt

Plant-Based Paella

by Caryn Dugan

Easy | 3 Servings

The ultimate one-pot meal! This plant-based riff on authentic Spanish Paella has deep layers of flavor that will have you scooping up the very last drop of goodness.

Ingredients

½ yellow onion, chopped
½ red bell pepper, chopped
1 poblano pepper, chopped
1 c homemade vegetable broth (recipe p. 124)
3 garlic cloves, minced
1 c fresh mushrooms, de-stemmed and roughly chopped
3 piquillo peppers, chopped
½ c cooked artichoke hearts, chopped
1/4 c green olives with pimentos, cut in half
1 c San Marzano tomatoes, roughly chopped
San Marzano tomato juice
1½ tsp smoked paprika
¼ tsp freshly ground black pepper
pinch saffron
16 oz. riced frozen cauliflower
½ c green peas
Italian parsley, to garnish

Directions

1. Preheat oven to 400°F.
2. Gather all ingredients.
3. To an oven safe, pre-heated skillet, add the onion, bell pepper and poblano pepper. Bring the heat down to medium-high and stir often.
4. When the onion becomes translucent, add in the garlic and continue to stir.
5. If the vegetables begin to stick, add in a tablespoon or so of the broth to deglaze.
6. After about 60 seconds, add in the mushrooms, piquillos, artichokes, green olives, tomatoes and juice, paprika, ground black pepper, and saffron. Stir well.
7. Add in rice and mix well again.
8. Add in 1/4 cup of the broth, stir and transfer to the oven.
9. Bake for 20 minutes, checking every 5 minutes or so to add more broth if it evaporates (but only it is looking really dry).
10. On the last 5 minutes, add the peas, lightly stir and place back in oven.
11. Garnish with parsley if using and serve from hot skillet.

Nutrition Per Serving 150 calories, 1.5g total fat, 0g sat fat, 130mg sodium, 28g carbohydrates, 7g fiber, 12g sugar, 9g protein

Ingredient Swaps: I used Chinese shiitake mushrooms (which look like crimini), but any mushroom with work. If you cannot find San Marzano, fire-roasted tomatoes are also good.

Tip or fact: San Marzano tomatoes are a type of plum tomato that are believed to be the best canned tomatoes in the world. Try them out and see if you agree!

Shopping list

Produce
- 1 yellow onion
- 1 red bell pepper
- 1 poblano pepper
- 3 garlic cloves
- fresh mushrooms
- 3 piquillo peppers
- Italian parsley

Packaged
- can cooked artichoke hearts
- green olives with pimentos
- San Marzano tomatoes

Refrigerated or Frozen
- riced frozen cauliflower
- green peas

Seasonings and Spices
- 1½ tsp smoked paprika
- ¼ tsp freshly ground black pepper
- pinch saffron

Potato & Vegetable Slow Cooker Casserole by Jyl Steinback

Easy | **8 Servings**

Potatoes and veggies slow cooked in a combination of savory spices with a touch of cinnamon sweet and some heat produce this flavor packed dish.

Ingredients

6 baking potatoes, sliced
1 large onion, sliced
2 large carrots, peeled and sliced
1 medium zucchini, sliced
1 yellow squash, sliced
11 oz. can Mexicorn, drained
1 c frozen peas, thawed and drained
1 c sliced fresh mushrooms
2½ c canned tomato sauce, low sodium
¼ c low sodium soy sauce
1 tsp dried thyme
1 tsp dry mustard
1 tsp dried basil
2 tsp chili powder
½ tsp ground cinnamon
⅛ tsp dried rosemary
2 Tbsp dried parsley

Directions

1. Gather all ingredients.
2. Layer potatoes, onion, carrots, zucchini, squash, Mexicorn, peas, and mushrooms in slow cooker.
3. Combine remaining ingredients and mix well.
4. Pour tomato mixture over vegetables.
5. Cover and cook on low heat for 10-12 hours or high heat for 5-6 hours in the oven.
6. Garnish with parsley if using and serve from hot skillet.

Nutrition Per Serving 240 calories, 1g total fat, 0g sat fat, 460mg sodium, 52g carbohydrates, 7g fiber, 8g sugar, 8g protein

Tip or fact: To reduce sodium even further (100mg), swap out canned Mexicorn for 1 can unsalted corn and ½ red and green bell pepper chopped

One Pot & One-Dish Meals

Shopping list

Produce
□ 6 baking potatoes
□ 1 large onion
□ 2 large carrots
□ 1 medium zucchini
□ 1 yellow squash
□ mushrooms

Packaged
□ 11 oz. can Mexicorn, drained
□ canned tomato sauce, low sodium
□ low sodium soy sauce

Refrigerated or Frozen
□ frozen peas

Seasonings and Spices
□ dried thyme
□ dry mustard
□ dried basil
□ chili powder
□ ground cinnamon
□ dried rosemary
□ dried parsley

Rustic Russet Casserole
by Jyl Steinback

Medium | **8 Servings**

Savor the Simplicity of this classic potato dish.

Ingredients

2 lbs russet potatoes
¼ c low-sodium vegetable broth
1 tsp potato starch
1 garlic clove
½ c gluten free breadcrumbs
2 medium green bell peppers
2 tsp tahini sauce
½ c coconut milk

Directions

1. Preheat oven to 350°F.
2. Gather all ingredients.
3. Peel potatoes and bake them on their own on a pan for 15 minutes. Remove potatoes and cut into slices.
4. Dice bell peppers and add them along with potatoes into even layer in glass pan.
5. Bake for 10 minutes.
6. Add coconut milk and tahini to a saucepan, and bring to a slight boil.
7. Whisk in potato starch along with veggie broth.
8. Add minced garlic and prepare to combine with vegetables.
9. Make a layer of potatoes and vegetables, and follow with a layer of sauce.
10. Add one more veggie layer and then one more of sauce. Then add breadcrumbs before baking.
11. Bake for 15-20 minutes or until the breadcrumbs brown and become crispy.
12. Serve and enjoy!

Nutrition Per Serving 170 calories, 4.5g total fat, 3.5g sat fat, 65mg sodium, 29g carbohydrates, 3g fiber, 2g sugar, 4g protein

Storage: Store in an airtight glass container in the refrigerator for 1-3 days.

Tip or fact: Potato storage facilities are kept at temperatures above 39°F as potato starch turns into sugar and alters the taste below this temperature!

Shopping list

Produce
- ☐ 2 lbs russet potatoes
- ☐ 1 garlic clove
- ☐ 2 medium green bell peppers

Packaged
- ☐ low-sodium vegetable broth
- ☐ potato starch
- ☐ gluten free breadcrumbs
- ☐ tahini sauce
- ☐ coconut milk

Spicy Black Bean and Sweet Potato Chili by Jyl Steinback

Medium | **Gluten Free** | **8 Servings**

Spice-up your traditional bowl of chili with this flavorful twist of spicy sweetness.

Ingredients

- 3-4 c canned low sodium black beans
- 3 cloves garlic, chopped
- 1 c onion, chopped
- 2-3 scallions, sliced
- 1-2 hot chili pepper, sliced
- 1 medium green pepper
- 3-4 c sweet potato, cooked and cubed
- 2 cans low sodium stewed tomatoes
- 1 can crushed tomatoes
- 1 c fresh tomatoes, sliced
- 2 tsp ground cumin
- 1 tsp dried oregano
- ¼ c fresh parsley or cilantro, minced

Directions

1. Gather all ingredients.
2. Bake or microwave the sweet potatoes until just firm.
3. When cool enough to handle, peel and cut into 3/4-inch dice. Set aside until needed.
4. Add ¼ cup of water in a large soup pot. Add the onion and garlic and sauté over medium heat until the onion is golden.
5. Add the beans, hot chili pepper, green pepper, the tomatoes, and seasoning.
6. Bring to a simmer and covered for 15 minutes.
7. Add the diced sweet potatoes and continue to simmer for 10 to 15 minutes or until the vegetables are tender.
8. Stir in the parsley or cilantro and scallions. If time allows, let stand off the heat for an hour or two, then heat through as needed.
9. Top each serving with extra parsley or cilantro, if desired.

Nutrition Per Serving 260 calories, 1g total fat, 0g sat fat, 420mg sodium, 53g carbohydrates, 15g fiber, 14g sugar, 12g protein

One Pot & One-Dish Meals

Tip or fact: Sweet potatoes are a superfood and they taste great! They can be substituted in virtually any recipe that calls for apples, squash or white potatoes.

Shopping list

Produce
- ☐ 3 cloves garlic
- ☐ 1 onion
- ☐ 2-3 scallions
- ☐ 1-2 hot chili pepper
- ☐ 1 medium green pepper
- ☐ 3-4 sweet potatoes
- ☐ 1 tomato
- ☐ fresh parsley or cilantro

Packaged
- ☐ 2 cans low sodium stewed tomatoes
- ☐ 1 can crushed tomatoes

Seasonings and Spices
- ☐ ground cumin
- ☐ dried oregano

Thai Cauli

by Carolina Maturana

Easy | **Gluten Free** | **4-5 Servings**

This one pot dish is simple and unique. Its ingredients combined are delicious and contain healthy facts and nutrients.

Ingredients

1 medium cauliflower head
1 medium zucchini
1 c mushrooms, sliced
1 medium yellow onion
1 Tbsp ginger
1-2 in fresh lemongrass stalk
1 garlic clove, minced
1 Tbsp coconut amino
1 Tbsp Thai chili paste
¼ c fresh Thai basil, cut into strips
¼ c fresh cilantro
1 tsp date syrup or coconut nectar
22 oz. can light coconut milk for cooking
1 c water
1 Tbsp lime juice
¼ tsp pink Himalayan salt

Shopping list

Produce

□ 1 medium cauliflower head
□ 1 medium zucchini
□ mushrooms
□ 1 medium yellow onion
□ fresh lemongrass
□ 1 garlic clove
□ 1 bunch Thai basil
□ 1 bunch fresh cilantro
□ 1 lime
□ 1-2 inches ginger

Packaged

□ coconut amino
□ Thai chili paste
□ date syrup or coconut nectar
□ 22 oz. can light coconut milk for cooking

Directions

1. Gather all ingredients.
2. Wash cauliflower, zucchini, mushrooms, cilantro and basil. Use a paper towel to gently dry basil and cilantro.
3. Cut zucchini in half and each piece in the middle length wise. Get rid of ends, cut into 1/3 inch half moons and put them in a bowl and set aside.
4. Slice mushrooms, put them in a cup and set aside.
5. Cut cauliflower into medium to small florets and set aside.
6. Peel ginger and mince.
7. Cut lemongrass into one inch approximately and mince.
8. Mince garlic.
9. Thinly chop cilantro leaves.
10. Remove basil leaves from stem and stack them. Roll them lengthwise and cut into thin strips. Set aside.
11. In a medium bowl combine date syrup, Thai chili paste, lime juice, coconut aminos, salt and mix well. Set aside.
12. Heat a large sauce pan medium to high. Make sure the pan is hot enough by testing with a little water. The water should form mercury like balls on the surface. Dry sauté onions, continuously stirring to prevent burning until they are translucent and have a little of a golden color.
13. Add mushrooms and zucchinis, combine and cook for 1 minute.
14. Add ginger, garlic and lemongrass and stir for 30 seconds to one minute.
15. Add date syrup, Thai chili paste, lime juice, coconut amino and salt mixture and stir.
16. Add cauliflower, water and can of coconut milk. Combine well and bring it to a boil.
17. Reduce heat to simmer and cover. Cook for 7-9 minutes until cauliflower is tender. For a thicker consistency remove lid after 5 minutes and cook for 5-7 minutes or until desired consistency.
18. Remove from heat and add basil, cilantro combine well and serve.
19. Save some cilantro to garnish. Can be served with brown rice, quinoa or enjoyed in a bowl.

Nutrition Per Serving 140 calories, 7g total fat, 5g sat fat, 380mg sodium, 19g carbohydrates, 3g fiber, 9g sugar, 4g protein

Tofu Stroganoff

by Carolina Maturana

Easy | **Gluten Free** | **4 Servings**

This is a satisfying one pot dish that everyone loves.

Ingredients

1 block organic firm tofu
½ medium onion, finely chopped
2 c mushrooms, sliced
2 garlic cloves, minced
¼ c low sodium tamari
2 tsp paprika
4 c water
8 oz. gluten free brown rice spiral pasta
1 c cashew sour cream (recipe p. 5)
1 Tbsp arrowroot slurry
¼ c fresh parsley, garnish
pepper, to taste

Directions

1. Gather all ingredients.
2. Make cashew sour cream. Recipe p. 5 (does not require overnight soak).
3. Remove excess water from tofu. Crumble into ground tofu and use paper or kitchen towel to remove remaining water. Set aside.
4. Heat a large sauce pan medium to high heat. Make sure the pan is hot enough by testing with a little water. The water should form mercury like ball on the surface. Dry sauté onions, continuously stirring to prevent burning until they are translucent and have a little of a golden color.
5. Add mushrooms and garlic cook for 2 minutes.
6. Add crumbled tofu and tamari. Cook for 5 minutes stirring the ingredients and add paprika.
7. Add 3½ cups of water, pasta, combine well and cover.
8. Lower heat to low and simmer for 15-20 minutes.
9. Add ½ cup of sour cream, arrowroot slurry and stir until it thickens.
10. Add desired amount of parsley and serve. Use remaining parsley to garnish.

One Pot & One-Dish Meals

Nutrition Per Serving 140 calories, 7g total fat, 5g sat fat, 380mg sodium, 19g carbohydrates, 3g fiber, 9g sugar, 4g protein

Storage: Serve and eat right after preparing.

Ingredient Swap: Cornstarch can be used instead of arrowroot. Arrowroot can be found with spices at the bulk department at some health stores. No need to buy a whole package.

Tip or fact: Gluten free pasta in general gets very dry and hardens when saved in the fridge for later.

Shopping list

Produce
☐ 1 medium onion
☐ mushrooms
☐ 2 garlic cloves
☐ fresh parsley

Packaged
☐ block organic firm tofu
☐ low sodium tamari
☐ gluten free brown rice spiral pasta

Seasonings and Spices
☐ pepper
☐ paprika
☐ arrowroot

Veggie Chili Skillet Meal
by Jyl Steinback

Easy | **4 Servings**

Veggie chili over couscous! Sounds good to me!

Ingredients
1 Tbsp low sodium vegetable broth
½ c frozen diced onions
16 oz. frozen broccoli, cauliflower, and carrots
8 oz. can low-sodium tomato sauce
1 tsp chili powder
⅛ tsp red pepper flakes
16 oz. can chili beans, drained
2 c cooked couscous

Directions
1. Gather all ingredients.
2. Add broth to a large nonstick skillet and heat over medium-high heat.
3. Add onions and frozen vegetables. Cook, stirring frequently for 7–8 minutes until vegetables are tender.
4. Add tomato sauce, chili powder, and red pepper flakes. Bring to a boil over high heat, then reduce heat to low and simmer 8–10 minutes.
5. Add beans, and heat 5 minutes.
6. Serve over cooked couscous.

Nutrition Per Serving 270 calories, 2g total fat, 0g sat fat, 440mg sodium, 29g carbohydrates, 4g fiber, 8g sugar, 12g protein

Ingredient Swap: Swap wheat for a gluten free grain – millet, etc.

Tip or fact: Dried herbs and spices lose their flavor and potency after about a year. It's best to buy them in the smallest possible amounts and store them in tightly closed bottles in a cool, dry place out of direct light.

Shopping list

Packaged
☐ low sodium vegetable broth
☐ 8 oz. can low-sodium tomato sauce
☐ 16 oz. can chili beans, drained
☐ couscous

Refrigerated and Frozen
☐ frozen diced onions
☐ 16 oz. frozen broccoli, cauliflower, and carrots

Seasonings and Spices
☐ chili powder
☐ red pepper flakes

Vegetarian's Dream Chili

by Jyl Steinback

Easy | **Gluten Free** | **6 Servings**

If you are dreaming of chili but don't have a lot of time for chopping, this is the recipe for you!

Ingredients

29 oz. canned petite-cut diced tomatoes, no added salt, do not drain

2 oz. canned chopped green chilies

1½ c cooked chickpeas (recipe p. 6).

1 zucchini, cubed

1 yellow squash, cubed

2 carrots, sliced

3 c frozen seasoning vegetables, thawed and drained

1-2 Tbsp chili powder

4 oz. can diced green chiles, do not drain

1 tsp minced garlic

1 Tbsp dried oregano

2 tsp ground cumin

Directions

1. Gather all ingredients.
2. Prepare the cooked chickpeas (recipe p. 6).
3. Combine all ingredients in slow cooker and mix well.
4. Cover and cook on low heat for 6-8 hours or high heat for 3-4 hours.
5. Serve warm in a bowl with a dollop of cashew sour cream (recipe p. 5).

Nutrition Per Serving 150 calories, 2g total fat, 0g sat fat, 290mg sodium, 28g carbohydrates, 8g fiber, 11g sugar, 6g protein

Tip or fact: For a full-meal deal, add ½ cup cooked brown rice, couscous, or lentils to Vegetarian's Dream Chili.

One Pot & One-Dish Meals

Shopping list

Produce
□ 1 zucchini
□ 1 yellow squash
□ 2 carrots
□ 1 tsp minced garlic

Packaged
□ 4 oz. can diced green chiles, do not drain
□ 29 oz. canned petite-cut diced tomatoes, no added salt, do not drain
□ 2 oz. canned chopped green chilies

Refrigerated and Frozen
□ frozen seasoning vegetables, thawed and drained

Seasonings and Spices
□ chili powder
□ dried oregano
□ ground cumin

Parsley

Thyme

Anise

Bay Leaf

Arugula

Mint

Sage

Vanilla

Perfect Pasta & Grains

Terragon

Rosemary

Brown Rice with Black-Eyed Peas
by Jyl Steinback

Easy | **Gluten Free** | **8 Servings**

This is a great dish for a potluck. Simple, wholesome and delicious.

Ingredients

1-4 Tbsp low sodium vegetable broth
1 c onion, chopped
¾ tsp garlic powder
16 oz. can low sodium diced tomatoes, undrained
½ tsp dried basil
¼ tsp dried thyme
3 c cooked brown rice
16 oz. can black-eyed peas, rinsed and drained
pepper, to taste

Directions

1. Gather all ingredients.
2. In a large nonstick skillet add 1 tablespoon vegetable broth and heat over medium-high heat.
3. Add onion. Cook, stirring frequently, until softened and transparent.
4. Sprinkle garlic powder over onion and cook 1 to 2 minutes.
5. Add tomatoes, basil and thyme. Cook over medium heat 5 to 7 minutes until heated through.
6. Add cooked rice and black-eyed peas. Season with pepper. Cover and cook over low heat 12 to 15 minutes.
7. Spoon rice mixture into non-stick microwave-safe casserole dish, cover and refrigerate until ready to serve.
8. Just before heating, add remaining vegetable broth (a tablespoon at a time) until casserole is moistened.
9. Heat in microwave on High 8 to 10 minutes for whole casserole or 1 to 2 minutes for individual servings, until heated throughout.

Nutrition Per Serving 150 calories, 1.5g total fat, 0g sat fat, 190mg sodium, 29g carbohydrates, 4g fiber, 2g sugar, 5g protein

Ingredient Swap: To reduce sodium even further, use dried black-eyed peas. Cooking instructions on p. 6.

Tip or fact: Store Basil in a glass of water at room temperature out of direct sunlight. The fresh leaves are the parts mostly used, but you may use the flower buds or garnish or in a salad.

Shopping list

Produce
☐ 1 onion

Packaged
☐ low sodium vegetable broth
☐ 16 oz. can low sodium diced tomatoes, undrained
☐ brown rice
☐ 16 oz. can black-eyed peas, rinsed and drained

Seasonings and Spices
☐ garlic powder
☐ dried basil
☐ dried thyme
☐ pepper

Curried Lentils and Spinach
by Jyl Steinback

Easy | **Gluten Free** | **4 Servings**

This is a meal in itself! A curry that brings together greens, a grain and beans in this savory slow cooked dish.

Ingredients
10 oz. frozen chopped spinach, thawed and drained
¾ c frozen chopped onions, thawed and drained
1 c dry lentils, boiled
¼ c dry converted rice
1 tsp crushed garlic
1½ tsp curry powder
¼ tsp chili powder
1 tsp ground ginger
¼ tsp ground turmeric
¼ tsp cayenne pepper
2 c low sodium vegetable broth
1 c no salt added petite-cut diced tomatoes, drained

Directions
1. Gather all ingredients.
2. Combine all ingredients except tomatoes in slow cooker and mix well.
3. Cover and cook on low heat for 6-7 hours or high heat for 3-3½ hours.
4. Top with tomatoes and serve.

Nutrition Per Serving 270 calories, 1g total fat, 0g sat fat, 160mg sodium, 52g carbohydrates, 10g fiber, 4g sugar, 17g protein

Ingredient Swap: Brown rice for converted rice.

Tip or fact: Converted rice is steamed before the husks are removed and is more nutritious than white rice.

Perfect Pasta & Grains

Shopping list

Packaged
☐ dry lentils
☐ dry converted rice
☐ low sodium vegetable broth
☐ no salt added petite-cut diced tomatoes

Refrigerated or Frozen
☐ frozen chopped spinach
☐ frozen chopped onions

Seasonings and Spices
☐ crushed garlic
☐ curry powder
☐ chili powder
☐ ground ginger
☐ ground turmeric
☐ cayenne pepper

Edamame and Citrus Packed Quinoa by Jyl Steinback

Easy | **Gluten Free** | **5 Servings**

This fun dish is a mixture plant nutritious heaven. Everything you will love.

Ingredients

4-5 c Chinese cabbage
2 clementine fruit
2 c broccoli, steamed and chopped
1 c frozen edamame, thawed
3-4 Tbsp scallions, chopped
1½ c raw quinoa, rinsed
3 Tbsp low sodium soy sauce
1-2 Tbsp fresh ginger
1 tsp sesame seeds
3 Tbsp lemon juice
pepper, to taste

Directions

1. Gather all ingredients.
2. Combine the quinoa with 3 cups water in a medium saucepan. Bring to a boil.
3. Lower the heat. Cover and simmer gently until the water is absorbed, about 15 minutes.
4. Meanwhile, add a dash of water to a non-stick stir-fry pan. Add the edamame, broccoli and bell pepper and stir-fry over medium-high heat for 2 to 3 minutes.
5. Add the lemon juice, bok choy, and scallions, and continue to stir-fry for 1 to 2 minutes, just until wilted.
6. Stir in the cooked quinoa and sesame seeds. Stir well.
7. Season to taste with teriyaki sauce, ginger, and pepper.
8. Stir in the clementine orange sections and serve at once.

Nutrition Per Serving 260 calories, 5g total fat, 0g sat fat, 400mg sodium, 43g carbohydrates, 7g fiber, 6g sugar, 13g protein

Tip or fact: To clean bok choy cut off the tough ends, fill your sink or a large bowl with cold water, and swish the pieces to dislodge dirt and grit, but don't soak. If the leaves are especially dirty, change the water once or twice. Give the greens a final rinse under cold running water, then drain.

Shopping list

Produce
☐ 1 head Chinese cabbage
☐ 2 clementine fruit
☐ 2 heads broccoli
☐ 1 bunch scallions
☐ fresh ginger
☐ 3 lemons

Packaged
☐ quinoa
☐ low sodium soy sauce
☐ sesame seeds

Refrigerated or Frozen
☐ frozen edamame

Seasonings and Spices
☐ pepper

Great Grains

by Jyl Steinback

Easy | **4 Servings**

Quinoa, barley and brown rice star in this dish. A perfect base for any bowl you want to build.

Ingredients

14.5 oz. can no salt added petite-cut diced tomatoes, drained
and liquid reserved

¼ c dry quinoa

¼ c dry barley

⅓ c dry brown rice

1 c frozen chopped onions,
thawed and drained

1 c frozen chopped green bell
peppers, thawed and drained

½ c carrot, chopped

15 oz. can low sodium red kidney
beans, drained

8 oz. can no salt added tomato
sauce

2 cloves garlic, minced

1½ c frozen whole kernel corn,
thawed and drained

1 tsp dried oregano

1 tsp dried basil

1 tsp garlic powder

⅛ tsp pepper

Directions

1. Gather all ingredients.
2. Drain tomatoes and reserve liquid.
3. Add enough water to tomato liquid to equal 2 1/2 cups.
4. Combine all ingredients with tomatoes and liquid in slow cooker and toss to mix.
5. Cover and cook on low heat for 8-10 hours or high heat for 4-5 hours.

Nutrition Per Serving 350 calories, 2g total fat, 0g sat fat, 210mg sodium, 73g carbohydrates, 15g fiber, 8g sugar, 13g protein

Tip or fact: The kidney bean got its name because of the shape of the bean closely resembles the kidneys.

Perfect Pasta & Grains

Shopping list

Produce
☐ 1 carrot
☐ 2 cloves garlic

Packaged
☐ 14.5 oz. can no salt
added petite-cut
diced tomatoes
☐ dry quinoa
☐ dry barley
☐ dry brown rice
☐ 15 oz. can low
sodium red kidney
beans
☐ 8 oz. can no salt
added tomato
sauce

Refrigerated or Frozen
☐ frozen chopped
onions
☐ frozen chopped
green bell peppers
☐ frozen whole kernel
corn

Seasonings and Spices
☐ dried oregano
☐ dried basil
☐ garlic powder
☐ pepper

Grilled Potatoes

by Jyl Steinback

Easy | **Gluten Free** | **4 Servings**

Quinoa, barley and brown rice star in this dish. A perfect base for any bowl you want to build.

Ingredients

2 large baking potatoes
2 large sweet potatoes
pepper, optional
cashew sour cream (recipe p. 5), optional
chopped chives, optional

Directions

1. Gather all ingredients.
2. Prepare a medium fire.
3. Wrap each potato in heavy-duty foil and pierce several times with fork through foil.
4. Grill 45 to 60 minutes, until potatoes are tender and soft.
5. Potatoes can be baked on the side while grilling other foods.
6. Serve with a little pepper if desired or top with cashew sour cream (recipe p. 5) and chives.

Nutrition Per Serving 200 calories, 0g total fat, 0g sat fat, 120mg sodium, 46g carbohydrates, 4g fiber, 4g sugar, 5g protein

Tip or fact: I (Jyl) eat a potato 3-4 times a week. The calorie density of potatoes is low and you would need to eat about 5 pounds to reach 2,000 calories. It is what you put into the potato. My favorite is sauté onions and wild mushrooms sometimes topped with cauliflower rice. It is the most important food crop in the world (behind wheat, maize, and rice).

Shopping list

Produce
☐ 2 large baking potatoes
☐ 2 large sweet potatoes
☐ 1 bunch chives, optional

Seasonings and Spices
☐ pepper, optional

Kale and Spinach Stuffed Pasta Shells
by Jyl Steinback

Easy | **5 Servings**

One of my all time favorite recipes when I am craving something steamy and savory.

Ingredients

4 cloves garlic
1 c kale
1 c onion
5 jumbo whole wheat pasta shells
4 c spinach
1 c zucchini
8 oz. firm tofu
3 c stewed tomatoes
1 Tbsp nutritional yeast
1 Tbsp oregano
1 Tbsp pepper

Directions

1. Preheat the oven to 350°F.
2. Gather all ingredients.
3. Cook shells in boiling water according to package directions.
4. Meanwhile, drain the tofu and pat dry with paper towels.
5. Crumble into the bowl of a food processor or high-speed blender along with the oregano, garlic and nutritional yeast. Process on high until smooth and "ricotta-like."
6. Stuff shells with 2 tablespoons of filling and place in a non-stick 9x13 inch pan. Repeat until all shells have been stuffed.
7. Pour the stewed tomatoes over shells.
8. Cover with foil and bake 25-30 minutes. Serve!

Nutrition Per Serving 330 calories, 5g total fat, 0.5g sat fat, 310mg sodium, 58g carbohydrates, 3g fiber, 4g sugar, 15g protein

Tip or fact: Carrots are such a fun vegetable. They are perfect in soups and casseroles, and they provide tremendous health benefits when eaten raw with a hummus.

Perfect Pasta & Grains

Shopping list

Produce
☐ 4 cloves garlic
☐ 1 bunch kale
☐ 1 onion
☐ 1 bunch spinach
☐ 1 zucchini

Packaged
☐ oregano
☐ pepper

Lentil Pilaf

by Jyl Steinback

Medium | **Gluten Free** | **6 Servings**

Colorful and flavorful.

Ingredients

¼ c green bell pepper, diced
¼ c red bell pepper, diced
½ c carrots, diced
½ c zucchini, diced
¼ c yellow squash, diced
1 Tbsp onion powder
¾ c dried lentils
1½ c low sodium vegetable broth
1 tsp minced garlic
3 c cooked brown rice

Directions

1. Gather all ingredients.
2. Heat a large nonstick skillet over medium-high heat.
3. Add peppers, carrots, zucchini, and squash to skillet. Sprinkle with onion powder and cook 5 to 7 minutes, stirring constantly, until vegetables soften.
4. Add lentils, vegetable broth, and garlic to skillet. Increase heat to high and bring mixture to a boil.
5. Immediately reduce heat to low, cover and simmer 10 to 15 minutes.
6. Serve immediately over warm rice.

Nutrition Per Serving 220 calories, 1.5g total fat, 0g sat fat, 45mg sodium, 42g carbohydrates, 5g fiber, 2g sugar, 9g protein

Tip or fact: When lentils are served with a grain they then become a complete protein. Lentils are loaded with lots of iron, folate, fiber and protein. They are naturally gluten free.

Shopping list

Produce
☐ 1 green bell pepper
☐ 1 red bell pepper
☐ 1 carrot
☐ 1 zucchini
☐ 1 yellow squash
☐ 1 clove garlic

Packaged
☐ dried lentils
☐ low sodium vegetable broth
☐ brown rice

Seasonings and Spices
☐ onion powder

Mushrooms 'n Barley

by Jyl Steinback

Medium | 6 Servings

An earthy mix of mushrooms onion and barley makes this dish a cold weather favorite.

Ingredients

3 c + 1 Tbsp low sodium vegetable broth
1 c mushrooms, chopped
1 c onion, chopped
1½ c dry pearled barley

Directions

1. Gather all ingredients.
2. In a large nonstick skillet add 1 tablespoon broth and heat over medium-high heat.
3. Add mushrooms and onion to skillet. Cook, stirring frequently, until vegetables are softened.
4. Pour in remaining broth and bring to a boil over high heat.
5. Stir in barley. Reduce heat to low, cover and simmer 40 to 45 minutes, until liquid is absorbed.
6. If not serving immediately, spoon mixture into shallow baking dish, cover and refrigerate.
7. When ready to serve, reheat in microwave oven on High 5 to 7 minutes, until heated through.

Nutrition Per Serving 200 calories, 0.5g total fat, 0g sat fat, 80mg sodium, 44g carbohydrates, 9g fiber, 3g sugar, 6g protein

Tip or fact: An excellent source of cholesterol-lowering fiber, one serving of pearled barley provides 11 percent of the RDA for iron as well as fair amounts of folate and niacin.

Perfect Pasta & Grains

Shopping list

Produce
□ mushrooms
□ 1 onion

Packaged
□ low sodium vegetable broth
□ dry pearled barley

No-Bake Lasagna Pasta

by Jyl Steinback

Medium | **6 Servings**

Love lasagna? Try this veggie-packed version with a noodle twist and the option for spicing it up.

Ingredients

8 oz. whole wheat rotini or fusilli
1 Tbsp low-sodium vegetable broth
1 onion, chopped
3 cloves garlic, sliced
8 oz. sliced white mushrooms
½ tsp salt
¼ tsp freshly ground pepper
14 oz. can diced tomatoes with Italian herbs
8 c baby spinach
½ tsp crushed red pepper, optional

Directions

1. Gather all ingredients.
2. Bring a large pot of water to a boil. Add pasta. Cook until just tender, about 10 minutes or according to package directions.
3. Drain and transfer to a large bowl.
4. Meanwhile, heat low-sodium vegetable broth in a large non-stick skillet over medium heat.
5. Add onion and garlic and cook, stirring, until soft and beginning to brown, about 3 minutes.
6. Add mushrooms, salt and pepper and cook, stirring, until the mushrooms release their liquid, about 4 to 6 minutes.
7. Add tomatoes, spinach and crushed red pepper (optional).
8. Increase heat to medium-high. Cook, stirring once halfway through, until the spinach is wilted, about 4 minutes.
9. Toss the sauce with the pasta and divide among 4 bowls.

Nutrition Per Serving 110 calories, 1g total fat, 0g sat fat, 450mg sodium, 23g carbohydrates, 4g fiber, 6g sugar, 6g protein

Tip or fact: Uncooked dry pasta can be kept for up to a year. Cooked pasta can be frozen and re-eaten within three months.

Shopping list

Produce
□ 1 onion
□ 3 cloves garlic
□ white mushrooms
□ baby spinach

Packaged
□ 8 oz. whole wheat rotini or fusilli
□ low-sodium vegetable broth
□ 14 oz. can diced tomatoes with Italian herbs

Seasonings and Spices
□ salt
□ freshly ground pepper

Pumpkin Spice Pilaf

by Jyl Steinback

| Easy | Gluten Free | 6 Servings |

With just the right touch of cinnamon and nutmeg this savory pumpkin pilaf will not only be fall staple but a family tradition at your Thanksgiving dinner.

Ingredients

1¾ c low sodium vegetable broth
1 c dry long grain brown rice
1 c canned unsalted pumpkin
½ tsp ground cinnamon
⅛ tsp ground nutmeg
2 Tbsp chopped green onion

Directions

1. Gather all ingredients.
2. In a large nonstick saucepan add 1 tablespoon of the broth to saucepan and heat over medium-high heat.
3. Add rice and cook, stirring constantly, until rice is coated.
4. Add remaining broth, pumpkin, cinnamon, and nutmeg. Bring to a boil over high heat.
5. Reduce heat to low, cover, and simmer 25–30 minutes until liquid is absorbed.
6. Stir in green onion and serve.

Nutrition Per Serving 130 calories, 1g total fat, 0g sat fat, 45mg sodium, 28g carbohydrates, 3g fiber, 2g sugar, 3g protein

Tip or fact: Ground cinnamon is composed of around 11% water, 81% carbohydrates, 4% protein, and 1% fat.

Perfect Pasta & Grains

Shopping list

Produce
☐ 1 bunch green onion

Packaged
☐ low sodium vegetable broth
☐ dry long grain brown rice
☐ canned unsalted pumpkin

Seasonings and Spices
☐ ground cinnamon
☐ ground nutmeg

Raisin Couscous and Lentils
by Jyl Steinback

Easy | **Gluten Free** | **2 Servings**

A medley of raisins, mint and tomato are what makes this Mediterranean side dish special.

Ingredients

2 c cooked couscous
1 c cooked lentils
½ c chopped fresh tomato
2 Tbsp raisins
1 tsp dried mint flakes
⅛ tsp black pepper
⅛ tsp cayenne pepper
¼ c cashew sour cream (recipe p. 5), optional

Directions

1. Preheat toaster oven to 400°F.
2. Gather all ingredients.
3. Cook lentils and couscous.
4. Combine couscous, lentils, tomato, raisins, mint, black pepper, and cayenne pepper and mix well.
5. Spoon into 1.5 quart casserole dish.
6. Cover with foil and bake 20-25 minutes, until heated through.
7. Top with cashew sour cream, if using.

Nutrition Per Serving 380 calories, 4g total fat, 0.5g sat fat, 15mg sodium, 68g carbohydrates, 12g fiber, 11g sugar, 17g protein

Tip or fact: Looks can be deceiving! Despite the fact the couscous looks, feels, and tastes like a grain, it's really pasta!

Shopping list

Produce
☐ 1 tomato

Packaged
☐ couscous
☐ lentils
☐ raisins

Seasonings and Spices
☐ mint flakes
☐ black pepper
☐ cayenne pepper

Red Beans and Rice

by Jyl Steinback

Easy | 6 Servings

Comfort food in a bowl.

Ingredients

1 lb. dry red kidney beans

29 oz. canned stewed tomatoes with bell pepper and onion, do not drain

½ c frozen chopped onions, thawed and drained

½ tsp garlic powder

⅛ tsp pepper

1 tsp dried basil

1 tsp dried thyme

⅛ tsp cayenne pepper

1½ c converted brown rice

½ c dry white wine

Directions

1. Gather all ingredients.
2. Place beans in large soup pot. Cover beans with water and bring to a boil.
3. Boil 10 minutes.
4. Reduce heat, cover, and simmer 90 minutes or until beans are tender.
5. Drain.
6. Combine all ingredients except rice and wine in slow cooker and mix well.
7. Cover and cook on high heat for 4 hours.
8. Reduce heat to low and cook 4 ½ hours.
9. Add rice and wine and cook 90 minutes.

Nutrition Per Serving 360 calories, 0g total fat, 0g sat fat, 400mg sodium, 70g carbohydrates, 16g fiber, 6g sugar, 18g protein

Tip or fact: Beans and rice has been a staple pairing for thousands of years. Why? Because in some cultures meat played a much smaller role in the diet and beans were a primary source of protein.

Perfect Pasta & Grains

Shopping list

Packaged

☐ 2 14.5 oz. cans stewed tomatoes with bell pepper and onion
☐ 1 lb. red kidney beans
☐ converted brown rice
☐ dry white wine

Refrigerated and Frozen

☐ 12 oz. pkg. frozen chopped onions

Seasonings and Spices

☐ garlic powder
☐ pepper
☐ dried basil
☐ dried thyme
☐ cayenne pepper

Shiitake Mushrooms and Brown Rice by Jyl Steinback

Easy | **Gluten Free** | **6 Servings**

Shitake mushrooms bring a rich buttery meaty flavor to this dish. Serve this alongside of any Asian themed dinner or potluck.

Ingredients

2 Tbsp low sodium vegetable broth
1 c sliced shiitake mushrooms
1 c asparagus, cut 1-inch pieces
¼ tsp garlic powder
3 c cooked brown rice
¼ c sliced green onion
¼ tsp lemon pepper

Directions

1. Gather all ingredients.
2. In a large nonstick skillet or wok add vegetable broth and heat over medium-high heat.
3. Add mushrooms, asparagus, and garlic powder.
4. Cook, stirring frequently, until vegetables are tender-crisp, about 1 to 2 minutes.
5. Add cooked rice, green onion, and lemon pepper.
6. Stir until ingredients are mixed.
7. Cook over medium heat until thoroughly heated.

Nutrition Per Serving 130 calories, 1g total fat, 0g sat fat, 10mg sodium, 27g carbohydrates, 3g fiber, 1g sugar, 4g protein

Tip or fact: Did you know a single Portabella mushroom can contain more potassium than a banana and they are made up of around 90% water.

Shopping list

Produce
☐ 1 shiitake mushrooms
☐ 1 bunch asparagus
☐ 1 bunch green onions

Packaged
☐ low sodium vegetable broth
☐ cooked brown rice

Seasonings and Spices
☐ garlic powder
☐ lemon pepper

Spicy Lentils on Brown Rice by Jyl Steinback

Easy | Gluten Free | 6 Servings

Green chiles spice up earthy lentils while fresh cilantro brightens the dish.

Ingredients

1½ c dry lentils
1 c chopped onion
2½ tsp minced garlic
½ c chopped fresh cilantro
2 Tbsp chopped green chiles
1½ tsp ground cumin
1 tsp ground coriander
14.5 oz. can petite diced tomatoes with green chiles, undrained
1 c green chile salsa
2 c water
3 c cooked brown rice

Directions

1. Gather all ingredients.
2. Rinse lentils and drain well.
3. Combine all ingredients except brown rice in large pot or Dutch oven.
4. Bring to a boil over high heat.
5. Reduce heat to medium-low, cover and cook 30-35 minutes, stirring frequently, until lentils are tender.
6. Serve over cooked brown rice.

Nutrition Per Serving 320 calories, 2g total fat, 0g sat fat, 540mg sodium, 61g carbohydrates, 8g fiber, 5g sugar, 16g protein

Tip or fact: Cumin is a type of flowering plant that belongs to the carrot family.

Perfect Pasta & Grains

Shopping list

Produce
☐ 1 onion
☐ 2 cloves garlic
☐ 1 bunch fresh cilantro
☐ 2 chopped green chiles

Packaged
☐ dry lentils
☐ 14.5 oz. can petite diced tomatoes with green chiles
☐ green chile salsa
☐ brown rice

Seasonings and Spices
☐ cumin
☐ ground coriander

Tomato Basil Steel Cut Oats
by Sharon Palmer

Easy | **1 Servings**

I'm in love with savory porridges. And this one is a genuine treat for the senses.

Ingredients

1 c steel cut oats, uncooked

3 c water

4 small heirloom tomatoes, sliced thinly

1 c diced baked tofu

½ c coarsely chopped walnuts

12 olives, drained green or black

½ c fresh basil, sliced

freshly ground black pepper, to taste

soymilk, plain, unsweetened, to taste

Directions

1. Gather all ingredients.
2. Bring water to a boil in a small pot and add oats.
3. Cook for about 20-25 minutes, to desired texture.
4. Divide oatmeal among 4 bowls.
5. Top each bowl with 1 small heirloom tomato, sliced, 2 tablespoons walnuts, 3 olives, and 2 tablespoons basil.
6. Garnish with dusting of black pepper and sea salt (if desired).
7. Serve with soymilk, as desired.

Nutrition Per Serving 350 calories, 17g total fat, 2g sat fat, 95mg sodium, 35g carbohydrates, 6g fiber, 4g sugar, 17g protein

Tip or fact: Make steel cut oats the day before and reheat the next morning—garnishing with the toppings—if you want to enjoy this meal in minutes.

Shopping list

Produce
- ☐ 4 small heirloom tomatoes
- ☐ 1 bunch fresh basil

Packaged
- ☐ steel cut oats
- ☐ baked tofu
- ☐ coarsely chopped walnuts
- ☐ green or black olives

Refrigerated or Frozen
- ☐ plain unsweetened soymilk

Vegetable Rice Pilaf
by Jyl Steinback

| Easy | Gluten Free | 6 Servings |

Pilafs make great bases for bowl dishes. Adding broccoli and some beans to make this a complete nutritious meal.

Ingredients

2 Tbsp + 1½ c nonfat vegetable broth, divided
1 medium onion, sliced
1 tsp minced garlic
1 tsp chili powder
2 tsp paprika
¼ tsp ground cinnamon
⅛ tsp ground nutmeg
⅛ tsp ground cloves
1½ c long grain rice
⅔ c + 2 Tbsp dry white wine
14.5 oz. can petite-cut diced tomatoes with roasted garlic and sweet onion, drained
¼ lb. sliced fresh mushrooms
1 medium zucchini, cubed
1 yellow squash, cubed

Directions

1. Gather all ingredients.
2. In a large nonstick skillet add 2 tablespoons broth to skillet and heat over medium-high heat.
3. Add onion and cook over medium-high heat, stirring frequently, until onions are lightly browned.
4. Add minced garlic, chili powder, paprika, cinnamon, nutmeg, and cloves.
5. Cook, stirring constantly, 1 minute.
6. Add rice and mix well.
7. Add remaining broth, wine, tomatoes, mushrooms, zucchini, and squash.
8. Bring to a boil over high heat.
9. Reduce heat to low, cover pan, and simmer 15-18 minutes until rice and vegetables are tender.

Nutrition Per Serving 150 calories, 1g total fat, 0g sat fat, 360mg sodium, 26g carbohydrates, 3g fiber, 8g sugar, 4g protein

Perfect Pasta & Grains

Tip or fact: Store whole cloves for up to 1 year in an airtight glass container or jar out of direct sunlight. Ground cloves lose their flavor very fast.

Shopping list

Produce
- □ 1 medium onion
- □ fresh mushrooms
- □ 1 medium zucchini
- □ 1 yellow squash

Packaged
- □ nonfat vegetable broth, divided
- □ long grain rice
- □ dry white wine
- □ 14.5 oz. can petite-cut diced tomatoes with roasted garlic and sweet onion

Seasonings and Spices
- □ chili powder
- □ paprika
- □ ground cinnamon
- □ ground nutmeg
- □ ground cloves

Vegetarian Hoppin' John with Okra by Sharon Palmer

Medium | **Gluten Free** | **6 Servings**

If you're looking for the perfect plant-powered recipe to add to your New Year's Day menu, look no further. This is also a great one dish meal for dinner or meal prep.

Ingredients

- 1½ c dried black-eyed peas
- 1 medium onion, diced
- 1 medium green bell pepper, diced
- 3 medium celery stalks, sliced
- 2 medium carrots, sliced
- 2 garlic cloves, minced
- ¼ tsp cayenne
- 1 tsp dried thyme
- 2 c low-sodium vegetable broth
- 6 c water
- 1 bay leaf
- ½ tsp smoked paprika
- 2 c sliced fresh or frozen okra
- 1 c uncooked long-grain brown rice

Directions

1. Gather all ingredients.
2. Soak the black-eyed peas overnight in enough cold water to cover them.
3. Drain the peas and set aside.
4. Add the onion, bell pepper, celery, carrots, garlic, cayenne, and thyme to a large heavy pot and sauté for 5 minutes.
5. Add the drained peas, broth, 3 cups of the water, bay leaf, and smoked paprika to the pot and bring to a boil.
6. Reduce the heat, cover, and simmer, stirring occasionally, for 1 hour.
7. About 30 minutes into the cooking time, start to prepare the rice.
8. If using a rice cooker, put the remaining 3 cups of water and the rice into the cooker and prepare according to the manufacturer's instructions. If cooking on the stovetop, bring 3 cups water to a boil in a medium saucepan. Add the rice and reduce the heat to a simmer. Cook, covered, until all the liquid is absorbed, 45 to 50 minutes.
9. After the peas and vegetables have cooked for an hour, add the okra to the mixture and cook for an additional 15 minutes.
10. Remove the bay leaf.
11. Serve the pea mixture immediately over the hot rice.

Nutrition Per Serving 300 calories, 2g total fat, 0g sat fat, 260mg sodium, 60g carbohydrates, 9g fiber, 8g sugar, 14g protein

Ingredient Swap: Substitute cooked barley, wheat berries, or quinoa for the brown rice for an interesting flavor variation.

Shopping list

Produce
- ☐ 1 medium onion
- ☐ 1 medium green bell pepper
- ☐ 3 medium celery stalks
- ☐ 2 medium carrots
- ☐ 2 garlic cloves
- ☐ 1 bay leaf
- ☐ okra

Packaged
- ☐ dried black-eyed peas
- ☐ low-sodium vegetable broth
- ☐ long-grain brown rice

Seasonings and Spices
- ☐ cayenne
- ☐ dried thyme
- ☐ smoked paprika

Zucchini Noodles

by Ashley Arpel Greenwald

Easy | **Gluten Free** | **2 Servings**

The reason my boyfriend stays with me. Ladies and gentlemen, I give you my zoodle recipe!

Ingredients

3 c zucchini noodles
1 Tbsp lemon juice
3 Tbsp minced garlic
3 Tbsp lemon juice
3 c unsalted tomato puree
2 Tbsp unsalted tomato paste
½ Tbsp malt vinegar
1 tsp ground cinnamon
⅛ tsp black pepper

Directions

1. Preheat oven to 400°F.
2. Gather all ingredients.
3. Place zucchini noodles in a large baking dish suited for casseroles. At least 3 quarts.
4. Pour 1 tablespoon lemon juice on noodles and mix with your hands.
5. Place in the oven and cook for 45 minutes.
6. While the noodles bake, mince garlic and place in a large saucepan along with 3 tablespoons lemon juice. Sauté on medium heat for 3 minutes.
7. Reduce to low heat and stir in tomato puree and tomato paste.
8. Add vinegar, cinnamon and black pepper.
9. Cover and let simmer for about 20 minutes, stirring occasionally. By the time the noodles are done, the sauce will be too.
10. When noodles are done, remove from oven. Transfer noodles to a colander to drain. The tips of the cooked noodles will be slightly browned/crisped.
11. Add the noodles to the saucepan still over low heat. Mix using tongs.
12. Remove sauced noodles from heat and serve immediately.

Perfect Pasta & Grains

Nutrition Per Serving 260 calories, 3g total fat, 0g sat fat, 115mg sodium, 47g carbohydrates, 11g fiber, 23g sugar, 9g protein

Storage: Store in an airtight glass container in the refrigerator for the following day's lunch or dinner.

Tip or fact: Look in the produce section for zucchini noodles. Most grocery stores sell in packages of 8-10 oz, and this recipe will require about 3 packages.

Shopping list

Produce
☐ 3 lemons
☐ 3 cloves garlic

Packaged
☐ zucchini noodles
☐ unsalted tomato puree
☐ unsalted tomato paste
☐ malt vinegar

Seasonings and Spices
☐ ground cinnamon
☐ black pepper

Parsley

Thyme

Anise

Bay Leaf

Arugula

Mint

Sage

Vanilla

Vibrant Veggies

Terragon

Rosemary

Dill

Baked Tomatoes

by Jyl Steinback

Easy | **2 Servings**

This is a great dish for a potluck. Simple, wholesome and delicious.

Ingredients

1 large tomato, halved
½-1 tsp Dijon mustard
2 Tbsp whole wheat breadcrumbs

Directions

1. Preheat oven to 350°F.
2. Gather all ingredients.
3. Place tomato halves, cut side up, non-stick pan.
4. Spread Dijon mustard on top and sprinkle with seasoned breadcrumbs.
5. Bake 10-12 minutes, until tomatoes are tender and crumbs are lightly browned.

Nutrition Per Serving 35 calories, 0g total fat, 0g sat fat, 40mg sodium, 7g carbohydrates, 1g fiber, 3g sugar, 2g protein

Tip or fact: Laugh and the whole body may be smiling! The World Laughter Tour, an organization that promotes the therapeutic effects of laughter, lists the following benefits of laughing: reduced stress, boosted immune system functioning, improved digestion, stabilized mood, inspired creativity, and a rested brain.

Shopping list

Produce
☐ 1 large tomato

Packaged
☐ Dijon mustard
☐ whole wheat breadcrumbs

Seasonings and Spices
☐ chili powder
☐ paprika
☐ ground cinnamon
☐ ground nutmeg
☐ ground cloves

Balsamic Portobello Steaks

by Jyl Steinback

Easy | **4 Servings**

Mushrooms on the grill ... soooo good! Try thinking outside your "lunchbox" and experiment by swapping standard balsamic vinegar with savory flavored ones.

Ingredients

4 large portobello mushrooms, cleaned and dried
1½ tsp garlic powder
¾ c balsamic vinegar
4 multigrain rolls, optional
4 slices tomato, optional
1 small red onion, sliced, optional
handful fresh spinach

Directions

1. Preheat grill.
2. Gather all ingredients.
3. Remove mushroom stems and store for use later chopped in a salad or freeze to make stock.
4. Place mushroom caps in shallow baking dish.
5. Sprinkle with garlic powder.
6. Spoon balsamic vinegar over mushrooms until well coated.
7. Let stand 10-15 minutes.
8. Place mushroom caps on non-stick foil on grill, close lid and cook 3-4 minutes, until tender.
9. Brush mushrooms with balsamic vinegar once during grilling.
10. Serve on multigrain rolls with sliced tomatoes, spinach and sliced onions.

Nutrition Per Serving 60 calories, 0g total fat, 0g sat fat, 20mg sodium, 12g carbohydrates, 1g fiber, 9g sugar, 2g protein

Vibrant Veggies

Tip or fact: Portobello, like other mushrooms, are virtually free of fat, sodium, and cholesterol yet provide essential fiber. One medium cap (about 4 ounces) only contains 40 calories.

Shopping list

Produce
☐ 4 large portobello mushrooms
☐ 1 tomato
☐ 1 small red onion
☐ 1 bunch fresh spinach

Packaged
☐ balsamic vinegar
☐ 4 multigrain rolls, optional

Seasonings and Spices
☐ garlic powder

Balsamic Zucchini Sauté

by Jyl Steinback

Easy | **Gluten Free** | **6 Servings**

We have just the recipe for all of those summer zucchini! Sauté those babies up with some red pepper flakes, garlic and balsamic vinegar. So easy and so good!

Ingredients

6 large zucchini, sliced
3 cloves garlic, chopped
¼ tsp red pepper flakes
1 Tbsp balsamic vinegar

Directions

1. Gather all ingredients.
2. Heat a nonstick skillet over medium-high heat.
3. Add zucchini and ½ garlic to hot skillet and sauté about 10 minutes, or until zucchini is softened.
4. Reduce heat to medium and add remaining garlic and pepper flakes.
5. Cook 1-2 minutes longer.
6. Remove from heat and cool to room temperature.
7. Sprinkle zucchini mixture with balsamic vinegar and serve.

Nutrition Per Serving 60 calories, 1g total fat, 0g sat fat, 25mg sodium, 11g carbohydrates, 3g fiber, 8g sugar, 4g protein

Tip or fact: This is another recipe where using a flavored vinegar could add a personal zest to your dish. Lemon, basil or even mint go well with zucchini.

Shopping list

Produce
☐ 6 large zucchini
☐ 3 cloves garlic

Packaged
☐ balsamic vinegar

Seasonings and Spices
☐ red pepper flakes

Cajun Fries

by Jyl Steinback

Easy | **Gluten Free** | **8 Servings**

Crispy spicy Cajun potato fries, what could be wrong with that? Serve them alongside of your favorite veggie burger from the burgers chapter.

Ingredients

4 large baking potatoes, cut into thin strips
4 tsp Cajun seasoning

Directions

1. Preheat oven to 425°F.
2. Gather all ingredients.
3. Prepare a medium-hot grill and add 5-8 tablespoons of water.
4. Lightly spray baking sheets with nonfat cooking spray.
5. Place potato strips in a single layer on baking sheets.
6. Sprinkle evenly with Cajun seasoning. Turn potatoes and season other side.
7. Bake potatoes in oven for 20 minutes.
8. Remove from oven and place on grill.
9. Cover grill and cook 15-20 minutes, until potatoes are browned and crispy.

Nutrition Per Serving 150 calories, 0g total fat, 0g sat fat, 20mg sodium, 32g carbohydrates, 3g fiber, 2g sugar, 4g protein

Tip or fact: Although it shares the same name, the sweet potato is a root vegetable and only loosely related to the potato.

Vibrant Veggies

Shopping list

Produce
☐ 4 large baking potatoes

Seasonings and Spices
☐ Cajun seasoning

Caponata
by Jyl Steinback

Easy | Gluten Free | 6 Servings

A delicious and versatile dip that can be served warm or cold as a dip or tossed with pasta.

Ingredients

¾ lb. eggplant, peeled and cut into ½ inch cubes
½ c chopped onion
¼ c chopped celery
1 c chopped tomatoes, drained
2 Tbsp red wine vinegar
1½ Tbsp unsalted tomato paste
¾ tsp date sugar
½ tsp garlic powder
⅛ tsp black pepper
⅛ tsp ground red pepper
1 tsp dried parsley
2 tsp dried basil
¾ tsp dried oregano
¾ tsp lemon juice

Directions

1. Gather all ingredients.
2. Heat a large nonstick skillet over medium-high heat.
3. Add eggplant, onion and celery to skillet and cook 5-6 minutes, until vegetables are tender.
4. Add tomatoes, vinegar, tomato paste, sugar, garlic powder, pepper and ground red pepper. Mix well.
5. Cover skillet and cook, stirring occasionally, over low heat, 5-6 minutes, until heated through.
6. Remove skillet from heat. Stir in parsley, basil, oregano and lemon juice. Mix well.
7. Spoon mixture into serving bowl. Cover and refrigerate 1-2 hours.
8. Let mixture stand at room temperature 20 minutes before serving.
9. Great with fat-free pita chips.

Nutrition Per Serving 35 calories, 0g total fat, 0g sat fat, 10mg sodium, 8g carbohydrates, 3g fiber, 4g sugar, 1g protein

Tip or fact: While we traditionally think of eggplants as an elongated purple veggie, eggplants come in a variety of shapes and colors, including purple, white, green and even striped.

Shopping list

Produce
☐ ¾ lb. eggplant
☐ 1 onion
☐ 1 bunch celery
☐ 1 tomato
☐ 1 lemon

Packaged
☐ red wine vinegar
☐ unsalted tomato paste
☐ date sugar

Seasonings and Spices
☐ garlic powder
☐ black pepper
☐ ground red pepper
☐ dried parsley
☐ dried basil
☐ dried oregano

Chickpea Curry

by Nele Liivlaid

Easy | **Gluten Free** | **4 Servings**

This tasty plant nutritious curry with tomatoes will make your meal filling and complete that is full of flavor and delicious.

Ingredients

2 small onions, finely dice
8 thin ginger slices
2 medium carrots, chop
4 smaller garlic cloves, crushed
2 tsp Indian spice mix (recipe p. 7)
2 tsp turmeric
24 oz. low sodium tomato puree
½ c coconut milk
1 c dry chickpeas, cooked, rinsed and drained (recipe p. 6)
black pepper, to taste

Directions

1. Gather all ingredients.
2. Start by making a batch of Indian Spice Mix (recipe p. 7).
3. Heat up a few tablespoons of water or broth in a non-stick skillet or large pan.
4. Add the onions, carrot and ginger. Sauté the veggies with the lid on until softened, about 3 minutes stirring every now and then.
5. Throw in crushed garlic cloves, the spice mix and turmeric, stir and cook for a few minutes. Add a few splashes of water as necessary.
6. Pour in tomato puree, mix and bring to boil. Reduce the heat and simmer for 10 minutes.
7. Add the coconut milk and chickpeas. Bring to boil and turn off the heat.
8. Season with black pepper.
9. For a more mushy result, take potato masher or fork and mash the chickpeas until the curry has thickened to desired consistency.
10. Garnish with fresh parsley or coriander.

Vibrant Veggies

Nutrition Per Serving 320 calories, 4.5g total fat, 1g sat fat, 200mg sodium, 60g carbohydrates, 15g fiber, 19g sugar, 15g protein

Ingredient Swap: Replace the spice mix and turmeric with any preferred unsalted curry powder or garam masala mix.

Tip or fact: Serve with chopped Romaine lettuce or steamed leafy greens (kale, chard, collard greens).

Shopping list

Produce
☐ 2 small onions
☐ ginger
☐ 2 medium carrots
☐ 4 cloves garlic

Packaged
☐ 24 oz. low sodium tomato puree
☐ coconut milk
☐ dry chickpeas

Seasonings and Spices
☐ Indian spice mix
☐ turmeric

"Grilled" Peppers and Onions by Jyl Steinback

Easy | **Gluten Free** | **4 Servings**

Grilled peppers and onions are a great topper for veggie burgers.

Ingredients

1lb. frozen pepper stir-fry mix
¼ c red wine vinegar
1 Tbsp Dijon mustard
2 tsp minced garlic, roasted
¼ tsp black pepper

Directions

1. Preheat broiler on high.
2. Gather all ingredients.
3. Spread pepper stir-fry mix on baking sheet.
4. Combine remaining ingredients in a small bowl and mix well.
5. Brush peppers with vinegar-mustard mixture.
6. Broil 3 minutes.
7. Turn peppers over, brush with sauce and broil 2 to 3 minutes, until browned.

Nutrition Per Serving 50 calories, 0.5g total fat, 0g sat fat, 55mg sodium, 8g carbohydrates, 0g fiber, 5g sugar, 1g protein

Tip or fact: You can substitute 3 fresh bell peppers and 1 onion for frozen stir-fry mix. Cut peppers and onion into thick strips or chunks and prepare as directed.

Shopping list

Produce
□ 1 clove garlic

Packaged
□ red wine vinegar
□ Dijon mustard

Refrigerated or Frozen
□ 1lb. frozen pepper stir-fry mix

Seasonings and Spices
□ black pepper

Grilled Veggie Kabobs
by Jyl Steinback

Easy | **Gluten Free** | **5 Servings**

Marinating your veggies before grilling as a brightness that makes your grilled veggies all the tastier!

Ingredients

Kabobs:

1 c broccoli, chopped
2 c eggplant, cubed
12 mushrooms, whole
1 c onion, chopped
2 c red, green peppers, chopped
2 medium yellow squash, sliced thick

Marinade:

¼ c balsamic vinegar or cider
3 Tbsp fresh lemon juice
1 tsp freshly ground black pepper
1½ tsp dried oregano
2 cloves garlic, chopped
½ tsp rosemary

Directions

1. Gather all ingredients.
2. Mix marinade ingredients in a small bowl, stirring to blend and set aside.
3. Place prepared vegetables in large lidded container. Pour in the marinade and mix with your hands or spoon. Make sure all veggies are coated with marinade.
4. Marinate in the refrigerator 1-4 hours. Stir occasionally.
5. When ready to cook, remove vegetables from marinade and thread onto kabob skewers. Leave a little space between the vegetables for air to circulate.
6. Grill directly on grill until all vegetables are golden and tender, 20-25 minutes.
7. Serve alone or over brown rice, quinoa or left over grain and enjoy!

Nutrition Per Serving 80 calories, 0.5g total fat, 0g sat fat, 15mg sodium, 17g carbohydrates, 5g fiber, 9g sugar, 4g protein

Tip or fact: Eggplant is actually characterized botanically as a fruit, although it is treated like a vegetable in cooking. It belongs to the nightshade family and closely related to potato and tomato.

Vibrant Veggies

Shopping list

Produce

☐ 1 head broccoli
☐ 1 eggplant
☐ 12 mushrooms
☐ 1 onion
☐ 1 red pepper
☐ 1 green pepper
☐ 2 medium yellow squash
☐ 2-3 lemons
☐ 2 cloves garlic

Packaged

☐ balsamic vinegar or cider

Seasonings and Spices

☐ black peppercorns
☐ dried oregano
☐ rosemary

Kasha Stuffed Portobello Mushrooms by Jyl Steinback

Easy | **4 Servings**

Yummy little morsels of goodness! These are perfect for entertaining or as a tasty little side.

Ingredients

1 c kasha (buckwheat oats), dry
4 portobello mushroom caps
2 c vegetable broth
3 c Swiss chard, chopped into small pieces
1 large red bell pepper, chopped into small pieces
1 shallot, chopped into small pieces
2 cloves garlic, minced
pepper, to taste

Directions

1. Preheat oven to 325°F.
2. Gather all ingredients.
2. Remove the stem and gills from the Portobello mushrooms. Gently rinse and wipe down with a paper towel.
3. Prepare the vegetable broth (recipe p.124) if using homemade.
4. Cook the kasha according to package directions. Use vegetable broth instead of water.
5. Heat a non-stick pan over a medium heat.
6. Add the shallot, bell pepper, Swiss chard, and pepper. Cover, stirring occasionally for 5 minutes.
7. Add garlic. Continue to cook until vegetables are tender but still a little firm.
8. Add cooked kasha to pan and stir.
9. Portion out kasha-vegetable mixture into Portobello mushroom caps and place on non-stick baking sheet.
10. Cook in oven for 10 minutes.
11. Season with pepper to taste.
12. Let cool and serve.

Nutrition Per Serving 262 calories, 5g total fat, 0g sat fat, 236mg sodium, 46g carbohydrates, 6g fiber, 3g sugar, 13g protein

Tip or fact: Cooking with low sodium broth is a great way to add flavor without adding excess calories and fat.

Shopping list

Produce
- [ ] 4 portobello mushrooms
- [ ] 1 head swiss chard
- [ ] 1 large red bell pepper
- [ ] 1 shallot
- [ ] 2 cloves garlic

Packaged
- [ ] kasha
- [ ] vegetable broth

Seasonings and Spices
- [ ] pepper

Polenta Fries with Marinara
by Kelley Williamson

Easy | **Gluten Free** | **4 Servings**

Beautiful and crispy fries with an Italian dream sauce.

Ingredients

1 package rolled polenta, any flavor

28 oz. canned tomato sauce, reduced sodium

14 oz. can diced tomatoes, unsalted

1 Tbsp garlic powder

½ tsp sea salt

1 c fresh basil, chopped

Directions

1. Preheat oven to 350°F.
2. Gather all ingredients.
3. On a cutting board, cut the polenta roll in half lengthwise and then cut each ½ in half lengthwise.
4. Lay each piece flat on the cutting board and then cut into four lengthwise strips and then cut the 4 strips in half.
5. Place on a parchment lined baking sheet and bake in the oven for about 30 minutes or until they turn a nice golden brown.
6. While baking, make the marinara sauce. Add all ingredients to a saucepan and simmer.
7. Pour the marinara sauce in a bowl and then place the polenta fries around the bowl.
8. Enjoy the dipping.

Nutrition Per Serving 150 calories, 3g total fat, 0g sat fat, 430mg sodium, 26g carbohydrates, 1g fiber, 13g sugar, 4g protein

Vibrant Veggies

Tip or fact: Everything is great dipped in a wonderful Italian marinara sauce. Add fresh vegetables and enjoy dipping raw and cooked items in the sauce.

Shopping list

Produce
☐ fresh basil

Packaged
☐ 1 package rolled polenta, any flavor
☐ 28 oz. canned tomato sauce, reduced sodium
☐ 14 oz. can diced tomatoes, unsalted

Seasonings and Spices
☐ garlic powder
☐ sea salt

Red Potatoes with Fresh Herbs by Jyl Steinback

Easy | **Gluten Free** | **4 Servings**

Fresh rosemary, parsley and chives give a boast of flavor to these roasted little red gems.

Ingredients

2 lbs. red new potatoes, halved
¼ c low sodium vegetable broth
1 Tbsp finely chopped parsley
1 Tbsp finely chopped rosemary
2 Tbsp finely chopped chives

Directions

1. Preheat oven to 450°F.
2. Gather all ingredients.
3. Arrange potatoes in a single layer in non-stick baking dish.
4. Pour broth over top and sprinkle with fresh parsley, rosemary and chives.
5. Bake 25-30 minutes until potatoes are cooked through.
6. Sprinkle with additional herbs before serving, if desired.

Nutrition Per Serving 160 calories, 0g total fat, 0g sat fat, 50mg sodium, 37g carbohydrates, 4g fiber, 3g sugar, 4g protein

Tip or fact: 1 tablespoon of fresh herbs is equivalent to 1 teaspoon of dried herbs.

Shopping list

Produce
☐ red new potatoes
☐ fresh parsley
☐ fresh rosemary
☐ fresh chives

Packaged
☐ low sodium vegetable broth

Roasted Brussels Sprouts

by Jyl Steinback

Easy | **Gluten Free** | **6 Servings**

Roasting Brussels sprouts brings out their nutty savory flavor.

Ingredients

1 lb. fresh Brussels sprouts
2-3 Tbsp low sodium vegetable broth
pepper, to taste

Directions

1. Preheat oven to 400°F.
2. Gather all ingredients.
3. Clean and prepare Brussels sprouts by cutting off stem, peeling off outer leaves and then cut in half.
4. In a large bowl, toss Brussels sprouts with vegetable broth
5. Place Brussels sprouts in a single layer on a non-stick baking sheet.
6. Cook until fork tender, about 35-40 min.
7. Add pepper to taste.

Nutrition Per Serving 35 calories, 0g total fat, 0g sat fat, 70mg sodium, 7g carbohydrates, 3g fiber, 2g sugar, 3g protein

Tip or fact: Select bright green, firm, and compact Brussels sprouts. Pass on those with wilted leaves or soft spots. Do not wash or trim sprouts before storing them.

Vibrant Veggies

Shopping list

Produce
☐ 1 lb. fresh Brussels sprouts

Packaged
☐ low sodium vegetable broth

Seasonings and Spices
☐ pepper

Roasted Curry Cauliflower with Peas by Diane Smith

Easy | **Gluten Free** | **4 Servings**

Here's a quick way to get your veggies with lots of flavor on the table in a flash.

Ingredients

1 head cauliflower leaves trimmed and broken into bite-sized pieces.
2 Tbsp almond or peanut butter
1 tsp curry powder
2 tsp water
½ c peas defrosted in warm water
⅓ c sliced almonds
¼ c parsley or cilantro, chopped
sea salt, to taste
pepper, to taste

Directions

1. Preheat oven to 400°F.
2. Gather all ingredients.
3. In a small bowl, mix the nut butter, curry powder, water, and salt and pepper.
4. Heat in the microwave for a few seconds to thin.
5. Place cauliflower in a large baking dish and squeeze lemon over.
6. Pour marinade over cauliflower and mix with clean hands.
7. Stir in the peas.
8. Place, uncovered, in the oven for 20-25 minutes or until tender.
9. Sprinkle sliced almonds over top and a sprinkling of parsley or cilantro.

Nutrition Per Serving 150 calories, 9g total fat, 1g sat fat, 65mg sodium, 14g carbohydrates, 6g fiber, 5g sugar, 7g protein

Tip or fact: You can use any of the beautiful colorful cauliflower in the market for this dish.

Shopping list

Produce
☐ 1 head cauliflower
☐ 1 bunch parsley or cilantro

Packaged
☐ almond or peanut butter
☐ sliced almonds

Refrigerated or Frozen
☐ frozen peas

Seasonings and Spices
☐ curry powder
☐ sea salt
☐ pepper

Roasted Vegetables

by Jyl Steinback

Easy | **Gluten Free** | **8 Servings**

Lemon spices and fresh parsley make theses roasted veggies pop!

Ingredients

½ lb. baby red potatoes, halved
10 oz. bag baby carrots
1 onion, peeled and sliced
1 small zucchini, cubed
4 cloves garlic, peeled
6 Tbsp low sodium vegetable broth
1 Tbsp grated lemon peel
½ tsp chili powder
½ tsp mustard seed
¼ tsp pepper
¼ c chopped fresh parsley

Directions

1. Preheat oven to 425°F.
2. Gather all ingredients.
2. In the non-stick baking dish combine potatoes, carrots, onion, zucchini, and garlic on baking sheet.
3. Combine broth, lemon peel, chili powder, mustard seed, and pepper in small bowl and mix well.
4. Pour broth mixture over vegetables and toss to coat.
5. Bake 25–30 minutes, stirring occasionally, until vegetables are tender and lightly browned.
6. Garnish with parsley before serving.

Nutrition Per Serving 45 calories, 0g total fat, 0g sat fat, 45mg sodium, 10g carbohydrates, 2g fiber, 3g sugar, 1g protein

Tip or fact: Roasted veggies can be served hot as a side or served at room temperature over a bed of greens as a salad.

Vibrant Veggies

Shopping list

Produce
☐ ½ lb. baby red potatoes
☐ 10 oz. bag baby carrots
☐ 1 onion
☐ 1 small zucchini
☐ 4 cloves garlic
☐ 1 lemon
☐ 1 bunch parsley

Packaged
☐ low sodium vegetable broth

Seasonings and Spices
☐ chili powder
☐ mustard seed
☐ pepper

Sweet and Sour Red Cabbage by Jyl Steinback

| Easy | Gluten Free | 6 Servings |

Warm spices, sweet apple and lemon juice come together to make this tasty slaw.

Ingredients
1 small onion, finely chopped
2 small apples, diced
4 c red cabbage, chopped
⅛ tsp ginger
½ tsp nutmeg
⅛ tsp lemon juice
2 Tbsp vinegar
pepper, to taste

Directions
1. Gather all ingredients.
2. Using a large saucepan, cook onion in small amount of water until tender.
3. Add remaining ingredients and cook, covered, until vegetables are tender. Stir occasionally.
4. Serve it warm as a side or cold as a topping to a part of a bowl, plant nutritious burger or mushroom sandwich.

Nutrition Per Serving 50 calories, 0g total fat, 0g sat fat, 65mg sodium, 12g carbohydrates, 3g fiber, 8g sugar, 1g protein

Storage: Store in fridge in airtight glass container for up to 5 days.

Tip or fact: The heaviest cabbage on record weighed 138 pounds and was presented at the Alaska State Fair in 2012.

Shopping list

Produce
☐ 1 small onion
☐ 2 small apples
☐ 2 heads red cabbage
☐ 1 lemon

Packaged
☐ vinegar

Seasonings and Spices
☐ nutmeg
☐ pepper

Sweet N Sour Edamame

by Ashley Arpel Greenwald

Easy | **Gluten Free** | **2 Servings**

Remember that Sweet N Sour sauce from a few chapters back? Edamame is the perfect companion and a great snack to share!

Ingredients

2 ½ c frozen edamame, cooked
¼ c unsweetened applesauce,
2 Tbsp low sodium soy sauce
½ Tbsp malt vinegar
1 Tbsp lemon juice

Directions

1. Gather all ingredients.
2. Cook edamame according to package instructions and set aside.
3. Place the remaining ingredients into a large saucepan and stir over low heat.
4. Cover and let simmer for 8 minutes, stirring occasionally.
5. Remove pan from heat and add the cooked edamame.
6. Stir to cover edamame and serve immediately.

Nutrition Per Serving 180 calories, 7g total fat, 0g sat fat, 590mg sodium, 16g carbohydrates, 8g fiber, 7g sugar, 18g protein

Tip or fact: Edamame is great source of protein, calcium and iron.

Vibrant Veggies

Shopping list

Produce
☐ 1 lemon

Packaged
☐ unsweetened applesauce,
☐ low sodium soy sauce
☐ malt vinegar
☐ lemon juice

Refrigerated or frozen
☐ frozen edamame

Teriyaki Cauliflower Wings

by Kelley Williamson

Easy | **Gluten Free** | **4 Servings**

Do you love Asian? Then you will love these wings.

Ingredients

Wings:
1 small head cauliflower, chopped to florets
1 Tbsp sesame seeds

Teriyaki Sauce:
½ c low sodium tamari
¼ c water
½ c coconut sugar
2 cloves garlic minced
1 Tbsp ginger, minced
2 Tbsp rice vinegar
1 Tbsp arrowroot

Directions

1. Preheat oven to 350°F.
2. Gather all ingredients.
3. Line a baking sheet with parchment paper.
4. Cut up the cauliflower florets to bite sized pieces and then place on the parchment lined baking sheet.
5. Bake in the oven for about 12 to 15 minutes or until a golden brown.
6. While the cauliflower wings are baking add all teriyaki sauce ingredients to a saucepan and simmer until thickened.
7. Set aside to cool slightly.
8. Pour ¼ cup of the teriyaki sauce into a bowl and then add the wings and mix well.
9. Place the wings on a plate and sprinkle with sesame seeds.
10. Enjoy warm!

Nutrition Per Serving 50 calories, 1g total fat, 0g sat fat, 310mg sodium, 9g carbohydrates, 1g fiber, 5g sugar, 2g protein

Storage: Store in fridge in airtight glass container.

Ingredient Swap: In place of teriyaki sauce, you can use a different sauce such as hot wings, Siracha, sambal oelek, etc.

Tip or fact: When you have a craving for hot wings or something teriyaki but don't want all the fried calories, then these wings are for you. Add a dipping sauce or just eat them right out of the bowl. The homemade teriyaki sauce has on 553 mg of sodium per ¾ cup.

Shopping list

Produce
☐ 1 small head cauliflower
☐ 2 cloves garlic
☐ ginger

Packaged
☐ low sodium tamari
☐ coconut sugar
☐ rice vinegar
☐ arrowroot
☐ sesame seeds

Unfried Beans

by Jyl Steinback

Easy | **Gluten Free** | **4 Servings**

This will be your go-to oil-free refried bean substitute you can't go without!

Ingredients

16 oz. can pinto beans, rinsed and drained
¼ c chunky-style salsa
1½ tsp onion powder
¼ tsp garlic powder
¼ tsp chili powder
¼ tsp ground cumin

Directions

1. Gather all ingredients.
2. In a 2-quart saucepan add all the ingredients.
3. Bring to a boil over medium-high heat, stirring frequently.
4. Reduce heat to low. Simmer 10-12 minutes, stirring occasionally.
5. Cool to room temperature.
6. Process bean mixture in food processor or blender until smooth.
7. Cover and refrigerate beans for up to 1 week.

Nutrition Per Serving 100 calories, 0.5g total fat, 0g sat fat, 290mg sodium, 19g carbohydrates, 6g fiber, 2g sugar, 5g protein

Storage: Store in fridge in airtight glass container up to 1 week.

Tip or fact: Canned beans provide most of the same benefits as dried ones; just ½ cup cooked pinto beans provide ½ the daily value for fiber for women.

Vibrant Veggies

Shopping list

Packaged
☐ 16 oz. can pinto beans, rinsed and drained
☐ chunky-style salsa

Seasonings and Spices
☐ onion powder
☐ garlic powder
☐ chili powder
☐ ground cumin

Vegetable-Stuffed Peppers

by Jyl Steinback

Easy | **Gluten Free** | **4 Servings**

Flavorful veggie goodness packed into a pretty packets. The area perfect side dish for entertaining.

Ingredients

4 large bell peppers
½ c cooked brown rice
15 oz. can whole kernel corn, drained
½ c chopped green onions
⅛ tsp garlic powder
⅛ tsp pepper
14.5 oz. can low sodium petite-cut diced tomatoes, do not drain
⅓ c dry red wine
6 oz. can unsalted Italian tomato paste with roasted garlic

Directions

1. Gather all ingredients.
2. Cut off tops of bell peppers and remove stems. Chop remaining portion of each top and set aside. Clean out the inside of peppers.
3. Over a small bowl, drain petite cut tomatoes. Set liquid aside.
4. Combine chopped pepper, rice, corn, green onions, garlic powder, and ¼ cup petite cut tomatoes (without liquid) and mix well.
5. Stuff mixture into peppers. Arrange peppers standing upright in slow cooker.
6. In another small bowl, Combine remaining tomatoes and liquid with wine and tomato paste. Mix well.
7. Pour mixture over and around peppers.
8. Cover and cook on low heat for 6-7 hours or high heat for 3-3½ hours.

Nutrition Per Serving 210 calories, 2g total fat, 0g sat fat, 220mg sodium, 39g carbohydrates, 7g fiber, 14g sugar, 6g protein

Tip or fact: Red bell peppers are actually green bell peppers that have been left on the vine to continue to ripen and red bell peppers have more than twice the vitamin C of a green pepper.

Shopping list

Produce
☐ 4 large bell peppers
☐ 1 bunch green onions

Packaged
☐ brown rice
☐ 15 oz. canned whole kernel corn
☐ 14.5 oz. can low sodium petite-cut diced tomatoes
☐ dry red wine
☐ 6 oz. can unsalted Italian tomato paste with roasted garlic

Seasonings and Spices
☐ garlic powder
☐ pepper
☐ 15.25

Parsley

Thyme

Anise

Bay Leaf

Arugula

Mint

Sage

Vanilla

Sensational Sweets

Terragon

Rosemary

Dill

Cinnamon

Banana Avocado Mousse

by Reuel Rodriguez

Easy | **Gluten Free** | **6 Servings**

Talk about a great treat for a mid-day treat.

Ingredients

7 ripe bananas
1 large ripe avocado
¼ c date sugar
¼ cacao powder
2 tsp ground cinnamon
¼ c unsweetened almond milk
1 Medjool date, pitted
1 Tbsp hemp seeds, garnish
crushed pistachios, garnish

Directions

1. Preheat oven to 375°F.
2. Gather all ingredients.
3. Place bananas on a baking sheet, leaving space between each. Bake for 15-20 minutes, until the skin splits and becomes black.
4. When done, remove bananas from oven and place each one on a cooling rack. Allow to cool for at least 20 minutes and then peel and set aside.
5. Use a spoon to scoop the insides of the avocado and place it in the bowl of a food processor or blender.
6. Add date sugar, cacao powder, cinnamon, almond milk and date. Process until completely combined.
7. Add peeled bananas two at a time, processing in between each until a creamy consistency is reached.
8. Pour mixture in 6 small ramekins or mason jars and top with garnish of choice. I love pistachios!
9. Serve immediately.
13. Best served warm with hugs and kisses!

Nutrition Per Serving 270 calories, 9g total fat, 1.5g sat fat, 15mg sodium, 48g carbohydrates, 8g fiber, 25g sugar, 5g protein

Storage: Store in an airtight glass container in the refrigerator for no longer than 1 day to preserve.

Ingredient Swap: Swap almond milk for any plant-based milk OR fresh orange juice to give it a unique flavor.

Tip or fact: This is a fun recipe that can elevate your next party or event!

Shopping list

Produce
☐ 7 ripe bananas
☐ 1 large ripe avocado
☐ 2 tsp ground cinnamon
☐ ¼ c unsweetened almond milk
☐ 1 Medjool date, pitted
☐ 1 Tbsp hemp seeds, garnish
☐ crushed pistachios, garnish

Packaged
☐ date sugar
☐ cacao powder
☐ Medjool date
☐ hemp seeds
☐ pistachios

Refrigerated or Frozen
☐ unsweetened almond milk

Seasonings and Spices
☐ ground cinnamon

Banana Soft Serve Ice Cream
by Ashley Arpel Greenwald

Easy | **Kid Friendly** | **Gluten Free** | **1-2 Servings**

Yes, you can tell me you love me now. Healthy, easy ice cream?! YES!

Ingredients
3 medium bananas, frozen
1 Tbsp vanilla extract

Directions
1. Gather all ingredients.
2. Peel and slice all 3 bananas.
3. Place slices in a glass container, cover and freeze for at least 2 hours or overnight.
4. When the bananas are completely frozen remove them from the freezer and transfer them to a blender or the bowl of a food processor.
5. Add vanilla extract and process until a smooth soft serve consistency is reached.
6. Scoop ice cream into a bowl and serve immediately.

Nutrition Per Serving 330 calories, 1g total fat, 0g sat fat, 0mg sodium, 81g carbohydrates, 9g fiber, 44g sugar, 4g protein

Storage: Store in an airtight glass container in the freezer.

Tip or fact: Top with banana chips for an added crunch.

Sensationa Sweets

Shopping list

Produce
☐ 3 medium bananas

Packaged
☐ vanilla extract

Blondie Brookies

by Ashley Arpel Greenwald

Medium | **Gluten Free** | **9 Servings**

The richness of a chocolate chip cookie with the decadence of a brownie! Blondie Chocolate Chip Cookie Brownies – Blondie Brookies

Ingredients

Chocolate Chip Cookie Base:

3 Tbsp coconut oil, melted
1 c oat flour
1 c blanched almond flour
2 Tbsp brown coconut sugar
½ tsp baking soda
3 Tbsp chunky peanut butter
2 Tbsp pure maple syrup
½ tsp almond extract
⅓ c cacao nibs

Chocolate Brownie Top:

⅓ c oat flour
⅓ c blanched almond flour
⅓ c unsweetened cocoa powder
⅓ c pure maple syrup
3 Tbsp coconut oil, melted
½ tsp almond extract

Directions

1. Preheat oven to 350°F.
2. Gather all cookie base ingredients.
3. Place coconut oil in a microwavable bowl and microwave for 30 seconds, until all coconut oil has melted into liquid. Pour into large mixing bowl.
4. Pour remaining cookie base ingredients except for the cacao nibs into a large mixing bowl. Mix with your hands.
5. Add cacao nibs and mix again. The mixture will be very crumbly.
6. Transfer mixture into baking dish. Use your hands to press the mixture down creating a thick cookie base that reaches each corner of the pan. Set aside.
7. Gather all brownie top ingredients.
8. Place coconut oil in a microwavable bowl and microwave for 30 seconds, until all coconut oil has melted into liquid. Transfer to medium mixing bowl and add all remaining brownie top ingredients. Mix.
9. When fully combined, transfer mixture into baking dish on top of the cookie base. Spread mixture evenly on top.
10. Place in oven and bake for 18 minutes.
11. When done baking, remove Brookies from oven and let sit for at least 30 minutes.
12. Slice and serve when completely cooled.

Nutrition Per Serving 270 calories, 18g total fat, 8g sat fat, 80mg sodium, 23g carbohydrates, 4g fiber, 10g sugar, 5g protein

Storage: Store in an airtight glass container.

Ingredient Swap: Swap peanut butter for nut butter of choice.

Tip or fact: Best served with our Banana Soft Serve Ice Cream! Recipe on p. 289.

Shopping list

Packaged

☐ coconut oil
☐ oat flour
☐ blanched almond flour
☐ brown coconut sugar
☐ baking soda
☐ chunky peanut butter
☐ pure maple syrup
☐ almond extract
☐ cacao nibs
☐ unsweetened cocoa powder

Cacao Chip Cookies

by Ashley Arpel Greenwald

Easy | **Kid Friendly** | **Gluten Free** | **12 Servings**

Plant basing something as classic as the chocolate chip cookie was nerve wracking. Could I do this? Will people like this? AM I CRAZY? OMG! You will love them!

Ingredients

1 c almond flour
1 c millet flour
½ c date sugar
⅓ c date syrup
2 Tbsp almond milk
½ tsp vanilla extract
1 c cacao chips

Directions

1. Preheat oven to 350°F.
2. Gather all ingredients.
3. Using a whisk, combine almond flour, millet flour and date sugar in a large mixing bowl.
4. Add date syrup, almond milk and vanilla extract. Whisk again.
5. Use your hands to mix in cacao chips.
6. Roll cookie dough into medium sized balls and place on a parchment or silicone lined cookie sheet. Use the palm of your hand to press down on each ball to flatten it ever so slightly as these cookies do not expand on their own.
7. Bake for 14 minutes. If you prefer a crispier cookie, bake for 15 minutes.

Nutrition Per Serving 180 calories, 9g total fat, 2.5g sat fat, 5mg sodium, 23g carbohydrates, 2g fiber, 11g sugar, 4g protein

Sensational Sweets

Storage: Store in an airtight glass container for up to 4 days.

Ingredient Swap: Swap millet flour for oat flour.

Tip or fact: Raw cacao nibs are the natural form of chocolate, free of additives such as milk, butter, oils, etc. Therefore, cacao nibs will not melt, even when placed in the oven.

Shopping list

Packaged
☐ almond flour
☐ millet flour
☐ date sugar
☐ date syrup
☐ vanilla extract
☐ cacao chips

Refrigerated or Frozen
☐ almond milk

Chocolate Cake and Frosting

by Ashley Arpel Greenwald

Medium | **Kid Friendly** | **10-12 Servings**

Decadent, romantic and oh so rich in chocolatey goodness! This scrumptious chocolate cake is anything but ordinary and will hypnotize you with every bite!

Ingredients

Cake Ingredients:

1¼ c whole wheat pastry flour
½ c tapioca flour
1 ½ c brown coconut sugar
¼ c unsweetened cocoa powder
1 tsp baking soda
¾ c extra virgin olive oil
1¾ c oat milk
½ tsp vanilla extract

Frosting Ingredients:

3 ripe large bananas
¼ c + 1 Tbsp pure maple syrup
4 Tbsp cocoa powder
1 tsp vanilla extract
⅛ tsp cream of tartar, optional

Directions

1. Preheat oven to 350°F.
2. Gather all ingredients.
3. Mix whole wheat pastry flour and tapioca flour together in a large mixing bowl.
4. Add brown coconut sugar and baking soda. Set aside.
5. Whisk olive oil and oat milk together in a medium bowl.
6. Pour wet mixture into dry mixture and whisk, completely combining.
7. Fill two 8 inch or three 6 inch round nonstick cake pans with cake batter.
8. Place in the oven and bake for 25 minutes. When the cake is done, you should be able to insert a fork or toothpick into the center and remove it cleanly.
9. Remove from oven and place in the refrigerator to chill completely (about 30 minutes) before applying frosting.
10. Place all frosting ingredients in a blender and blend on high. If you'd like thicker frosting, include the cream of tartar.
11. Refrigerate until ready to use.
12. Frost cake. Slice and enjoy!

Nutrition Per Serving 350 calories, 15g total fat, 2.5g sat fat, 135mg sodium, 55g carbohydrates, 5g fiber, 26g sugar, 4g protein

Ingredient Swap: Can swap oat milk with plant based free milk of choice. Can swap brown coconut sugar for maple sugar.

Tip or fact: Before frosting the cake, turn each cake layer upside down and gently slice the edges off. Flip the cake right side up and slightly slice off the dome center if your cake has one. This process gives you a flat and clean cake surface to evenly distribute the frosting.

Shopping list

Produce
☐ 3 ripe large bananas

Packaged
☐ whole wheat pastry flour
☐ tapioca flour
☐ brown coconut sugar
☐ unsweetened cocoa powder
☐ baking soda
☐ extra virgin olive oil
☐ vanilla extract
☐ pure maple syrup
☐ cocoa powder

Refrigerated or Frozen
☐ oat milk

Seasonings and Spices
☐ cream of tartar, optional

Chocolate Marshmallows

by Ashley Arpel Greenwald

| Medium | Kid Friendly | Gluten Free | 16 Servings |

Soft and chewy chocolate marshmallows to make your little ones burst with happiness!

Ingredients

1 can unsalted garbanzo beans
½ Tbsp almond extract
½ tsp cream of tartar
1 Tbsp unsweetened cocoa powder
¾ c water
1 Tbsp agar powder
1 c brown coconut sugar

Directions

1. Preheat oven to 250°F.
2. Gather all ingredients.
3. Open can of garbanzo beans and drain out all liquid over a medium size bowl. This liquid is aquafaba. Transfer garbanzo beans to a sealed container and place in the refrigerator, saving them for another recipe.
4. Pour ½ cup of aquafaba into a large mixing bowl and add almond extract, cream of tartar and cocoa powder. Mix using an electric mixer until a thick and fluffy consistency is reached. Set aside.
5. In a small pot over medium heat, bring water and agar powder to a boil. When mixture begins to thicken, add coconut sugar. Continue to stir over medium heat for 2 minutes.
6. After 2 minutes, remove sugar mixture from heat and pour into aquafaba mixture. Use electric mixer on high to combine. Mix for another 3-5 minutes.
7. Immediately pour mixture into a nonstick 9x6 or 8x8 baking dish. Let sit at room temperature for at least 30 minutes.
8. After 30 minutes, remove marshmallow block from baking dish and slice into small individual cubes.
9. Place cubes in a larger baking dish so that they are not touching each other and bake for 20 minutes. When done, turn the oven off, but do not remove the marshmallows.
10. Let them sit for another 20 minutes in the diluting heat.
11. Best served in warm unsweetened vanilla almond milk.

Sensational Sweets

Nutrition Per Serving 130 calories, 0.5g total fat, 0g sat fat, 25mg sodium, 26g carbohydrates, 2g fiber, 16g sugar, 3g protein

Storage: Store in an airtight glass container for up to 3 days.

Tip or fact: You can use agar powder to thicken other foods like certain soups and even ice cream! You can find agar powder at health food stores, Asian markets and online.

Shopping list

Packaged
☐ 1 can unsalted garbanzo beans
☐ almond extract
☐ unsweetened cocoa powder
☐ brown coconut sugar

Seasonings and Spices
☐ cream of tartar
☐ agar powder

Insanely Delicious Cinnamon Rolls by Nele Liivlaid

Medium | **Gluten Free** | **9-10 Servings**

So excited to share ... beyond delicious.

Ingredients

Dough Ingredients:

⅛ c psyllium husks
½ c water
8.8 oz. unsweetened soymilk
1 Tbsp apple cider vinegar
¼ tsp alcohol free vanilla extract
3.5 oz. oat flour
3.5 oz. coconut flour
2 Tbsp date sugar
1 Tbsp cinnamon
½ tsp Himalayan salt
1 tsp aluminum-free baking powder

Filling Ingredients:

4.2 oz. nut butter
1½ Tbsp coconut nectar or agave
¼ tsp Himalayan salt
1 Tbsp cinnamon
1 Tbsp date sugar
1½ Tbsp + 1 tsp mesquite powder
3½ Tbsp + ¼ tsp unsweetened coconut milk

Shopping list

Packaged

☐ psyllium husks
☐ apple cider vinegar
☐ alcohol free vanilla extract
☐ oat flour
☐ coconut flour
☐ date sugar
☐ aluminum-free baking powder
☐ nut butter
☐ coconut nectar or agave
☐ mesquite powder

Refrigerated or Frozen

☐ unsweetened soymilk
☐ unsweetened coconut milk

Seasonings and Spices

☐ cinnamon
☐ Himalayan salt

Directions

1. Gather dough ingredients.
2. Pour psyllium husks and water into a small bowl and mix. Let sit for 10 minutes.
3. Pour soymilk, apple cider vinegar and vanilla extract into a medium bowl and mix. Let sit for 10 minutes.
4. Pour oat flour, coconut flour, date sugar, cinnamon, salt and baking powder into a large mixing bowl and mix.
5. Pour both wet mixtures into the dry mixture and mix, creating a dough.
6. Cover dough and place in the refrigerator for at least 30 minutes. Dough can be left in the refrigerator overnight if need be.
7. Preheat oven to 390°F.
8. Mix all filling ingredients together in a large mixing bowl. Let sit at room temperature for 5 minutes so the mesquite powder can absorb the liquid.
9. Remove dough from refrigerator and transfer to a parchment lined cutting board. Place another sheet of parchment on top of dough ball and roll out using a rolling pin. Roll the dough into about 11×13.8 inch rectangle and remove top parchment paper.
10. Spread filling evenly onto dough.
11. Slowly roll dough into a tight spiral, releasing the parchment paper as you progress.
12. Slice spiraled log into 9-10 rolls and place each on a parchment lined baking sheet.
13. Place sheet in oven and bake for 23-25 minutes, or until rolls are golden brown.
14. Let cool a bit before eating.

Nutrition Per Serving 210 calories, 9g total fat, 3g sat fat, 210mg sodium, 26g carbohydrates, 6g fiber, 8g sugar, 6g protein

Tip or fact: These cinnamon rolls go extremely well with caramel sauce or chocolate sauce.

Key Lime Pie Parfait

by Ashley Arpel Greenwald

| Medium | Kid Friendly | Gluten Free | 4 Servings |

Tangy, sweet and creamy! The perfect midday pick me up!

Ingredients

2 medium avocados
½ c + 2 Tbsp lime juice
2 Tbsp pure maple syrup
2 Tbsp coconut cream
½ tsp vanilla extract
½ c unsalted/peeled pistachios
½ c pitted dates

Directions

1. Gather all ingredients.
2. Place pistachios in the bowl of a food processor or blender. Process until the nuts are ground. Pour into a medium bowl and set aside.
3. Place pitted dates in the bowl of a food processor or blender. Process until a thick paste consistency is achieved.
4. Scoop into medium bowl containing pistachios and begin mixing together using your hands. Your mixture will have a cookie dough consistency. When completely combined, set aside.
5. Cut both avocados in half lengthwise so that each pit is exposed. Use a large spoon to scoop out pits from both avocados. Discard pits.
6. Scoop out the flesh of both avocados into the bowl of a food processor or blender. Add lime juice and blend until pureed.
7. Add remaining ingredients and blend for 2-3 minutes.
8. There are a plethora of different glasses/bowls to choose from when it comes to creating this parfait. Feel free to use what you already have in your pantry, however, make sure it is shallow enough so you can eat out of it.
9. Fill the glass with 2 tablespoons of crust mixture. Use your hands to firmly press the mixture into the glass.
10. Fill the remainder of the glass with filling mixture.
11. Repeat process with all glasses.
12. Top with sliced lime or pistachio crumbles and serve immediately.

Sensational Sweets

Nutrition Per Serving 370 calories, 23g total fat, 4.5g sat fat, 15mg sodium, 42g carbohydrates, 10g fiber, 25g sugar, 6g protein

Tip or fact: Use the filling of this parfait as a hair masque! Avocados are rich in fatty amino acids that will lock in moisture while the lime juice will refresh and brighten color!

Shopping list

Produce
☐ 2 medium avocados
☐ 5-6 limes
☐ 5 dates

Packaged
☐ pure maple syrup
☐ vanilla extract
☐ unsalted/peeled pistachios

Refrigerated or Frozen
☐ coconut cream

Maple Marshmallows

by Ashley Arpel Greenwald

Medium | **Gluten Free** | **16 Servings**

I am not the only person who pretended the marshmallows in my hot cocoa were cotton candy clouds, right?

Ingredients

1 can unsalted garbanzo beans
1 Tbsp vanilla extract
½ tsp cream of tartar
¾ c water
1 Tbsp agar powder
1 c maple sugar

Directions

1. Preheat oven to 250 °F.
2. Gather all ingredients.
3. Open can of garbanzo beans and drain out all liquid over a medium size bowl. This liquid is aquafaba. Transfer garbanzo beans to a sealed container and place in the refrigerator, saving them for another recipe.
4. Pour ½ cup aquafaba into a large mixing bowl and add vanilla extract and cream of tartar. Mix using an electric mixer until a thick and fluffy consistency is reached. Set aside.
5. In a small pot over medium heat, bring water and agar powder to a boil. When mixture begins to thicken, add maple sugar. Continue to stir over medium heat for 2 minutes.
6. After 2 minutes, remove sugar mixture from heat and pour into aquafaba mixture. Use electric mixer on high to combine. Mix for another 3-5 minutes.
7. Immediately pour mixture into a nonstick 9x6 or 8x8 baking dish. Let sit at room temperature for at least 30 minutes.
8. After 30 minutes, remove marshmallow block from baking dish and slice into small individual cubes.
9. Place cubes in a larger baking dish so that they are not touching each other and bake for 20 minutes.
10. When done, turn the oven off, but do not remove the marshmallows. Let them sit for another 20 minutes in the diluting heat.
11. Best served in hot cocoa!

Nutrition Per Serving 170 calories, 0g total fat, 0g sat fat, 20mg sodium, 37g carbohydrates, 2g fiber, 25g sugar, 3g protein

Storage: Store in an airtight glass container for up to 3 days.

Tip or fact: Agar powder is a tasteless alternative to gelatin that is free of gluten. You can find agar powder in health food stores, Asian markets and online.

Shopping list

Packaged
☐ 1 can unsalted garbanzo beans
☐ vanilla extract
☐ maple sugar

Seasonings and Spices
☐ cream of tartar
☐ agar powder

Peanut Butter Banana Pudding
by Ashley Arpel Greenwald

Easy | **Gluten Free** | **2 Servings**

Fuel your body in the morning with this protein packed pudding!

Ingredients

2 medium ripe bananas
4 Tbsp creamy peanut butter
¼ c unsweetened almond milk
½ tsp ground cinnamon

Directions

1. Gather all ingredients.
2. Peel both bananas and place them in a blender or the bowl of a food processor.
3. Add remaining ingredients and process until completely blended.
4. Serve immediately.
5. Top with sliced almonds, raisins or cacao nibs for some crunch.

Nutrition Per Serving 150 calories, 9g total fat, 1.5g sat fat, 80mg sodium, 17g carbohydrates, 2g fiber, 9g sugar, 4g protein

Storage: Store in an airtight glass container for 1 day.

Tip or fact: The two most popular types of cinnamon are Ceylon and Cassia. It comes from the bark of a tree which grows up to 60 feet tall.

Sensational Sweets

Shopping list

Produce
☐ 2 medium ripe bananas

Packaged
☐ creamy peanut butter

Refrigerated or Frozen
☐ unsweetened almond milk

Seasonings and Spices
☐ ground cinnamon

Shortbread Cookies

by Ashley Arpel Greenwald

Medium | **Kid Friendly** | **Gluten Free** | **10-12 Servings**

Ever so sweet. Ever so decadent. Ever so subtle. These shortbread cookies will become a staple at your parties, book club and all other get togethers!

Ingredients

2 c millet flour
½ c date syrup
½ c creamy almond butter
1 tsp vanilla extract

Directions

1. Preheat oven to 350°F.
2. Gather all ingredients.
3. Line a cutting board with parchment paper. Set aside.
4. Using your hands, mix all ingredients together in a large bowl until completely combined.
5. Roll all dough into a ball and place on the lined cutting board.
6. Place another piece of parchment on top of the dough and roll out with a rolling pin. About ½ inch high.
7. Remove top layer of parchment and use a cookie cutter to cut out cookies.
8. Place cookies on a parchment lined cookie sheet.
9. Use a fork to gently press down on the edges of each cookie, creating a border.
10. Bake for 12-14 minutes.

Nutrition Per Serving 180 calories, 8g total fat, 1g sat fat, 30mg sodium, 23g carbohydrates, 2g fiber, 4g sugar, 5g protein

Storage: Store in an airtight glass container for 3 days.

Ingredient Swap: Swap millet flour with oat flour or almond flour.

Tip or fact: Shortbread is a traditional Scottish biscuit usually served with tea, so grab your kettle and start pouring! It's tea time! Shortbread is naturally crumbly, but if you'd like a softer cookie, add 2 tbsp applesauce to dough mixture prior to rolling into a ball and placing on cutting board.

Shopping list

Packaged
☐ millet flour
☐ date syrup
☐ creamy almond butter
☐ vanilla extract

Sticky Strawberry Donuts

by Ashley Arpel Greenwald

Medium | **Kid Friendly** | **Gluten Free** | **12 Servings**

You DoNut understand ... this recipe is divine!

Ingredients

Donut Ingredients:

¼ c frozen strawberries, pureed
1 can garbanzo beans, unsalted
½ c unsweetened almond milk
½ c extra virgin olive oil
1 Tbsp lemon juice
2 c sweet white rice flour
1 c maple sugar
1½ tsp baking powder

Glaze Ingredients:

1 can garbanzo beans, unsalted
2 Tbsp strawberry puree
½ tsp vanilla extract
3 Tbsp maple sugar
¼ tsp cream of tartar

Shopping list

Produce
☐ 1 lemon

Packaged
☐ 2 cans garbanzo beans, unsalted
☐ ½ c extra virgin olive oil
☐ sweet white rice flour
☐ maple sugar
☐ baking powder
☐ vanilla extract

Refrigerated or Frozen
☐ frozen strawberries
☐ unsweetened almond milk

Seasonings and Spices
☐ cream of tartar

Directions

1. Preheat oven to 375°F.
2. Defrost strawberries for at least 10 minutes.
3. Gather remaining donut ingredients.
4. Open can of garbanzo beans and drain out all liquid over a medium size bowl. This liquid is aquafaba. Transfer garbanzo beans to a sealed container and place in the refrigerator, saving them for another recipe.
5. Measure and pour ¼ cup + 1 tablespoon aquafaba into a large mixing bowl. Add almond milk and olive oil. Mix with a whisk and set aside.
6. Place lemon juice and 8-10 defrosted strawberries in the bowl of a food processor or blender and process until completely pureed. Pour into aquafaba mixture and whisk thoroughly.
7. Add sweet white rice flour, maple sugar and baking powder. Whisk again.
8. Use a spoon to scoop mixture out of the bowl and into a nonstick donut pan. Fill each donut cup just under its full capacity. (A little more than ¾ high)
9. Place pans in the oven and bake for 15 minutes.
10. When donuts are done, remove from oven and allow them to cool for at least 20 minutes.
11. While the donuts are baking, gather the glaze ingredients.
12. Measure out 1/2 cup aquafaba into a large mixing bowl. If you don't have enough from the donuts, open another can of garbanzo beans.
13. Add remaining glaze ingredients into the large mixing bowl.
14. Mix with an electric hand mixer until a smooth whipped cream consistency is reached. (About 5-6 minutes)
15. Once the donuts have cooled enough, spread glaze on top of each donut and serve immediately.

Sensational Sweets

Nutrition Per Serving 260 calories, 10g total fat, 1g sat fat, 10mg sodium, 41g carbohydrates, 1g fiber, 13g sugar, 2g protein

Storage: Store in an airtight glass container in the refrigerator for 1 day.

Ingredient Swap: Swap sweet white rice flour for flour of choice, but be cautious as some flours are not gluten free.

Strawberry Soft Serve Ice Cream
by Ashley Arpel Greenwald

| Easy | Kid Friendly | Gluten Free | 2 Servings |

Bring the tropics into your kitchen with this sweet and tangy dessert!

Ingredients
3 medium bananas, frozen
½ c strawberries, frozen
1 Tbsp vanilla extract

Directions
1. Gather all ingredients.
2. Peel and slice all 3 bananas.
3. Place slices in a glass container, cover and freeze for at least 2 hours or overnight.
4. When the bananas are completely frozen remove them from the freezer and transfer them to a blender or the bowl of a food processor.
5. Add frozen strawberries and vanilla extract and process until a smooth soft serve consistency is reached.
6. Scoop ice cream into a bowl and serve immediately.

Nutrition Per Serving 350 calories, 1.5g total fat, 0g sat fat, 5mg sodium, 88g carbohydrates, 11g fiber, 47g sugar, 4g protein

Storage: Store in an airtight glass container in the freezer.

Tip or fact: We are always told bananas are high in potassium, but did you know that strawberries are too? Strawberries are also full of Vitamin C which supports immune health and clear skin! Sign me up!

Shopping list

Produce
☐ 3 medium bananas

Packaged
☐ vanilla extract

Refrigerated or Frozen
☐ frozen strawberries

Very Berry Crumble

by Ashley Arpel Greenwald

Medium | **Kid Friendly** | **5-6 Servings**

There's something about this crumble that makes me instantly think of the holiday season! Share a slice with someone you love!

Ingredients

Filling Ingredients:
2½ c frozen strawberries
1 c frozen blackberries
½ c brown coconut sugar
½ tsp vanilla extract
1 tsp lemon juice
4 Tbsp chia seeds

Crust & Topping Ingredients:
1 c + 1 Tbsp whole rolled oats
1 c + 1 Tbsp whole wheat pastry flour
½ c brown coconut sugar
1 Tbsp ground cinnamon
¾ c + 1 Tbsp cashew butter

Directions

1. Preheat oven to 350°F.
2. Gather all filling ingredients.
3. Place frozen strawberries and blackberries in a large skillet and sauté over medium heat. Cover for 6-8 minutes, stirring occasionally.
4. When fruit is tender and its juices begin to bubble, add ½ cup brown coconut sugar. Continue to heat for 10 minutes. Cover and stir occasionally.
5. After 10 minutes, remove mixture from heat and transfer to the bowl of a food processor blender. Process until pureed.
6. Pour mixture into a medium bowl and add vanilla extract, lemon juice and chia seeds. Mix and set aside for 20 minutes.
7. Gather crust and topping ingredients.
8. Pour 1 cup whole rolled oats, 1 cup whole wheat pastry flour and ½ cup brown coconut sugar into a medium sized mixing bowl. Add cinnamon and ¾ cup cashew butter. Mix with your hands.
9. Split crumble mixture in half. Pour 1 half of crumble mixture into a nonstick casserole dish and press down firmly. I used a 9x6 casserole dish.
10. Evenly pour and spread entire fruit mixture on top.
11. Lastly, add 1 tablespoon each of whole rolled oats, brown coconut flour and cashew butter to remaining crumble mixture. Mix with your hands and place on top of fruit filling.
12. Place in oven and bake for 1 hour.
13. Best served warm with hugs and kisses!

Sensational Sweets

Shopping list

Produce
□ 1 lemon

Packaged
□ brown coconut sugar
□ vanilla extract
□ chia seeds
□ whole rolled oats
□ whole wheat pastry flour
□ cashew butter

Refrigerated or Frozen
□ frozen strawberries
□ frozen blackberries

Seasonings and Spices
□ ground cinnamon

Nutrition Per Serving 390 calories, 7g total fat, 1g sat fat, 20mg sodium, 74g carbohydrates, 12g fiber, 28g sugar, 9g protein

Storage: Store in an airtight glass container in the refrigerator for 2 days.

Parsley

Thyme

Anise

Bay Leaf

Arugula

Mint

Sage

Vanilla

Charming Chocolates

Terragon

Rosemary

Dill

Cinnamon

Ginger

Almond Joy Energy Bites

by Kelley Williamson

Easy | **Kid Friendly** | **Gluten Free** | **10 Servings**

Ooohey Gooey Chocolate. Enjoy fresh or frozen!

Ingredients

1 c rolled oats
1 tsp vanilla
2 Tbsp cacao powder
2 Tbsp coconut flakes
2 Tbsp agave syrup
2 Tbsp maple syrup

Directions

1. Gather all ingredients.
2. In a large bowl mix all ingredients and then place (covered) in the refrigerator and let chill for 1 hour or so.
3. Bring out the bowl and then with your hands or a small ice cream scoop and make small balls with the ingredients.
4. Place on a parchment linked baking sheet.
5. Either eat them fresh or place in the freezer on a parchment lined baking sheet.
6. After frozen, place in an airtight glass container, and enjoy as a frozen candy bar.

Nutrition Per Serving 120 calories, 2g total fat, 1g sat fat, 0mg sodium, 21g carbohydrates, 2g fiber, 9g sugar, 3g protein

Storage: Store in an airtight glass container in the freezer.

Ingredient Swap: Add any ingredients that your kids would like, nuts, peanut butter or dried fruit.

Tip or fact: Remember to make many different flavors and freeze them. This is a great snack for when you are tired and hungry or when your kids come home from school.

Shopping list

Packaged
□ rolled oats
□ vanilla
□ cacao powder
□ coconut flakes
□ agave syrup
□ maple syrup

Banana Caramel Chocolates
by Laura Salyer

Easy | **Gluten Free** | **2-3 Serving**

A healthy, plant nutritious alternative to a popular favorite candy bar.

Ingredients

Banana Date Caramel:
12 Medjool dates, pitted
1 medium banana
2 Tbsp peanut butter
½ vanilla pod, scraped
2 Tbsp water or any plant-based milk
1 Tbsp flax meal
Toasted Pecan Garnish:
12 whole toasted pecans, optional

Chocolate Coating:
7 ½ Tbsp coconut oil
5 Tbsp unsweetened cacao powder
4 Tbsp pure maple syrup
pinch sea salt

Shopping list

Produce
□ 1 medium banana

Packaged
□ 12 Medjool dates, pitted
□ peanut butter
□ flax meal
□ 12 whole toasted pecans
□ coconut oil
□ unsweetened cacao powder
□ pure maple syrup

Refrigerated or Frozen
□ plant-based milk, optional

Seasonings and Spices
□ 1 vanilla pod
□ sea salt

Directions

1. Preheat oven to 350°F broil.
2. Gather all ingredients.
3. Combine pitted dates, banana, peanut butter (or other nut/seed butter of choice), vanilla bean paste, water, and flax meal in the bowl of a food processor. Process until smooth. If too dry, add ½ tablespoon at a time of liquid of choice until smooth consistency is reached.
4. Once smooth, scrape caramel into a greased glass dish or silicone baking mold and cover. Place in freezer for at least 2 hours.
5. Spread pecans on baking sheet and place in oven. Broil for 2-3 minutes, watching very closely to avoid burning.
6. Remove pecans from oven when slightly browned and fragrant. Set aside to cool.
7. Heat coconut oil in a small saucepan over low heat for 45 seconds or place in a microwavable bowl and melt in the microwave for 30 seconds. Heat until oil is completely liquified.
8. Add cacao powder and maple syrup. Stir until completely smooth. Set aside.
9. Remove caramel from freezer and turn out onto a large parchment lined cutting board.
10. Slice caramel into desired size and/or shape. Recipe usually makes 8-10 small caramels.
11. Once sliced, use a for or toothpick to gently dip each caramel into the chocolate coating.
12. Place back on parchment paper and top with toasted pecans and sea salt.
13. Once garnished, place caramel candies back in the freezer for 10-20 minutes, until desired hardness is achieved.

Charming Chocolates

Nutrition Per Serving 250 calories, 15g total fat, 9g sat fat, 50mg sodium, 30g carbohydrates, 3g fiber, 23g sugar, 2g protein

Storage: Store in an airtight glass container in the refrigerator for up to 3 days, or frozen for up to a month, but make sure to keep them in the refrigerator until you are ready to serve as the coconut oil coating may melt relatively quickly.

Tip or fact: Swap peanut butter for cashew butter sunflower butter. It is also possible to leave these ingredients out altogether, and then the banana-date flavor will shine through. Swap cacao powder with cocoa powder.

Chocolate Bread

by Jyl Steinback

Easy | **8 Servings**

Wow! This bread is beyond amazing!

Ingredients

2 tsp yeast
3½ c bread flour
1 tsp date sugar
1 tsp Himalaya salt
2 Tbsp unsweetened cocoa powder
1½ c chocolate almond milk
1 banana
½ c oatmeal
¼ c applesauce
¾ c craisins
¾ c chocolate chips

Directions

1. Gather all ingredients.
2. Add ingredients in the order suggested by the bread machine manufacturer and follow baking instructions provided in the manual.

Nutrition Per Serving 260 calories, 4.5g total fat, 2g sat fat, 150mg sodium, 51g carbohydrates, 3g fiber, 16g sugar, 8g protein

Storage: Freeze but be sure to slice the bread first.

Ingredient Swap: You can swap any dried fruits.

Tip or fact: When cooking with date sugar, replace brown or white sugar 1:1 in recipes. If baking with date sugar, you will need to reduce the flour amount sometimes up to 25% to account for the fiber in dates.

Shopping list

Produce
☐ 1 banana

Packaged
☐ yeast
☐ bread flour
☐ date sugar
☐ unsweetened cocoa powder
☐ oatmeal
☐ applesauce
☐ craisins
☐ chocolate chips

Refrigerated or Frozen
☐ chocolate almond milk

Seasonings and Spices
☐ Himalaya salt

Chocolate Chia Seed Pudding
by Reuel Rodriguez

| Easy | Kid Friendly | Gluten Free | 6 Servings |

This pudding recipe is not only great to make for kids, but it's also packed with nutrients!

Ingredients
¼ c cacao powder
½ tsp ground cinnamon
1½ c oat milk
3-5 Tbsp date syrup
¼ c chia seeds
½ Tbsp alcohol free vanilla extract

Directions
1. Gather all ingredients.
2. Mix cacao powder and cinnamon in a small bowl.
3. Slowly add milk and mix until a paste is formed.
4. Mix in 3 tablespoons date syrup. If sweet enough, do not add more. If not sweet enough, add remaining 2 tablespoons.
5. Finally, add chia seeds and vanilla extract. Mix thoroughly.
6. Cover and refrigerate for at least 4 hours. Enjoy.

Nutrition Per Serving 190 calories, 4.5g total fat, 0g sat fat, 45mg sodium, 35g carbohydrates, 6g fiber, 22g sugar, 4g protein

Storage: Store in an airtight glass container in the refrigerator for up to 3 days.

Ingredient Swap: Swap oat milk for coconut milk for a creamier consistency.

Tip or fact: For a tiny little seed, chia is packed with great nutrition, like fiber, iron and calcium.

Charming Chocolates

Shopping list

Packaged
☐ cacao powder
☐ date syrup
☐ chia seeds
☐ alcohol free vanilla extract

Seasonings and Spices
☐ ground cinnamon

Chocolate Protein Balls

by Carolina Maturana

Easy | **Gluten Free** | **6-7 Servings**

Ooohey Gooey Chocolate. Enjoy fresh or frozen!

Ingredients

1 c whole grain oats
1 c unsalted pumpkin seeds
3/4 c unsweetened cacao powder
1 c pitted Medjool dates

Directions

1. Gather all ingredients.
2. Place oats and pumpkin seeds into a blender or the bowl of a food processor and pulse until completely ground.
3. Add cacao powder and dates. Pulse until a mixture is formed that sticks together like dough.
4. Carefully transfer mixture from food processor to a parchment lined cutting board.
5. Use your hands to divide and roll dough into small bite size pieces. If the dough is too sticky, add more oats 1 tablespoon at a time.
6. Plate and serve immediately.

Nutrition Per Serving 230 calories, 4g total fat, 0.5g sat fat, 0mg sodium, 44g carbohydrates, 7g fiber, 17g sugar, 8g protein

Storage: Store in an airtight glass container in the refrigerator for up to 2 days.

Shopping list

Packaged
☐ whole grain oats
☐ unsalted pumpkin seeds
☐ unsweetened cacao powder
☐ pitted Medjool dates

Chocolate Pudding

by Ashley Arpel Greenwald

| Easy | Kid Friendly | Gluten Free | 2 Servings |

Chocolate pudding just got healthy. Hide from your kids!

Ingredients

2 medium ripe bananas
4 Tbsp creamy peanut butter
¼ c unsweetened almond milk
¼ c unsweetened cocoa powder
¼ tsp vanilla extract

Directions

1. Gather all ingredients.
2. Peel both bananas and place them in a blender or the bowl of a food processor.
3. Add remaining ingredients and process until completely blended.
4. Serve immediately.

Nutrition Per Serving 160 calories, 90g total fat, 2g sat fat, 80mg sodium, 20g carbohydrates, 4g fiber, 9g sugar, 5g protein

Storage: Store in an airtight glass container in the refrigerator for 1 days.

Tip or fact: Best served as a dip or frosting for Ashley's Cacao Chip Cookies, recipe on p. 291!

Charming Chocolates

Shopping list

Produce
☐ 2 medium ripe bananas

Packaged
☐ creamy peanut butter
☐ unsweetened cocoa powder
☐ vanilla extract

Refrigerated or Frozen
☐ unsweetened almond milk

Chocolate Soft Serve Ice Cream by Ashley Arpel Greenwald

| Easy | Gluten Free | 2 Servings |

Ice cream is a way of life!

Ingredients

3 medium bananas, frozen
¼ c unsweetened cocoa powder
1 Tbsp vanilla extract

Directions

1. Gather all ingredients.
2. Peel and slice all 3 bananas.
3. Place slices in an airtight glass container, and freeze for at least 2 hours or overnight.
4. When the bananas are completely frozen remove them from the freezer and transfer them to a blender or the bowl of a food processor.
5. Add cocoa powder and vanilla extract and process until a smooth soft serve consistency is reached.
6. Scoop ice cream into a bowl and serve immediately.

Nutrition Per Serving 380 calories, 4g total fat, 2g sat fat, 10mg sodium, 94g carbohydrates, 17g fiber, 44g sugar, 8g protein

Tip or fact: Studies have shown that eating chocolate can improve your mood!

Shopping list

Produce
☐ 3 medium bananas

Packaged
☐ unsweetened cocoa powder
☐ vanilla extract

Gooey Banana Chocolate Brownies by Ashley Arpel Greenwald

Easy | **16 Servings**

📷

Ladies and gentlemen, I give you your date this Friday night!

Ingredients

2 medium ripe bananas
1 c spelt flour
1 c unsweetened cocoa powder
1 tsp baking soda
½ tsp cinnamon
1 c maple syrup
1 c unsweetened almond milk
¼ c olive oil

Directions

1. Preheat oven to 350°F.
2. Gather all ingredients.
3. Blend both bananas in a blender or food processor until pureed.
4. Pour banana puree into a large bowl and mix in spelt flour, cocoa powder and the rest of the dry ingredients. Use a wooden spoon.
5. Add all wet ingredients and mix thoroughly.
6. Pour mixture into a medium nonstick baking pan (11x9x2) and bake for 20-22 minutes.
7. Remove from oven and wait 15 minutes before slicing and devouring.
8. Best served warm with hot cocoa!

Nutrition Per Serving 140 calories, 5g total fat, 1g sat fat, 270mg sodium, 26g carbohydrates, 3g fiber, 15g sugar, 2g protein

Charming Chocolates

Storage: Store in an airtight glass container in the refrigerator for up to 2 days.

Ingredient Swap: Swap spelt flour for whole wheat flour.

Tip or fact: Olive oil is very high in oleic acid which is helpful in reducing blood pressure.

Shopping list

Produce
☐ 3 medium ripe bananas

Packaged
☐ spelt flour
☐ unsweetened cocoa powder
☐ baking soda
☐ maple syrup
☐ olive oil

Refrigerated or Frozen
☐ unsweetened almond milk

Seasonings and Spices
☐ cinnamon

Gluten Free Chocolate Chip Cookies
by Nele Liivlaid

| Easy | Gluten Free | 20 Servings |

These cookies are perfect for those (frequent) occasions when you desperately need to have a very chocolaty bite. Believe me, you won't be disappointed!

Ingredients

- 1.8 oz. cacao paste
- 2 Tbsp coconut puree
- 6 Tbsp + 2 tsp oat bran
- ½ c rolled oats
- ¼ tsp Himalayan salt
- 2 tsp cinnamon
- 2 Tbsp cocoa powder
- ½ c carob powder
- 3 Tbsp date sugar
- ½ c + ⅕ c oat milk

Directions

1. Preheat oven to 350°F.
2. Gather all ingredients.
3. In a bowl, mix together the dry ingredients: oat bran, jumbo oats, carob, cocoa powder, salt, cinnamon and date sugar.
4. Add oat milk and mix well. Let soak for half an hour until you have a thick mass.
5. Melt ⅔ of the cacao mass and mix it with coconut puree.
6. Chop the reminder ⅓ of the cacao mass.
7. Combine together chopped cacao mass, melted cacao mass/coconut puree and oatmeal mix.
8. Form 20 cookies (about 0.7 oz. each) and place them on baking sheet lined with parchment paper. They will stick a bit to your fingers!
9. Bake for 16 minutes.
10. Remove from oven and let cool.

Nutrition Per Serving 50 calories, 2.5g total fat, 1.5g sat fat, 25mg sodium, 7g carbohydrates, 2g fiber, 2g sugar, 1g protein

Storage: Store in an airtight glass container in the refrigerator for up to 2 days.

Ingredient Swap: Feel free to use dark chocolate chips instead of chopped cacao paste.

Tip or fact: You might melt all the cacao mass and combine it with oatmeal mixture. This way the batter wouldn't stick to your fingers at all! You may add more or less date sugar depending on how sweet you like them.

Shopping list

Packaged
- ☐ cacao paste
- ☐ coconut puree
- ☐ oat bran
- ☐ rolled oats
- ☐ cocoa powder
- ☐ carob powder
- ☐ date sugar

Refrigerated or Frozen
- ☐ oat milk

Seasonings and Spices
- ☐ Himalayan salt
- ☐ cinnamon

Tangy Orange Munchkins
by Jyl Steinback

| Easy | Kid Friendly | Gluten Free | 10-12 Servings |

Take a couple of these on the road for a quick energizing bite!

Ingredients
½ Tbsp orange zest
½ c raw almonds, crushed
2 c Medjool Dates, pitted
½ c raw cacao powder
1 Tbsp chia seeds
3 Tbsp fresh orange juice

Directions
1. Gather all ingredients.
2. Use a fruit zester to grate the skin of the orange into a small bowl. Set aside.
3. Pour crushed almonds into a medium bowl and set aside.
4. Place all dates in a blender or bowl of a food processor. Process until a paste is formed. If paste begins to stick to the walls of the bowl, scrape it down in between pulses.
5. Add cacao powder, chia seeds, and orange juice. Process again for about 1-2 minutes until completely combined.
6. Transfer mixture to a medium sized bowl.
7. Use your hands to form individual balls and gently roll each one in the bowl of chopped almonds, coating completely.
8. Place on a large dish.
9. Continue this process until the mixture is gone and serve immediately.

Charming Chocolates

Nutrition Per Serving 150 calories, 5g total fat, 0g sat fat, 0mg sodium, 26g carbohydrates, 4g fiber, 20g sugar, 3g protein

Storage: Store in an airtight glass container in the refrigerator for up to 2 days.

Ingredient Swap: Swap crushed almonds for crushed unsalted pistachios.

Tip or fact: Great source of energy!

Shopping list

Produce
☐ 1 orange

Packaged
☐ raw almonds
☐ Medjool Dates
☐ raw cacao powder
☐ chia seeds

Refrigerated or Frozen
☐ fresh orange juice

Nibbles In The Classroom

Nibbles in the Classroom are quick and easy recipes for kids to get involved in the kitchen, or in this case, the classroom. We've developed these kid-friendly recipes with minimal preparation skill requirements and maximum kid fun. We commonly hear that kids do not like veggies or they are picky eaters. This partially explains why most kids (and adults too) are not eating the recommended levels of fruits, veggies, nuts, seeds, whole grains and legumes. Failure to make these recommendations can lead to nutrition deficiencies which is even more impactful on growth and development for kids and young adults.

It is important to know that kids respond better to trying new things when they are involved in the decisions, so why not take some time to help make health more fun. Facts about kids:

- If a child helps grow fruits and vegetables, they are more curious about what it will taste like and are more likely to try it.
- If a child helps shop for fruits and vegetables, they are more likely to eat it when prepared at home.
- If a child is given the opportunity to create a dish, they are more likely to try it.

See a theme here? When kids are involved in food decisions, it can lead to knowledge and a lifetime of healthy behaviors.

Today, close to half (40%) of calories for ages 2 to 18 years is from added sugar and solid fats, also known as empty calories? The leading sources of calories include soda, fruit drinks, desserts (think ice cream and cookies) and pizza.1 Furthermore, 30% of the vegetables consumed by children ages 2 to 18 years is in the form of French fries or potato chips,2 which has no nutritional benefit from eating a potato after it is processed out. Our dishes will help increase essential nutrition at meal and snack time to help growing bodies. It can also reduce extra calories that kids do not need from foods devoid of nutrition. You will be surprised to see some desserts also included, but know that they also bring nutrition from the ingredients we use. Afterall, we know kids like dessert. Let's give them what they want with the bonus of good nutrition. Now that is thinking outside of the lunchbox!

When it comes to food allergies, we know that some schools and parents are struggling with nuts of any kind. Not to worry. We purposely created recipes to not include peanuts or tree nuts (unless of course you choose to add them on your own). When shopping for ingredients, we also recommend looking at allergen statements to ensure that the ingredients in our recipes are truly free of nut.

Happy nibbling on these delicious and plant nutritious recipes!

Sources

1. Reedy J, Krebs-Smith SM. Dietary sources of energy, solid fats, and added sugars among children and adolescents in the United States. Journal of the American Dietetic Association, Volume 110, Issue 10, Pages 1477-1484, October 2010. Available at: http://www.ncbi.nlm.nih.gov/pubmed/20869486.

2. Vital Signs Weekly: Fruit and Vegetable Intake Among Children — United States, 2003–2010. Weekly. August 8, 2014 / 63(31);671-676 On August 5, 2014, this report was posted as an MMWR Early Release on the MMWR website (http://www.cdc.gov/mmwr). As viewed on June 2, 2019 at: https://www.cdc.gov/mmwr/preview/mmwrhtml/mm6331a3.htm

Ants on a Log

by Ashley Arpel Greenwald

| Easy | Kid Friendly | Gluten Free | 3 Servings |

A classic snack with a little twist to make it 100% nut free!

Ingredients

1 celery stalk
3 Tbsp sunflower butter
2 Tbsp unsweetened raisins

Directions

1. Gather all ingredients.
2. Cut each celery stick into thirds creating little logs.
3. Fill each log with ½ teaspoon sunflower butter. If you prefer more, go for it!
4. Top sunflower butter with 3-4 raisins and enjoy!

Nutrition Per Serving 120 calories, 9g total fat, 1g sat fat, 65mg sodium, 9g carbohydrates, 1g fiber, 5g sugar, 3g protein

Ingredient Swap: Swap raisins for craisins and really have a party!

Tip or fact: Did you know that one "stick" from a full celery stalk is called a leafstalk?!

Nibbles in the Classroom

Shopping list

Produce
☐ 1 celery stalk

Packaged
☐ unsweetened raisins

Refrigerated or Frozen
☐ sunflower butter

Apple Donuts

by Ashley Arpel Greenwald

Easy | **Kid Friendly** | **Gluten Free** | **6 Servings**

A fun and fast no bake donut? Yes, please!

Ingredients

2 Granny Smith apples
2 lemons, juiced, optional
4 Tbsp sunflower butter
½ c dried blueberries
½ c cacao nibs
4 Tbsp favorite jam, optional

Directions

1. Gather all ingredients.
2. A parent, guardian or teacher should remove the core of both apples with a corer.
3. The adult will then use a large serrated knife to slice apples from top to bottom creating a round donut shape with a hole in the middle. 2 apples makes about 10-12 donut slices
4. If preparing at home to take somewhere, slice both lemons in half crosswise and squeeze each half 3-4 times over a small bowl to release the juice. Use a basting brush to spread the lemon juice on both sides of the apple donut. It is so fun to use your fingers as a basting brush. Be creative and have fun. The lemon juice is to prevent the apples from browning.
5. Place apple donuts in a covered glass container and place in the refrigerator until school time.
6. Spread sunflower butter on one side of each apple donut slice.
7. Top sunflower butter with dried blueberries, cacao nibs and jam if using.
8. Devour!

Nutrition Per Serving 130 calories, 6g total fat, 2.5g sat fat, 20mg sodium, 16g carbohydrates, 3g fiber, 10g sugar, 1g protein

Tip or fact: Did you know Granny Smith apples that stay on the tree until the leaf drops have a sweeter flavor and due to the high acid content, these apples do not turn brown after cutting as quickly as most other apple do.

Shopping list

Produce
☐ 2 Granny Smith apples
☐ 2 lemons

Packaged
☐ dried blueberries
☐ cacao nibs
☐ favorite jam, optional

Refrigerated or Frozen
☐ sunflower butter

Apple Turtles

by Ashley Arpel Greenwald

Medium | **Kid Friendly** | **Gluten Free** | **4 Servings**

Turtles are naturally slow creatures, but I bet you'll devour these yummy nibbles very fast!

Ingredients

2 Granny Smith apples
2 lemons, juiced, optional
½ c green grapes
¼ c cacao nibs
4 Tbsp unsalted sunflower butter

Directions

1. Gather all ingredients.
2. A parent, guardian or teacher should cut apples in half midway and set aside.
3. If preparing at home to take somewhere, slice both lemons in half crosswise and squeeze each half 3-4 times over a small bowl to release the juice. Use a basting brush to spread the lemon juice on both sides of the apple donut. It is so fun to use your fingers as a basting brush. Be creative and have fun. The lemon juice is to prevent the apples from browning.
4. Pour sunflower butter into a shallow dish and set aside.
5. Slice 3 grapes in half. Dip the flat side of the sliced grapes into sunflower butter and stick them to the apples creating arms, legs a tail and head for the turtle.
6. Dip 2 small cacao nibs in the sunflower butter and stick them to the "head grape" creating eyes.
7. Name your turtle. I named mine Mr. Green!
8. Eat immediately.

Nibbles in the Classroom

Nutrition Per Serving 230 calories, 14g total fat, 4g sat fat, 0mg sodium, 23g carbohydrate, 6g fiber, 13g total sugar, 3g protein

Tip or fact: Granny Smith apples are very tart. If you want, swap in another type of sweeter apple, like a gala or a yellow delicious.

Shopping list

Produce
☐ 2 Granny Smith apples
☐ 2 lemons
☐ green grapes

Packaged
☐ cacao nibs

Refrigerated or Frozen
☐ unsalted sunflower butter

Chocolate Bananas

by Jyl Steinback

| Easy | Kid Friendly | Gluten Free | 1 Serving |

The sweetest treat for anytime.

Ingredients

1 banana
2 Tbsp chocolate syrup no sugar

Directions

1. Gather all ingredients.
2. Take the banana and peel it – slice banana and put it into an airtight glass container and freeze.
3. When ready to eat, take it out of the freezer and drizzle the sugar free syrup over the bananas and enjoy.

Nutrition Per Serving 210 calories, 1g total fat, 0g sat fat, 30mg sodium, 52g carbohydrates, 3g fiber, 34g sugar, 2g protein

Storage: Store in an airtight glass container in the freezer.

Tip or fact: Did you know that the inside of a banana peel can help relieve itching from bug bite? Try it on your next mosquito bite!

Shopping list

Produce
☐ 1 banana

Packaged
☐ chocolate syrup no sugar

Chocolate & Fruit Covered Frozen Bananas by Kelley Williamson

Easy | **Kid Friendly** | **Gluten Free** | **8 Servings**

Hearty but Healthy all in one bite.

Ingredients

4 bananas

8 oz. chocolate chips, no dairy and very little oil

¼ c unsweetened shredded coconut

½ c strawberries

½ c blueberries

Directions

1. Gather all ingredients.
2. Slice the bananas crosswise and then skewer with either a popsicle stick or a heavy bamboo skewer and then place on a parchment lined baking sheet and freeze for at least 3 hours. You can also make this recipe by not freezing, but fun when frozen.
3. In a small mixing bowl, add the chocolate chips and melt in a microwave until creamy. You will want to microwave the chips right before you use them otherwise they harden and you will need to microwave again.
4. Prepare the fruit by dicing into small pieces and placing into separate bowls.
5. Place the unsweetened shredded coconut into a small bowl.
6. Take the bananas and first dip into the chocolate and spoon on chocolate if needed. Then quickly decorate with fruit and coconut and then place back on the parchment lined baking sheet.
7. Enjoy as soon as decorated.

Nibbles in the Classroom

Nutrition Per Serving 220 calories, 10g total fat, 7g sat fat, 0mg sodium, 36g carbohydrates, 4g fiber, 26g sugar, 2g protein

Storage: Store in an airtight glass container for 1-2 days in the freezer.

Ingredient Swap: Add in all types of dried or fresh fruit to make this more of a chocolate fruit treat. You can choose your favorite fruit or berry.

Tip or fact: Bananas are related to ginger. More than 1,000 varieties of bananas grow in 150 countries so enjoy your frozen banana treat with chocolate and your favorite fruit.

Shopping list

Produce
- [ ] 4 bananas
- [ ] blueberries
- [ ] strawberries

Packaged
- [ ] 8 oz. chocolate chips, no dairy and very little oil
- [ ] unsweetened shredded coconut

Chocolate Truffles

by Ashley Arpel Greenwald

| Easy | Kid Friendly | Gluten Free | 8 Servings |

This NUT FREE snack will certainly bring a smile to a child's face ... even when they are at school!

Ingredients

1 c sunflower butter
¾ c pure maple syrup
5 Tbsp unsweetened cocoa powder
4 Tbsp oat flour
½ c cacao nibs

Directions

1. Gather all ingredients.
2. In a large bowl, mix all ingredients together using your hands.
3. Place bowl in the refrigerator for 20 minutes to cool and firm mixture.
4. After 20 minutes remove bowl from refrigerator and use your hands to roll dough into small individual balls and place on a large plate. Plate does not need to be parchment lined.
5. Refrigerate for at least 1 hour to firm.

Nutrition Per Serving 340 calories, 22g total fat, 4g sat fat, 115mg sodium, 34g carbohydrates, 5g fiber, 22g sugar, 8g protein

Ingredient Swap: Swap sunflower butter for nut butter of choice if no nut allergies are present.

Tip or fact: It takes 3 pounds of sunflower seeds to make one jar of sunbutter.

Shopping list

Packaged
☐ sunflower butter
☐ pure maple syrup
☐ unsweetened cocoa powder
☐ oat flour
☐ cacao nibs

Chocolate-Vanilla Swirl Chia Pudding
by Kelley Williamson

| Easy | Kid Friendly | Gluten Free | 4 Servings |

Talk about the perfect arts and crafts project!

Ingredients

Vanilla Pudding:
2 Tbsp chia seeds
1 c unsweetened soy milk
1 tsp vanilla
1 tsp agave

Chocolate Pudding:
2 Tbsp chia seeds
1 c unsweetened soy milk
1 tsp cacao powder

Garnish:
1 medium ripe banana

Directions

1. Gather all ingredients.
2. Place chia seeds in a medium mixing bowl. Top with remaining vanilla pudding ingredients and mix thoroughly using a wooden spoon. Cover with plastic wrap and place in the refrigerator for at least 2 hours.
3. Place chia seeds in a medium mixing bowl. Top with remaining chocolate pudding ingredients and mix thoroughly using a wooden spoon. Cover with plastic wrap and place in refrigerator for at least 2 hours.
4. After 2 hours have passed and the mixtures have thickened, remove both from the refrigerator.
5. Use a tablespoon to scoop 1 tbsp vanilla pudding into a small serving bowl. Now do the same with chocolate. Repeat this process 3-5 times, or until bowl is full.
6. Top with sliced banana and other fruit of choice.

Nutrition Per Serving 310 calories, 11g total fat, 1.5g sat fat, 130mg sodium, 41g carbohydrates, 9g fiber, 20g sugar, 12g protein

Nibbles in the Classroom

Storage: Store in an airtight glass container in the refrigerator for up to 2 days.

Ingredient Swap: Swap soy milk for almond milk or oat milk.

Tip or fact: Enjoy this for breakfast with the gingerbread granola or in the afternoon as a snack.

Shopping list

Produce
☐ 1 medium ripe banana

Packaged
☐ chia seeds
☐ vanilla
☐ agave
☐ cacao powder

Refrigerated or frozen
☐ unsweetened soy milk

Cinnamon Raisin Oatmeal Banana Bread by Jyl Steinback

Easy | **Kid Friendly** | **12 Servings**

A meal in a bread. I eat a slice every day. Won't you join me please . . .

Ingredients

2 tsp yeast
3½ c bread flour
1 tsp date sugar
1 tsp Himalayan salt
1 tsp cinnamon
½ c oatmeal
1½ c water
1 banana
¾ c craisins
¼ c applesauce
¼ c raisins
½ c almonds, optional

Directions

1. Gather all ingredients.
2. Cut banana in 4 and add along the sides of the breadmaker.
3. Add ingredients in the order suggested by the bread machine manufacturer and follow baking instructions provided in the manual.

Nutrition Per Serving 240 calories, 3.5g total fat, 0g sat fat, 130mg sodium, 45g carbohydrates, 3g fiber, 10g sugar, 8g protein

Storage: Slice the bread and then freeze.

Ingredient Swap: You can swap any dried fruits or nuts.

Tip or fact: I love this bread every morning with avocado and tomato. Please share what is your favorite way to eat it. It Is beyond amazing.

Shopping list

Produce
☐ 1 banana

Packaged
☐ yeast
☐ bread flour
☐ date sugar
☐ oatmeal
☐ craisins
☐ applesauce
☐ raisins
☐ almonds, optional

Refrigerated or Frozen
☐ Himalayan salt
☐ cinnamon

Coo-Coo for Coconut Bites
by Kelley Williamson

Easy | Kid Friendly | Gluten Free | 10 Servings

Enjoy just after making or frozen!

Ingredients
1 c whole rolled oats
1 tsp alcohol free vanilla extract
2 Tbsp cacao powder
2 Tbsp coconut flakes
2 Tbsp agave
2 Tbsp pure maple syrup

Directions
1. Gather all ingredients.
2. Place all ingredients into a large mixing bowl and use your hands or a spatula to combine.
3. Cover large bowl and place in refrigerator to chill for at least 1 hour.
4. After at least 1 hour, remove bowl from refrigerator and, once again, use your hands to scoop and roll mixture into individual balls.
5. When done rolling, place each ball on a parchment lined baking sheet.
6. Can be eaten instantly or placed in a freezer and eaten completely frozen!

Nutrition Per Serving 70 calories, 1g total fat, 0.5g sat fat, 0mg sodium, 12g carbohydrates, 1g fiber, 6g sugar, 2g protein

Storage: Store in an airtight glass container in the freezer.

Tip or fact: This is a great snack for when you are tired and hungry or when your kids come home from school.

Nibbles in the Classroom

Shopping list

Packaged
- [ ] whole rolled oats
- [ ] alcohol free vanilla extract
- [ ] cacao powder
- [ ] coconut flakes
- [ ] agave
- [ ] pure maple syrup

Eye Popping Fruit Kabobs

by Kelley Williamson

Easy | **Kid Friendly** | **Gluten Free** | **4 Servings**

Fruit on a skewer that you can take anywhere and enjoy.

Ingredients

1 lime
1 Tbsp agave syrup
1 tsp water
1 c strawberries
2 medium bananas

Directions

1. Gather all ingredients.
2. Slice the fruit into 1 inch pieces and be creative on how you slice the fruit. You can do rounds on the bananas or large diagonal slices, etc.
3. In a small bowl mix together the water and then zest in the rind of the lime and then juice the lime into the same bowl. Mix well.
4. After the skewers are made drizzle on the lime juice mixture and enjoy.

Nutrition Per Serving 90 calories, 0g total fat, 0g sat fat, 0mg sodium, 22g carbohydrates, 3g fiber, 13g sugar, 1g protein

Storage: Store in an airtight glass container in the refrigerator for 1-2 days.

Ingredient Swap: Add all types of fruit like grapes, watermelon, blackberries, kiwi, etc., especially ones that are in season.

Tip or fact: Fruit is wonderful on a hot day or as a sweet treat anytime of the day. Enjoy fruit on the go by placing them on a skewer and adding a lime drizzle.

Shopping list

Produce
- ☐ 2 medium bananas
- ☐ strawberries
- ☐ 1 lime

Packaged
- ☐ agave syrup

Fruit Bears

by Ashley Arpel Greenwald

| Easy | Kid Friendly | Gluten Free | 12 Servings |

Let's give a new meaning to playing with our food!

Ingredients

1 loaf whole grain bread
2 jars sunflower butter
2 bananas
3 c strawberries
1 c blueberries

Directions

1. Gather all ingredients.
2. Place 4 slices of bread on a cutting board. Use a circular cookie/dough/biscuit cutter or a glass cup to cut out circles from the bread. 1 bread slice usually produces 2 circle cut outs.
3. Spread sunflower butter on each circle.
4. Peel bananas and discard peels. Use a butter knife to slice peeled bananas into small circles.
5. Place 1 banana circle on the bottom center of each bread circle, sunflower butter side up.
6. Slice remaining banana circles in half, creating the "bear" ears.
7. Use two blueberries as eyes and one as a nose.
8. Slice strawberries into very thin "smiles" and place just under the blueberry nose.
9. Continue process so every child in class has at least 1-2 bears.
10. Eat with best friends!

Nibbles in the Classroom

Nutrition Per Serving 270 calories, 14g total fat, 1.5g sat fat, 180mg sodium, 31g carbohydrates, 2g fiber, 9g sugar, 4g protein

Tip or fact: Did you know according to some studies, blueberries have been part of the human diet for at least 13,000 years.

Shopping list

Produce
- 2 bananas
- strawberries
- blueberries

Packaged
- 1 loaf whole grain bread

Refrigerated or Frozen
- 2 jars sunflower butter

Healthy Popcorn Balls

by Jyl Steinback

Easy | Kid Friendly | Gluten Free | 8-10 Servings

These will remind you of your childhood and Halloween but a healthier version.

Ingredients

4 c popped popcorn, no oil
½ c rolled oats
¼ c chia seeds
½ c dates
1 Tbsp applesauce
1 tsp cinnamon

Directions

1. Gather all ingredients.
2. Pop the popcorn according to microwave instructions and set aside to cool.
3. In a large bowl add in the oats, chia seeds and cinnamon. Mix well.
4. Add in the popcorn and mix.
5. Smash the dates in a bowl and then mix with the applesauce to make it a thick liquid.
6. Add date mixture to the popcorn and then, if you are willing, put on a pair of gloves and then mix the ingredients with your hands. This will help to make sure that the date mixture is covering each piece of popcorn.
7. Form into small 2 inch balls, place on a baking sheet or in a bowl and enjoy.
8. These can be refrigerated until ready to enjoy.

Nutrition Per Serving 110 calories, 2g total fat, 0g sat fat, 45mg sodium, 22g carbohydrates, 2g fiber, 9g sugar, 2g protein

Storage: Store in an airtight glass container in the refrigerator for 1-2 days.

Ingredient Swap: You can add any other types of seeds or use agave instead of brown rice syrup. You can also add in dried cranberries or other types of low fat fruits.

Tip or fact: By adding in ground flax seeds and chia seeds you add in omega-3 fatty acids.

Shopping list

Packaged
☐ popcorn, no oil
☐ rolled oats
☐ chia seeds
☐ dates
☐ applesauce

Seasonings and Spices
☐ cinnamon

No Bake Chocolate Millet Crispy Treats
by Kelley Williamson

Easy | **Kid Friendly** | **Gluten Free** | **15 Servings**

Remember you Mom's No Bake Cookies? Then you will love these!

Ingredients
1 c chocolate chips, no dairy and very little oil
¼ c unsweetened shredded coconut
1¼ c puffed millet

Directions
1. Gather all ingredients.
2. In a large mixing bowl, add the chocolate chips and melt in a microwave until creamy. Remember to melt the chocolate chips right before you need them otherwise the chocolate will harden and you will need to place back in the microwave.
3. Fold in the shredded coconut and puffed millet and stir quickly but mix well.
4. Using a cookie scoop, scoop out each ball and then place on a parchment lined baking sheet, cover with Reynolds wrap and refrigerate after you make all the balls.
5. Enjoy immediately or refrigerate in an airtight glass container.

Nutrition Per Serving 110 calories, 2g total fat, 0g sat fat, 45mg sodium, 22g carbohydrates, 2g fiber, 9g sugar, 2g protein

Nibbles in the Classroom

Storage: Store in an airtight glass container in the refrigerator for 1-2 days.

Ingredient Swap: Add in all types of dried fruit to make this more of a chocolate fruit treat. You can also use other puffed cereal if you cannot find puffed millet.

Tip or fact: Puffed millet is a type of grain, usually sold as a breakfast cereal. In addition to being low in fat, millet is also gluten-free, making it a nutritious option for people who are gluten-intolerant or who have celiac disease.

Shopping list

Packaged
☐ chocolate chips, no dairy and very little oil
☐ unsweetened shredded coconut
☐ puffed millet

Seasonings and Spices
☐ cinnamon

No Bake Whole Grain Bars
by Ashley Arpel Greenwald

Easy | **Kid Friendly** | **Gluten Free** | **32 Servings**

Quick and easy classroom fun!

Ingredients

1 c sunflower butter
4-5 Tbsp pure maple syrup
3 c whole grain cereal
½ c cacao nibs, optional

Directions

1. Gather all ingredients.
2. Line an 8x8 baking pan with parchment paper. Set aside.
3. Pour sunflower butter and maple syrup into a large mixing bowl. Mix.
4. Pour cereal and cacao nibs on top of sunflower mixture and use either wooden spoon or hands to combine.
5. Transfer mixture into prepared pan and firmly press it in, spreading the mixture into each corner.
6. Cover and refrigerate for at least 1 hour.
7. Remove pan from refrigerator and lift parchment paper out of pan. Slice into squares and serve!

Nutrition Per Serving 90 calories, 6g total fat, 1g sat fat, 40mg sodium, 8g carbohydrates, 1g fiber, 3g sugar 2g protein

Tip or fact: Not all whole grain cereals are equal. Make sure to look for whole grain as the first ingredient and look for at least 3g fiber per serving on the Nutrition Facts label.

Shopping list

Packaged
☐ pure maple syrup
☐ whole grain cereal
☐ cacao nibs, optional

Refrigerated or Frozen
☐ sunflower butter

Peanut Butter Protein Balls

by Nele Liivlaid

Easy | **Kid Friendly** | **Gluten Free** | **20 Servings**

These rich and healthy grain-free plant based peanut butter protein balls that use no refined sugars or oils are so easy to throw together!

Ingredients

4 Tbsp coconut flour
3 Tbsp nut protein powder or fat-reduced nut flour
¼ tsp ginger powder
¼ tsp Himalayan salt
1 Tbsp + 1 tsp baobab powder
4 Tbsp carob powder
2 Tbsp cocoa powder
3.2 oz. additive-free peanut butter
3.5 oz. additive-free plant milk
2 Tbsp date sugar
1.06 oz. goji berries
0.2 oz. cacoa nibs

Directions

1. Gather all ingredients.
2. Coarsely chop the goji berries. Put aside.
3. Add all the ingredients (except the berries and cocoa nibs) into food processor and process until dough ball forms. It happens quite quickly and sticks together really well.
4. Add chopped goji berries and pulse for a few times – enough to mix the berries into dough, but not to process them too much.
5. Take a 0.6 oz. piece of dough and then stick one side of it into cocoa nibs. After that you're ready to roll it into a ball or any other preferred shape.
6. Refrigerate the protein balls for a couple of hours or overnight and enjoy!

Nutrition Per Serving 60 calories, 3g total fat, 1g sat fat, 50mg sodium, 7g carbohydrates, 2g fiber, 3g sugar, 2g protein

Nibbles in the Classroom

Ingredient Swap: If you're allergic to peanuts, use any nut or seed butter instead.

Tip or fact: Baobab powder is there for its vitamin C content and sour taste. If you don't have any sour tasting powders (rose-hip, acai, blackcurrant, sea buckthorn, camu camu), then add a bit of lemon juice (add less plant milk to the batter) or zest.

Shopping list

Packaged

☐ coconut flour
☐ nut protein powder
☐ baobab powder
☐ carob powder
☐ additive-free peanut butter
☐ date sugar
☐ goji berries
☐ cocoa nibs

Refrigerated or frozen

☐ additive-free plant milk

Seasonings and Spices

☐ ginger powder
☐ Himalayan salt
☐ cocoa powder

Popcorn in the Classroom

by Ashley Arpel Greenwald

Medium | **Kid Friendly** | **Gluten Free** | **10 Servings**

Bring the movie theatre to school!

Ingredients

Popcorn:
⅓ c popcorn kernels
½ tsp extra virgin olive oil

Popcorn Seasoning:
1 c nutritional yeast flakes
1 tsp onion powder
½ tsp smoked paprika
½ tsp mustard powder

Directions

1. Gather all ingredients.
2. Place popcorn kernels in a small mixing bowl and add olive oil. Mix with hands.
3. Pour all kernels into a brown paper lunch bag. Fold the top of the bag over twice to seal kernels.
4. Place bag in microwave and cook for 1½ minutes.
5. Pour nutritional yeast, onion powder, smoked paprika and mustard powder into an airtight glass container. Seal and shake vigorously.
6. When popcorn is cooked, remove from microwave and pour popped popcorn into the container. Once again, shake vigorously making sure the yeast mixture is distributed evenly.
7. Serve immediately.

Nutrition Per Serving 45 calories, 1g total fat, 0g sat fat, 15mg sodium, 7g carbohydrates, 2g fiber, 0g sugar, 4g protein

Storage: Store in an airtight glass container for up to 2 days.

Tip or fact: Popcorn kernels can pop up to 3 feet in the air.

Shopping list

Packaged
☐ popcorn kernels
☐ extra virgin olive oil
☐ nutritional yeast flakes

Seasonings and Spices
☐ onion powder
☐ smoked paprika
☐ mustard powder

Raw Gingerbread Granola Apple Parfaits
by Kelley Williamson

Easy | **Kid Friendly** | **Gluten Free** | **4 Servings**

Gingerbread granola and apples. Who can resist?

Ingredients

Gingerbread Granola:
1 Tbsp applesauce
½ c orange juice
6 dates, smashed
2 c rolled oats
1 tsp ground dried ginger
½ tsp cinnamon
½ tsp nutmeg
½ tsp allspice
sea salt, to taste

Creamy Parfait:
½ c Tofutti cream cheese
½ c vanilla soy yogurt

Apples:
2 apples, cored and sliced

Directions

1. Gather all ingredients.
2. Mash the dates and then mix all ingredients for the granola together and set aside
3. Mix all ingredients for the creamy parfait in a small bowl using a whisk and set aside.
4. Slice the apples in very small diced pieces.
5. Place the small diced apples in either a glass.
6. Add granola on top and press down and then add parfait mixture on top.
7. Continue with apples, granola and creamy parfait mixture and then add a sprinkling of granola on top and an apple on the side (if wanted).

Nutrition Per Serving 370 calories, 9g total fat, 2.5g sat fat, 200mg sodium, 63g carbohydrates, 7g fiber, 27g sugar, 9g protein

Storage: Store in an airtight glass container in the refrigerator for 1 day.

Ingredient Swap: Add all types of fruit especially different ones that are in season.

Tip or fact: What a wonderful way to enjoy in season fruit but also gingerbread granola which will remind you of the holiday seasons up and coming.

Nibbles in the Classroom

Shopping list

Produce
☐ 2 apples

Packaged
☐ applesauce
☐ 6 dates
☐ rolled oats

Refrigerated or frozen
☐ orange juice
☐ Tofutti cream cheese
☐ vanilla soy yogurt

Seasonings and Spices
☐ ground dried ginger
☐ cinnamon
☐ nutmeg
☐ allspice
☐ sea salt

Rawlicious Granola

by Kelley Williamson

Medium | **Kid Friendly** | **Gluten Free** | **4-6 Servings**

Yummy granola that can be made in just a few minutes.

Ingredients

1 c rolled oats
⅓ c unsweetened coconut flakes
½ c ground flax seeds
½ c Lilly's chocolate chips
½ c dates, smashed
1 Tbsp unsweetened applesauce
1 Tbsp chia seeds
1 tsp vanilla extract

Directions

1. Gather all ingredients.
2. Stir all ingredients in a bowl until thoroughly mixed.
3. Cover and chill in the refrigerator or enjoy right away.

Nutrition Per Serving 280 calories, 13g total fat, 7g sat fat, 10mg sodium, 39g carbohydrates, 7g fiber, 21g sugar, 6g protein

Storage: Store in an airtight glass container in the refrigerator for 2-3 days.

Ingredient Swap: Add all types of seeds and dried fruit.

Tip or fact: A bowl of oatmeal for breakfast provides energy and fuel all morning long but now you can enjoy oatmeal any time of the day.

Shopping list

Packaged
- rolled oats
- unsweetened coconut flakes
- ground flax seeds
- Lilly's chocolate chips
- dates, smashed
- unsweetened applesauce
- chia seeds
- vanilla extract

Smoothie Bowl

by Reuel Rodriguez

| Easy | Kid Friendly | Gluten Free | 2 Servings |

This easy fruit smoothie bowl is not only easy to make with kids, but it tastes absolutely amazing!

Ingredients

1 oz. dried acai packet
1 banana
½ c frozen, unsweetened strawberries
½ c coconut milk
1 Tbsp hemp seeds
Optional Toppings:
½ c strawberries
¼ c flaked coconut
1 sliced kiwi
⅓ c blueberries

Directions

1. Gather all ingredients.
2. Combine ingredients in blender.
3. Pulse until desired consistency.
4. Pour into a bowl and enjoy.

Nutrition Per Serving 310 calories, 16g total fat, 5g sat fat, 50mg sodium, 40g carbohydrates, 10g fiber, 21g sugar, 3g protein

Storage: Store in an airtight glass container in the refrigerator for up to 1 day.

Ingredient Swap: Orange juice can be substituted instead of coconut milk. Any fruit can be used for optional toppings.

Nibbles in the Classroom

Shopping list

Produce
□ 1 banana
□ strawberries, optional
□ 1 kiwi, optional
□ blueberries, optional

Packaged
□ 1 oz. dried acai packet
□ hemp seeds
□ flaked coconut, optional

Refrigerated or frozen
□ frozen, unsweetened strawberries
□ coconut milk

Sunny Banana Sandwiches

by Ashley Arpel Greenwald

| Medium | Kid Friendly | Gluten Free | 12 Servings |

Sometimes I wish I could go back to kindergarten so I can play with my food and have it be socially acceptable.

Ingredients

Strawberry Flax Jam:
2 Tbsp flaxseeds
4 Tbsp cold water
2 ½ c fresh strawberries
2 Tbsp maple sugar, optional
Sandwiches:
1 jar unsalted sunflower butter
2 large ripe bananas

Directions

1. Gather all jam ingredients.
2. Place flaxseeds and water in the bowl of a food processor or blender. Let sit for at least 5 minutes, until most of the water has been absorbed by the flaxseeds.
3. Top flaxseed mixture with fresh strawberries and maple sugar, if using. Pulse on high until completely pureed.
4. Transfer jam to a glass jar with a cover and place in the refrigerator to keep chilled.
5. Gather sandwich ingredients.
6. Pour strawberry jam onto a shallow dish. Set aside.
7. Pour sunflower butter onto a separate shallow dish. Set aside.
8. Peel 1 banana and discard peel. Use a butter knife to slice peeled banana into small circles.
9. Dip each banana circle into the strawberry jam and place on a flat surface or plate, jam side facing up. Do not cover entire banana circle with jam, only the top that you dip in.
10. Peel second banana and discard peel. Slice peeled banana into small circles.
11. Dip each banana circle into the sunflower butter and place on top of jam covered banana circles, creating a tiny sandwich.
12. Eat immediately so the bananas do not brown.

Nutrition Per Serving 180 calories, 9g total fat, 1g sat fat, 0mg sodium, 24g carbohdyrates, 3g fiber, 16g sugar, 4g protein

Tip or fact: Ask the class what happens when you mix water with flaxseeds and let it sit for 5 minutes. Then show them the results.

Shopping list

Produce
☐ strawberries
☐ 1 large ripe bananas

Packaged
☐ flaxseeds
☐ maple sugar

Refrigerated or Frozen
☐ sunflower butter

Sweet Cream and Fruit

by Reuel Rodriguez

Easy | **Kid Friendly** | **Gluten Free** | **4 Servings**

Who can resist a fruit dipping sauce with strawberries and apples?

Ingredients

1 box silken tofu, drained
5 Medjool dates, chopped
1 tsp vanilla extract
1 tsp agave syrup
4 strawberries, sliced
10 grapes
1 apple, sliced

Directions

1. Gather all ingredients.
2. In a blender or food processor add all ingredients and blend until smooth.
3. While blending cut up your favorite fruit into bite sized pieces.
4. Place the sweet cream into a bowl and then add the fruit around the bowl. Enjoy.

Nutrition Per Serving 120 calories, 3g total fat, 0g sat fat, 0mg sodium, 20g carbohydrates, 2g fiber, 15g sugar, 6g protein

Storage: Store in an airtight glass container in the refrigerator.

Ingredient Swap: Add different flavors to the sweet cream or add different topping such as coconut flakes nuts, etc.

Tip or fact: Enjoy for breakfast or as a late night snack. There is nothing better than fresh fruit. Good for you and good for your body.

Nibbles in the Classroom

Shopping list

Produce
☐ 4 strawberries
☐ 10 grapes
☐ 1 apple

Packaged
☐ 1 box silken tofu, drained
☐ 5 Medjool dates, chopped
☐ vanilla extract
☐ agave syrup

Veggie Faces

by Ashley Arpel Greenwald

Easy | **Kid Friendly** | **Gluten Free** | **24 Servings** 📷

Who needs picture day when you can create a self portrait?

Ingredients

22-24 slices whole grain bread
8 oz. hummus
1 large cucumber
20 cherry tomatoes
20 baby carrots
20 sugar snap peas
5 c unsalted popcorn

Directions

1. Gather all ingredients.
2. Place 4 slices of bread on a cutting board, sideways so that you have a vertical rectangle slice as opposed to a horizontal. Top each slice with hummus.
3. Use a butter knife to slice cucumbers into circles. Place 2 cucumber circles on the bottom of each bread slice, creating eyes on top of the hummus.
4. Slice cherry tomatoes in half and use each half to cover the cucumber eyes as pupils.
5. Use a baby carrot as the nose and a sugar snap pea as the smile.
6. Place a handful of popped popcorn atop the face for hair and voila! You have created a friendly snack!
7. Continue process so every child in class has at least 1 slice of bread.
8. Eat with best friends!

Nutrition Per Serving 150 calories, 2.5g total fat, 0g sat fat, 160mg sodium, 26g carbohydrates, 1g fiber, 5g sugar, 2g protein

Ingredient Swap: This is where your creativity can really come into play! Use your imagination! What is your favorite vegetable? Does it look like a nose? A smile? Go crazy and switch things up!

Tip or fact: Silly creations with foods can lead to more kids trying fresh fruits and vegetables. Get creative and have fun!

Shopping list

Produce
☐ 1 large cucumber
☐ 20 cherry tomatoes
☐ 20 baby carrots
☐ 20 sugar snap peas

Packaged
☐ 1 loaf whole grain bread
☐ unsalted popcorn

Refrigerated or Frozen
☐ 8 oz. hummus

Watermelon Pizza Party

by Kelley Williamson

Easy | **Kid Friendly** | **Gluten Free** | **6-8 Servings**

How enjoyable to have a pizza party with all fruit that everyone can enjoy.

Ingredients

8 2 in. slice of watermelon
2 c soy vanilla yogurt
2 c Tofutti cream cheese
4 c each assorted fruits: strawberries, blueberries, raspberries, blackberries, kiwi, bananas, peaches, etc.

Directions

1. Gather all ingredients.
2. Slice a 2-inch slice of watermelon in a circle. Set on a plate large enough to hold the watermelon slice.
3. In a bowl mix the Tofutti and the yogurt and using a whisk, until smooth and creamy.
4. With your table knife spread on the cream cheese mixture on the watermelon slice and then with the table knife, make small indentations into the cream cheese to form triangle slices so that you can stay within the lines with you are placing the fruit on the watermelon slice.
5. Arrange the fruits in any order on top of the cream cheese.
6. Cut into wedges after decorating and enjoy.

Nutrition Per Serving 310 calories, 12g total fat, 4g sat fat, 250mg sodium, 48g carbohydrates, 3g fiber, 32g sugar, 6g protein

Nibbles in the Classroom

Storage: Store in an airtight glass container in the refrigerator for 1-2 days.

Ingredient Swap: Add all types of fruit on this pizza to make it fun and colorful. You can also make the fruit match the colors for holidays.

Tip or fact: Watermelons are almost entirely water, which makes them a refreshing treat on a hot day. They are loaded with all kinds of nutrition also.

Shopping list

Produce
☐ 1 watermelon
☐ strawberries, optional
☐ blueberries, optional
☐ raspberries, optional
☐ blackberries, optional
☐ kiwi, optional
☐ banana, optional
☐ peaches, optional

Refrigerated or Frozen
☐ soy vanilla yogurt
☐ Tofutti cream cheese

hot pepper

eggplant

onion

carrot

tomato

peas

melon

beet

bush pumpkin

cucumber

cabbage

brocoli

radish

lettuce

pepper

zucchini

cauliflower

chinese

corn

pepper

pimpkin

bean

spinach

mushroom

garlic

parsley

potato

celery

artichoke

asparagus

Legumes
beans

green bean

wax bean

green peas

snow peas

chick peas

lentis

scarlet runner bean

roman bean

adzuki bean

ladiad bean

lupine

mung bean

black-eyed pea

pinto bean

Lima bean

split peas

red kidney bean

black gram

black bean

flageolet

yard-long bean

soybeans

broad beans

7 Days of Meals

	Breakfast	Lunch	Dinner	Snacks	Desserts	Appetizers
DAY 1	Banana Blueberry Bread + Juice/ Smoothie of Choice	Summer Salad with Miso Lime Dressin	Big Bold Chili + Cornbread	Protein Balls	Shortbread Cookies	Hummus + Pita Crisp Crackers
DAY 2	Chocolate Chai Scones	Quinoa Chickpea Burger + Cheesy Vegan Sauce	One Pot Thai Coconut Curry Tofu	Popcorn Balls	Rustic Apple Pie	Vegan Spinach Dip
DAY 3	Easy Breakfast Cookies + Brighten Up Juice	Lentil Pea Corn Stew	Plant Based Paella + Golden Wedge Lettuce Wrap	Gingerbread Granola Apple Parfait	Strawberry Ice Cream	Heirloom Tomato Olive Bruschetta
DAY 4	Tofu Scramble	Oooh La La Nachos	Lentil Loaf + Red Potatos and Herbs	Peanut Butter Banana Pudding	Very Berry Crumble	Guacamole
DAY 5	Strawberry Lime Smoothie + Brown Rice Fruit Bread	Buddha Bowl	Vegetarian Pizza + Spicy Quinoa Salad	Polenta Fries	Key Lime Parfait	Teriyaki Cauliflower Wings
DAY 6	Apple Porridge	Egg Salad on Bread	Tofu Stroganoff + Balsamic Zucchini	"Cheese" Fondue	Chocolate Cake + Frosting	Touch of Spice Lentil Dip and Carrot/ Celery Sticks
DAY 7	Cocoa Raspberry Pancakes + Juice or Smoothie of Choice	Open Faced Black Bean Quesadilla	Cheezy Veggie Divan Over Brown Rice	Chocolate Protein Balls	Blondie Brookies	Tofu Lettuce Wraps

Index

Shape Up Us

Shape Up US is a 501c3 non-profit corporation is dedicated to "Building A Healthier Future" and empowering children and families to lead healthier, happier lives. Shape Up US provides teachers, children, parents and communities at large with educational tools to create healthy, lifelong habits to improve their overall wellness. With a focus on over-all health, physical exercise, nutrition, and mental and emotional well being, we accomplish our mission of building healthy futures for our children through a three-pronged approach of: AWARENESS! EDUCATION! ACTION!

AWARENESS! Shape Up Us Presents Health and Wellness Expos – A nationwide movement dedicated to Healthy Communities - Free State-by-State Wellness Expos that get thousands of participants on-board the wellness bandwagon-- to further promote health and prevent chronic disease, Shape Up US partners with host communities to provide a day of fun to promote health and prevent chronic disease across the spectrum of ages, races, genders and ethnicities. https://youtu.be/VLvFVlDFvFQ

EDUCATION! The Hip Hop Healthy Heart Program for Children™ is a K-6th grade comprehensive "Whole Child" wellness literacy education curriculum that has been created to "Build A Culture of Health" through our educational system. This program provides our children with the tools to flourish and be resilient! To guide them to blossom into their full potential (mentally, physically and emotionally). We are teaching through Personalized Learning by grouping our program K-3 and 4th-6th. This allows each child to learn at their own pace and in their own "Best" way. This program flows from teacher, to student, to family, to community. It provide an on-line curriculum and resources that "Transforms Our Children" through a Train-The-Trainer model that will "Positively" affect ALL who Engage in this program. It is the Solution To Lifestyle and Behavioral Changes!

ACTION! Clap4Health!℠ A National Fitness Campaign and Fundraiser--Using Clapping, as its method of delivery to get ACTIVE, GET HEALTHY and BE HAPPY!. Clap4Health! is an innovative solution to bringing wellness and physical education back into the schools and children's households. The benefits of clapping are based on the Acupressure Theory. "Our body has 340 known pressure points, 28 of which are in our hands." This is why many children and adults love to clap. It makes you happy! This program is being implemented across the nation to teach the benefits of keeping fit, active, healthy and happy.

COOKBOOK! "Think Outside The Lunchbox" Cookbook - 250 Plant Nutritious Recipes That The Whole Family Will Love Introduction by Dr. Scott Stoll and Foreword by Keegan Kuhn.

100% of Jyl's profits from the sale of "Think Outside The Lunchbox" Cookbook will go back to Shape Up Us.

www.ShapeUpUs.org

Sharing Stories

Nele Liivlaid's Story

I am in better shape now at 40 years old than I was at 20. This isn't because I diet or have an intense fitness regime: it's because I have adopted a healthy lifestyle. And I want to help YOU live a happy, healthy life too by making sensible choices.

I am passionate about promoting a healthy and sustainable lifestyle. I advocate for proper nutrition plus being active, something I know a lot about now, but I wasn't always this way. When I was in my early 20s I struggled with an eating disorder. I'd say I was slightly bulimic. I didn't have a clue about what to eat and thought the less I ate, the skinnier I would be. After adopting whole foods plant-based diet (WFPBD) at age 33 as well as walking and doing yoga, I am at peace with food and my body today.

How did I come to that? Well, it was back in 2012 when my best friend went to study nutrition and through her new information started to flow in. To be honest, I was quite sceptical in the beginning believing that meat really was essential for my health.

Then, however, I began to read The China Study (that my friend had suggested). I was staying home with my almost 2-year-old at the time. So, I could read the book every day when he was asleep. Then, in the evening I'd give an update to my husband who was also very sceptical at first asking all kinds of inconvenient questions. However, finally we were both convinced and at the same page about the necessity to transition ourselves to plant-based eating.

For a while already we'd both been feeling that dairy was not for us and thus this was the first food group we kicked out of our menu. Next came meat, then eggs and finally fish. When I started to insert all my meals into nutritional database, I was amazed of the quantities I could eat on WFPBD. I've always liked to eat a lot, so that made me super happy. I also discovered how wrong my conceptions of proper nutrition had been. I still remember when I thought eating a huge pear would make me fat!

My husband has been the beneficiary of making the switch to healthier eating after being hospitalized with gallstones for a second time. The surgeon told him it was absolutely necessary to cut him open in order to treat the problem. He refused and instead started eating my WFPBD meal plans. He got rid of his symptoms and lost 15 kilos (33 pounds) in six months.

However, my story doesn't end there. I too screwed up, even with WFPBD! I started eating too much of high glycemic foods, such as dried and fresh fruit as well as baked grains in combination with high-fat foods (nuts and seeds). Having a history with antibiotics it didn't take long before I developed Candida overgrowth. However, I choose to ignore the symptoms not to give up my favourite foods. Can you relate? I finally pulled myself together and left the comfort zone yet once again to start Candida diet in August 2016 after 2 years of postponing. So, the research began again – I found a lot of information on Candida diet online and purchased a few thorough books as well, but what I didn't find was a diet suitable for vegans. Consequently, I took all the information I'd gathered from my research and started to compile a balanced meal plan that'd cover all the macros as well as micros.

At first it was only for myself, but as time went by and I saw that the meal plan is working and also sharing my journey through my blog and social media, people started to inquire about it. So, as the demand grew, I developed the plan further and asked a few people to try it out. I was so glad to see that they were really happy with the results, so more and more people have tried it with equally positive outcome. By now, vegan Candida meal plans and balanced blood sugar on WFPBD has become my niche!

After being on my own health journey for so long, seeing others battle with well being and weight makes me sad. I often hear people blame their "bad" genes for being overweight. But that's just an excuse. As the mother of a young boy, I know it's tough trying to read up on healthy foods and take the time to prepare good meals. That's one of the reasons I started my blog Nutriplanet.org.

I put information about proper nutrition, exercise and healthy minds directly into your hands through articles, blog posts, tutorial videos, recipes and shopping/eating out guidance. I compile my health and nutrition research, knowledge and certificate in Plant Based Nutrition into ready-to-use tips for you to plug into everyday living.

This stuff is not secret but it's something I believe big business would prefer you didn't know. I think companies are profiting from not being concerned about people's health and the environment. Breaking the chain of illness and getting people moving means making informed choices and reversing the idea that good food can't be tasty. I love to eat and anything I prepare needs to taste delicious.

When I started looking into healthy lifestyles and eating, I knew I had to tell others about what I discovered. I knew I had to share the connection between health and nutrition so people could take their well-being into their own hands before it was too late. That's what my work is about: a hub for you to fuel your body and mind throughout your journey on Earth.

"'Think Outside The Lunchbox' is about considering eating a whole food, plant-based diet that will provide the body with nutrients to support a healthy immune system and the overall health for the entire body at the cellular level."
- Jerry Casados, NTP, McDougall Starch Solution Certified Instructor, Co-founder Plant-Base Summit

"In our vision to make Midland the healthiest community in Texas, we've realized that our approach has to be holistic in both philosophy and application. That means we have to take a leadership role in ensuring our community knows the importance of food, exercise, stress management, spirituality and social engagement in obtaining optimal health. We also have to make sure we're delivering a consistent message to both children and adults so the whole family can take this journey together. We know that the healthiest community's in the world approach health in this same, holistic fashion, instilling these key values in their children as soon as their old enough to understand them. Resources like this only help support this kind of whole health, whole family approach."
- Marcy Madrid, Vice President, Community Health Midland Health

The time has come to make the food we serve our families important. Yes, That's every meal. In a world where fast food giants are finally making room for plant-based menu options, Jyl and Ashley are generating kid-friendly fare that everyone at home will appreciate. Thinking Outside The Lunchbox includes a broad selection of clean, whole food, plant-based, recipes that are dedicated to the delectable. Choose from gluten free, oil free, dairy-free, soy-free, and/or nut-free recipes that are as nourishing as they are delicious! Ashley and Jyl, I give my highest praises: Double Yay and Double Yum!
- Meryl A. Fury, MS, RN, President/CEO, Plant Based Nutrition Movement